*Understanding Contemporary
Irish Fiction and Drama*

Understanding Modern European and Latin American Literature

James Hardin, Series Editor

volumes on

UNDERSTANDING

Contemporary Irish Fiction and Drama

Margaret Hallissy

The University of South Carolina Press

© 2016 University of South Carolina

Published by the University of South Carolina Press
Columbia, South Carolina 29208

www.sc.edu/uscpress

Manufactured in the United States of America

25 24 23 22 21 20 19 18 17 16
10 9 8 7 6 5 4 3 2 1

Library of Congress Cataloging-in-Publication Data
can be found at http://catalog.loc.gov/.

ISBN 978-1-61117-662-9 (cloth)
ISBN 978-1-61117-663-6 (ebook)

This book was printed on recycled paper with
30 percent postconsumer waste content.

To Jack Mallon, Courtney Casey, and Gracie Mallon
looking forward

Contents

Series Editor's Preface

Understanding Modern European and Latin American Literature has been planned as a series of guides for undergraduate and graduate students and nonacademic readers. Like the volumes in its companion series *Understanding Contemporary American Literature,* these books provide introductions to the lives and writings of prominent modern authors and explicate their most important works.

Modern literature makes special demands, and this is particularly true of foreign literature, in which the reader must contend not only with unfamiliar, often arcane artistic conventions and philosophical concepts, but also with the handicap of reading the literature in translation. It is a truism that the nuances of one language can be rendered in another only imperfectly (and this problem is especially acute in fiction), but the fact that the works of European and Latin American writers are situated in a historical and cultural setting quite different from our own can be as great a hindrance to the understanding of these works as the linguistic barrier. For this reason the *UMELL* series emphasizes the sociological and historical background of the writers treated. The philosophical and cultural traditions peculiar to a given culture may be particularly important for an understanding of certain authors, and these are taken up in the introductory chapter and also in the discussion of those works to which this information is relevant. Beyond this, the books treat the specifically literary aspects of the author under discussion and attempt to explain the complexities of contemporary literature lucidly. The books are conceived as introductions to the authors covered, not as comprehensive analyses. They do not provide detailed summaries of plot because they are meant to be used in conjunction with the books they treat, not as a substitute for study of the original works. The purpose of the books is to provide information and judicious literary assessment of the major works in the most compact, readable form. It is our hope that the *UMELL* series will help increase knowledge and understanding of European and Latin American cultures and will serve to make the literature of those cultures more accessible.

J. H.

Introduction

It all begins with the land. Upon it, the characters live and move and have their being. In fiction and drama, where action happens is intricately bound up with what happens, to whom, because of whom, and why. Setting explains, literally, where the characters are coming from. Unlike the United States, whose vast tracts of underpopulated land often served as both a magnet for the adventurous and a safety valve for the malcontent, Ireland is a place of, in William Butler Yeats's words, "little room." From at least the sixteenth century, the question of who owned the land, and by what right, underlies all of Ireland's history and much of its literature. Landowners, predominantly British in origin and Anglican in religion, dominated the native Celts for generations, leaving behind a heritage of resentment which persisted even after landholding arrangements had changed. The confinement of the lower classes to the smaller, less fertile, less desirable plots of land, which they had little time to cultivate because of their duty work on the landlord's land, led directly to the Irish dependence on the potato as the main, and often the only, element of the diet. So it was that, when the potato crop failed in 1845, mass starvation and mass emigration robbed the land of its inhabitants.

Whether in times of famine or relative prosperity, regions of Ireland in which the plays or fiction are set bear their own symbolic freight. A major dichotomy exists in Irish writing between the city and the country. Here there are similarities to the United States, wherein in some political circles the non-coastal, non-urban sections of the country are described as, and apparently believed by some to be, "the heartland." A similar notion of the country in Ireland, as being closer than the city to pure, authentic, Irish values, also prevails. The countryside, particularly the remote areas in the west, is perceived as less contaminated by contact with the modern world, more traditional in values. The city is seen as the locus of worldly values, but also of accomplishment of all sorts: educational, economic, artistic. City folk see themselves as sophisticated, worldly-wise, Europeanized and/or Americanized, open to change and to cultural diversity. Urbanites scorn the "culchies," rural people, who scorn the urbanites in turn.

Another great spatial divide is that between Northern Ireland and the Republic of Ireland. The relationship of Ireland to England is a long and, to the "Republican" supporter of Irish independence, sad tale. The term *Republican* in Irish political discourse is unrelated to the Republican Party in the United States; an Irish Republican is one who advocates for or approves of separation from the United Kingdom. Since 1922 the larger portion of Ireland has achieved its separationist goal and is indeed a separate country from Northern Ireland, which remains part of the United Kingdom. This division of an island that is so small to begin with has political, social, economic, and religious consequences. Although at the time of this writing (2015) relative peace prevails, hostilities have simmered for years, erupting sporadically into violence. At issue is the continuing existence of two separate countries on one island, with all the historical memory that arrangement involves.

Collective memory is preserved and transmitted via storytelling. The storytelling custom arose in the countryside as community entertainment during the long, dark winter nights before electrification introduced other absorbing, but isolating, forms of entertainment. Storytelling customs survive in modern Irish literature in the form of episodes in fiction and drama. When any play, short story, or novel, Irish or not, incorporates a smaller narrative into the larger narrative, this story-within-the-story poses technical issues requiring close literary analysis: the relationship of the two narratives to each other, and the suitability of the particular tale to the particular teller and audience. In an Irish work, the tale-telling situation also connects both teller and tale to a long and strong tradition. The Irish custom preserved and transmitted the community's sense of its own history, sometimes a family's, sometimes the tribe's. At the same time, the paradoxical secretiveness of an otherwise loquacious people is often demonstrated in stories not told, in crucial details suppressed, in questions that beg to be answered but are not.

Traditionally, folk tales were told in the native language; thus the storytelling tradition is intimately bound up with the fate of the Irish language in Ireland. Language in Ireland, like land ownership, is a contentious issue, pitting the language of the natives against that of the conquerors, and exacerbating tensions between the two groups. In an effort to maintain their cultural identity, the Irish long resisted the suppression of their language. But as in the United States, knowledge of English opened doors of opportunity. The advantages to the Irish of mastering a language that provided access not only to British culture but to other English-speaking countries had to be weighed against the loss of a key component of Irish culture.

Historical events moved the Irish, willingly or not, toward English as the predominant language. In 1832, with the advent of the National School System, a blow was dealt to the Irish language in that speaking Irish was forbidden in the schools, the use of English mandated, resulting in a generation of children whose primary language was not that of their parents. The Great Famine beginning in 1845 meant that large numbers of the Irish-speaking, especially in the west, either died or emigrated. Post-Famine, the prospect of emigration encouraged Irish speakers to learn English in hopes of employment in England or Canada or Australia or the United States. Most, but not all, Irish emigrants to the United States spoke English, giving them a leg up in the areas of employment, education, and general psychological adjustment. Whether in Ireland or elsewhere, the American dialect of English would eventually predominate, one of many indicators of the cultural influence of the United States.

As mentioned earlier, by the mid-nineteenth century, the great bulk of the Irish population had become dependent on the potato. Unlike some other crops which required large acreages to flourish, such as the crops grown in the western United States, the potato would grow on small plots, and small plots were all the Irish had after much of the arable land had been distributed to the landlords. A so-called lazy crop that, once planted, required little attention, the potato could be grown on the small parcels of rocky land available to tenants and "small" farmers. While the lazy crop ripened, tenants worked on the landlords' land in exchange for the rental fees on their own patches. The potato had the further advantage of being a healthful and convenient food, easy to cook; roasted or boiled, with milk or butter, the potato makes for a dull but nourishing meal. It could not, however, be stored from season to season. Thus while the Irish peasantry increased in number, they were unable to plan for lean years; even in good years, hungry months often preceded the ripening of the crops. If the crops failed, those months extended into years.

Potato blights had happened before the Great Famine, a fact that should have alerted the government in London to make preparations for future crop failures. But when in 1845 a fungus attacked the potato crops, and was more widespread, virulent, and recurrent than previous blights had been, subsistence became starvation, almost literally overnight. Ireland being part of the British Commonwealth at the time, help from the mother country might well have been expected, and, in historical retrospect, should have been forthcoming. But not only were no effective strategies in place to distribute food to the poor, there was no general agreement that it was the government's responsibility to do so. Perhaps this was a matter to be handled by religious institutions, or private charity? Perhaps the problem should be handled at the most local level, by the landlords themselves? As the authorities dithered, the Irish starved.

Some landlords, rather than continue to support an increasingly unproductive tenantry, chose to pay their passage money to Canada or New York or Boston. And some landlords were themselves forced into bankruptcy and emigrated too, doing their part to swell the emigrant tide. They crossed the Atlantic on the so-called famine ships, hastily repurposed former slavers and cargo vessels whose owners saw in the misery of the Irish people the opportunity for a quick profit. Sick and starving, many emigrants died at sea. Those who survived, many of them unskilled laborers, were greeted with scant enthusiasm. Descendants of some of these Famine emigrants would become captains of industry (the Fords) and political leaders (the Kennedys). At the time, however, they must have seemed an unpromising lot, in their great numbers, with their strange accents, their unfamiliar religion, and their tendency to pack together in urban enclaves. Worse, many were sick, posing the realistic threat of actual, not merely metaphorical, contamination of the "native" stock, that is, those whose forebears had emigrated a little sooner.

Back in Ireland, the Famine, and the ineptitude and/or callousness with which the British government responded to it, fueled already-existing hostilities, ultimately leading to political independence for the Republic of Ireland seventy years later. One giant step along this path was the Easter Rising of 1916. Small-scale but fervent revolutionary movements, often celebrated in song and story, had kept the issue of independence alive for several hundred years. The most dramatic of these occurred when a small group of armed rebels, inspired at least in part by the rhetoric of the American Revolution, seized the General Post Office in Dublin to protest the British government's presence in Ireland. In a military sense, the rebellion was hopeless: poorly planned, eccentrically led, ill-equipped, disorganized. The leaders' hope, that the seizure of the GPO would trigger a national uprising, proved to be unfounded. Even many Dubliners did not support the rebellion, in fact were Loyalists or supporters of British rule. Such people, and their descendants, found that their actions or inactions in 1916 had placed them on the wrong side of history. As a political act, the Rising was a failure, but as political theater it was flawless, scripting leading roles for men and women who saw themselves as combining the ancient spirit of Celtic Ireland with the sacrificial victimhood of Jesus Christ.

Irish hostility pre- and post-Rising focused not only on the British but on the descendants of those British who had settled in Ireland several centuries earlier: the Anglo-Irish. From the time of the Tudor monarchs in the sixteenth century, the British government had distributed lands in Ireland as a reward for service to the British Crown. The native Celtic population, however, regarded these lands as their own, thus not in the power of the British government to bestow. Thus began a troubled situation: the descendants of these Tudor grantees, termed the Anglo-Irish, lived in relative splendor, but on land which the Irish regarded as stolen, albeit long ago. Even in the heyday of British occupation, these great estates were often inherited by men who had no sense of responsibility for them or skill in maintaining them. Following the establishment of the Republic in 1922, a period of unrest ensued, in which hostility against the two-country solution was directed toward the Anglo-Irish, beneficiaries of past oppression even if not themselves oppressors. In the violence following the 1922 Anglo-Irish Treaty, many of these estates were destroyed, or the families driven out of Ireland, or both.

The symbol of Anglo-Irish dominance or Ascendancy was the so-called Big House (its size and grandeur magnified by contrast with the humble cottages of the native Celts). The literature they produced themselves, and that was written about them, chronicled the elegant, artistic, and intellectual life of a leisured and cultured class. At the same time, fictional critiques of that lifestyle presented the Anglo-Irish as decadent, unworthy heirs even to their less-than-illustrious forebears. As political changes led to the creation of the Republic of Ireland, the Big House often became the target of revolutionary violence, because of the bad old days it represented. The fate of the Anglo-Irish inspired a fictional subgenre: the Big House novel.

Meanwhile in the North, the old divisions still caused tension. Violence in the aftermath of the 1921 treaty continued long after; the two-state solution is regarded by some as problematic to this day, nearly one hundred years later. In Northern Ireland, politics, economics, social class, and religion are all intertwined. While in life exceptions to all generalizations are to be found, in literature a Loyalist political position is often associated with membership in the Protestant Church of Ireland, and Republican politics often are associated with Catholicism. Religious alliances exacerbate political hostility; socioeconomic resentments pit haves against have-nots. The inability of the two major groups to live trustingly with each other triggers acts of violence, which themselves require retribution, which in turn leads to more violence. Peace breaks out in certain areas and for limited periods of time; but resentments linger, and with them the potential for further Troubles. Political unrest either lies just below the surface, as in the rural areas of the North, or manifests itself in plain sight in urban areas like Belfast, in the working-class neighborhoods of which the signs of division are obvious and ugly.

A tourist in Ireland will generally see only the more pleasant aspects of Irish life, one of which is the pub. Along with the customary beverages come other traditions: *craic* or lively conversation, music, and dancing. The conviviality of the pub scene as depicted in Irish music and film masks a serious underlying problem, however. Alcohol consumption marks rites of passage; neither wedding nor wake is complete without a drop or two of the "water of life." Drinking in groups, especially according to the rules of "buying rounds," affirms one's membership in a community, especially for men. The sociable atmosphere of the pub is, however, often a veneer over the darker side of the Irish love affair with alcohol. The all-too-familiar consequences of addiction are manifest in Ireland as elsewhere: marital problems, unplanned pregnancy, domestic violence, disease, accidents, unemployment. Whether the stereotype of the drunken Irishman has any truth to it or not is a matter for alcohol researchers; but in fiction and drama, the way the Irish drink, and the way they behave when they drink, is depicted as deeply rooted in Irish culture.

When the weight of all these traditions bears too heavily, when Ireland seems to offer only confinement and restriction, America beckons as a land of freedom and opportunity in which one can fashion a new self. This perception of the United States encouraged emigration in the past and is so reflected in the literature. In the nineteenth century, the ocean voyage was so difficult that few ever made the journey home again. To the people back home, these emigrants were as if dead to them, a fact acknowledged in the custom of the American wake, in effect a funeral for a living person on the eve of his or her departure. Even if the emigrant did return, as he or she is exhorted to do in the emigrant ballad Americans know best, "Danny Boy," it would often be after such a long time that loved ones would be dead. As transportation improved, the possibility of returning, either to visit or to stay, became a reality; and at least some of the loved ones would still be alive. But no matter how achingly those in Ireland had longed for those who left, the returnees often came home to resentment. They were seen as dramatically changed, as Yanks, as "too" American, as different from family and friends and from their (perhaps imagined) former selves.

The attitude of the non-emigrants to the emigrants is complicated. When the emigrant departed, perhaps forever, there was grief as if at a death. But then there also was the not-easily-suppressed suspicion that perhaps the emigrants had reached for the winning ticket in life's lottery, leaving the others behind in more than the geographical sense. This fear often evolved into hostility toward the returnees, which manifested itself in disapproval of their new American ways. Not quite Irish anymore, this new species, the returned Yank, seemed to belong nowhere. The effort to reintegrate such hybrids into Irish society often took the form of snarky critiques of their perceived strange ways. For the Yanks themselves, the conflict between the desire for self-definition, which once attracted them to America, and the desire for traditionalism and familiarity, which made them nostalgic for Ireland, would never end on either side of the ocean. The Yanks had in fact changed, and irrevocably.

With this general overview in mind, we now turn to each event or theme in more detail, examining works of modern fiction and drama that depend upon a writer's interpretation of the past. A caveat is in order here. To study a country through its art is an indirect process, not to be confused with studying its history. Historians do not look at the past through the filter of art, yet even they often disagree about what happened and why. Every event discussed herein has been the subject of detailed study by historians, and admits of multiple interpretations. The study of drama and works of fiction such as are discussed here, fiction which incorporates interpretations of history, involves looking back at the past through the eyes of a particular writer at a particular time. The literary artist is not writing history, nor is the critic who discusses the artist. Whether that artist has his or her historical analysis right or not—or whether the artist was right at one time, but is no longer—is not the point for the student of literature. What is the point is to try to understand how the Irish experience is seen by a particular mind at a particular point in time, and how that affects the reader's understanding of a particular work. Literature reflects not so much history itself as the writer's viewpoint on history. While any viewpoint might be, in James Joyce's description of Irish art in *Ulysses,* a "cracked lookingglass," to the reader of literature, the cracks reflect their own sort of light. To extend Joyce's metaphor, it is now time to examine the structure upon which this mirror depends.

Chapter 1

"Nothing can happen nowhere"

A Place in the World

"Nothing can happen nowhere. The locale of the happening always colours the happening, and often, to a degree, shapes it."[1] Novelist Elizabeth Bowen (1899–1973), in "Notes on Writing a Novel" (1945), points to the significance of setting in drama and fiction; where action happens is intricately bound up with what happens (plot), who causes it to happen (characterization), and what key idea or impression the work conveys (theme). Just as the reader of a historical novel set in the American South during the Civil War (say, Margaret Mitchell's *Gone with the Wind*) is expected to know that "the South" is shorthand for a set of beliefs and behaviors, readers of Irish writing need to know what various places mean—for they certainly do *mean*. The physical setting not only provides a stage set or a backdrop for the activities of the characters, but also explains, literally, where they are coming from. While writers often ring changes upon conventions regarding place, it is important to understand what those conventions are, so as to see when they are being altered and for what purpose.

First and most obvious, Ireland is an island. Dictionary definitions of the word *island* include elements such as the following:

Small, not big enough to be called a continent;
Surrounded by water, therefore taking part of its sense of itself from the
   ocean that surrounds it;
Isolated, insulated, insular, from the Latin *insula* (island), with all the
   connotations of limitation included in these terms.

Small and isolated though it is, the land mass of Ireland contains two countries. The 1920 Government of Ireland Act divided Northern Ireland, which is part of the United Kingdom (UK), from the larger Republic of Ireland, which was once part of the UK but is now an independent country. This arrangement, regarded as imperfect even by those who signed the original treaty, was long a cause of political unrest, particularly in the North. The terms *Loyalist* and *Unionist* refer to those who advocate the current arrangement, who are loyal to, and therefore wish to be united with, the UK. In contrast the term *Republican* or *Nationalist* refers to those who support Ireland's existence as a political entity separate from Great Britain. A third category, actually a subcategory of Republicanism, encompasses those who are not satisfied with the division established by the 1922 Anglo-Irish Treaty and who believe that the Republic of Ireland should encompass the whole island. This outcome would require the severance of ties between Northern Ireland and the UK, and the expansion of the Republic to include what is now Northern Ireland. For complex religious and cultural reasons, this presents a difficult problem. And while in Irish life all these definitions are the subject of disagreement and admit of subtleties, as political categories do in any country, the reader of Irish literature must at minimum understand the broad outlines of these political differences.

One matter that requires clarification is the fact that some parts of Ireland located in the geographical north are not a part of the political entity called Northern Ireland. For example County Donegal, on the northwest coast of Ireland, is part of the Irish Republic. When such locations are referred to here, the reader should understand that "the north of Ireland" does not equal "the North" or "Northern Ireland"; the prior conventions of capitalization should help make clear this important distinction between directional north and political North.

While there are many Catholics in Northern Ireland and Protestants in the Republic, in general the political distinction suggests a religious one as well, in that Unionists or Loyalists in Northern Ireland tend to be Protestant, while Republicans (who may live in the North) tend to be Catholic. The political loyalty is a tribal one as well, in that Protestant Loyalists tend to feel affiliation to England, the English language, and to English ways in general, while Republican Catholics tend to identify Irishness with the Celtic past and even with the Irish language.

However, the Protestant/Loyalist versus Catholic/Nationalist alignment is not absolute. Shades of opinion have existed throughout Ireland's history, so there are Protestant Nationalists and Catholic Loyalists. Another term with which the reader should be familiar is *Anglo-Irish,* describing people who live in Ireland (and whose ancestors may have lived there for generations as well) but who some regard as "really" English in that they are descendants of the Planters, the Englishmen granted lands in Ireland by the British Crown, beginning in the mid-sixteenth century. From the point of view of the native Celtic population, such people will always be interlopers, will never be Irish, no matter how long their families have lived in Ireland. From the point of view of some Anglo-Irish, however, they already are Irish and have been for centuries.

Another piece of geographical shorthand is that the eastern coast of Ireland (site of Dublin, the capital of the Republic), is often identified with progress, with Europe (in the literature of the past) and the European Union (in more recent fiction), therefore with the modern and forward-looking in general. The west, on the other hand, is often identified with the traditional, with Celtic folklore, and with the Irish language. Therefore in a work of literature, unless there is evidence of a different authorial intention, the movement from Dublin to the west of Ireland will usually connote a return to traditional ways. Readers of James Joyce's story "The Dead," from his 1914 short-story collection *Dubliners,* or those who have seen the film directed by John Huston, will remember the discussion between the protagonist, Gabriel Conroy, and Miss Ivors. Her Nationalist political stance is made clear by her criticism of Gabriel for refusing her invitation to vacation in the Aran Islands, off the coast of Galway, where he can reconnect with his own country, language, and past. His preference for all things European, thus for taking his holidays in "France or Belgium or perhaps Germany," earns him her contempt; his identification with the English language and with British culture makes him a "West Briton" in her eyes.[2] Were Gabriel to agree to visit the Aran Islands, he would, she believes, learn to identify with Ireland, rather than England or the European continent, and the Irish past. Joyce is not the only writer to identify movement from east to west in Ireland this way; it is a convention of Irish literature in general.

If travel west is identified with a return to traditional Irish ways, "the movement westward in space figures simultaneously as a movement backwards in time."[3] The fact that the areas of Ireland where the Irish language is spoken on an everyday basis, the Gaeltacht, are mostly in the west adds to the association of this part of the country with what some define as the true Irish character. If one were to ask "what is 'authentic' and what is 'typical' in Ireland," the answer would be by no means clear, but "one traditional answer sees the rural elevated above the urban as a sign of Irishness."[4] This sentiment was articulated during a St. Patrick's Day radio speech in 1943 by Éamon de Valera (1882–1975), then president of the Republic of Ireland, and it is crucial to understanding this association between Ireland and the countryside:

> The Ireland that we dreamed of would be the home of a people who
> valued material wealth only as the basis for right living, of a people
> who, satisfied with frugal comfort, devoted their leisure to the things
> of the spirit—a land whose countryside would be bright with cosy
> homesteads, whose fields and valleys would be joyous with the sounds
> of industry, with the romping of sturdy children, the contest of athletic

youth and the laughter of happy maidens; whose firesides would be fo-
rums for the wisdom of serene old age. The home, in short, of a people
living the life that God desires that men should live.[5]

What de Valera was doing in this speech was attempting to preserve the past,
freezing what he defined as the national character as it existed in a (perhaps
imaginary) Golden Age.

If geography equals authenticity, that situation is rendered more complicated by the fact that, especially in the west, tourism is a major industry, and
those who visit the west as tourists—some from other countries, some from the
urbanized eastern parts of Ireland itself—want a specific kind of Irish experience: "Rural Ireland offers an ideal retreat for the metropolitan mind exhausted
by the rigours of the 'real' world. You may observe the comely maidens and
athletic youths, the fine old women and the pensive old men, in their natural
environment."[6] These words echo de Valera's with a satirical spin, suggesting
that the money to be made in the tourist trade is so significant that the inhabitants of the rural west, far from being the simple peasantry of song and story,
are sophisticated manipulators of their own image. In modern times the equation west = rural = traditional = authentic might well break down; the visitor
cannot be sure that what is seen represents anything like a true Irish experience.
If even the Irish cannot define that satisfactorily for themselves, tourists—and
readers—cannot be faulted for their confusion. Since authenticity seems to be
a problem in Irish culture, why would it not be a problem in its literature?
One cannot automatically assume that peasants are virtuous and city dwell-
ers vicious; but one also cannot read these characters without the country/city
stereotypes in mind.

Pondering the vexed question of what constitutes genuine Irishness, journalist Fintan O'Toole tells the story of a 1963 opening of a "spanking new high
tech factory complex." New though it was, "this factory was draped in green
shamrock-spangled curtains, and the curtains were being held aside by a little
Irish leprechaun in a red nightcap and big buckled shoes. It was in many ways a
perfect image of modern Irish culture: an increasingly urban and industrialized
reality made palatable, both to ourselves and to those whom we wish to attract,
by being wrapped up in harmless rural folksy images."[7] If, as O'Toole believes,
the Irish are falsifying their own culture to themselves, so much the more must
the reader who is not Irish watch out for a certain ambiguity in the depiction
of rural people and their ways. The Irish in Ireland might be doing what newspaper writer and observer of the Irish American scene Maureen Dezell feels
that many Irish Americans do, which is conjuring up what she calls "Eiresatz,"
phony cultural elements.[8]

Having taken note of the smaller world of the fiction—north or south, east
or west, urban or rural—and how that world shapes the characters, the reader

is ready to respond to the smaller levels of setting, the specific details of the place in which the story or drama is set. Whether it be house, pub, store, or any other location, this setting will in some way reflect the larger world of the fiction. In these Irish stories, certain streams of images recur. For one thing the weather, not one of Ireland's better features, is often a backdrop to the kind of action taking place. The landscape, with its rugged and barren beauty, might compare or contrast with the nature of the characters living thereupon. Above all the sea defines the island, as does the ocean voyage, real or imagined, the promise or threat of which has loomed so large in Ireland's history.

When the fiction is set on a particular piece of land, especially a farm, or when the land itself is a central issue in a story, the reader must see this against the backdrop of the historical antagonisms summed up in the phrase "the Irish land question." The land question can be divided into two interrelated sub-questions: Who owns the land? And by what right? The colonization of Ireland by England and the consequent redistribution of land ownership lie beneath the modern significance of land in modern Irish literature. Experts have analyzed Irish agriculture, but for the general reader the key fact is that on this small island the soil is not uniformly cultivable. Tourists love to visit the Burren, in County Clare, a rocky, barren landscape that looks like the surface of the moon. Scenic, yes, for those driving by on their way to a nice dinner; but tracts of land such as these must have looked very different to those who had to wrest a living out of the land. Quality of soil—even the mere presence of soil rather than rock—meant the difference between prosperity, subsistence, and starvation. Similarly the size of the piece of land can make its owner a "strong" farmer, something like an agribusinessman, as opposed to a smallholder, a tenant farmer, or a migratory farm worker.

In addition to horticultural factors, historical and political factors also lie behind the passion for land that is reflected in drama and fiction. Land ownership has been a contentious issue for centuries. Beginning with the Tudor monarchs in the sixteenth century, the "Plantation" system parceled out Irish land to Englishmen as a reward for service to the Crown. From the Nationalist perspective, that land was never the British Crown's to give; it belonged to the native Celtic population, which regarded this land as theirs by hereditary right, even as the Planters regarded the land as theirs by law and by conquest. Under British rule the native Irish former owners, or their descendants, often became tenants on the same piece of land that they had once owned, sometimes answerable to an absentee landlord who delegated law enforcement and rent collecting to an on-site middleman. The effort of some of these tenants and their supporters to reclaim lands they believed were unjustly alienated is a strong theme in Irish history. Land is always fraught with symbolic significance. Therefore when the setting is a rural one, and the characters are farmers, their love for the land is the most overpowering force in their lives; to the land all else must be sacrificed.

In the time leading up to the watershed event of Irish history, the Great Famine beginning in 1845, land came to be held in smaller and smaller plots. Partible inheritance, dividing the land among heirs, allowed the sons of the family to marry young and to raise families on portions of the original, larger, family homestead. But this custom had serious consequences. Because the plots of land were so small, only a crop that can be raised in limited space, and on poor land, was feasible. Thus developed the Irish dependence on the potato. Because the potato is nutritious and can serve as the staple of a healthy diet, when the potato flourished, the population grew as well, to an estimated eight million before the Famine. Then when the potato blight hit, the farmers were not properly situated, with their marginal, less fertile plots of land, to switch to another, unblighted crop. The consequence was mass starvation and mass emigration, which, demographers estimate, reduced the population of Ireland by about half. From this demographic disaster, the population of Ireland has never recovered. Modern writers of fiction such as William Trevor and Joseph O'Connor examine the legacy of that Great Famine.

The Famine, and the depleted population thereafter, had further consequences with regard to land ownership. According to historian Paul Bew, "the Irish experience has been of foreign conquest, poverty and oppression. The most obvious and significant feature of social life was the existence of a mainly Protestant landlord class extracting rent from a mainly Catholic peasantry."[9] Several other factors aggravated the landlord-tenant relationship: the practice of rack-renting, or charging excessive rent; eviction or the threat of eviction (the latter of which, historian Kerby Miller says, was "alarmingly frequent" and highly effective),[10] and the inability of the tenant to achieve an ownership stake in land that he nevertheless regarded as his own. This led to political and social unrest and the formation of rural organizations with three basic demands: security of tenure, a fair rent, and the right to sell land.

During the course of the latter half of the nineteenth century, and under pressure from agrarian violence, the British Parliament passed a series of Land Acts, which cumulatively "involved a transfer of the greater part of Ireland from the landlord to the peasant class."[11] The degree of change achieved is illustrated by the difference between an early law and a late one. The Landlord and Tenant Act of 1860 "was based on the view that land is exclusive property of the landlord, and that the tenant's interest is simply that of an individual who has agreed to pay a certain remuneration for the use of the land for a limited period"; accordingly the law tightened up the rules under which landlords could evict tenants for nonpayment of rent.[12] In contrast the Land Law Act of 1881 guaranteed tenants the "three F's," issues that had been long under contention: "a *fair rent*," "*fixity of tenure*," and "*free sale* of his interest in his holding."[13] Finally under the Purchase of Land Act of 1885, the tenants became the sole owners of the land.[14] What happened in the intervening years to loosen the hold of the British landlord class over the land was the formation of agrarian protest movements that, often through violence, asserted the rights of the native Irish over the Anglo-Irish. The issue can be summed up thus: "Was the soil of Ireland for supporting the largest number in a sufficiency of comfort, or was it to provide a very much smaller number with a great and unnecessary abundance?"[15] The answer, to the native Irish, was the former.

Land ownership also has a psychological dimension in Irish literature, in that it stands as a metaphor for male maturity. After the Famine, to prevent recurrence of at least some of the conditions that led to it, the custom of primogeniture began to replace partible inheritance. The eldest son of a family inherited the full parcel of land, but he could not marry until he did inherit. The inheritance factor, coupled with the Irish Catholic Church's strict sexual morality, led to long periods of celibacy until one's parents were dead, because most land passed from owner to owner via inheritance, not sale. On those rare occasions when pieces of land were available for sale, the hunger for that land often became obsession.

If land itself were not enough of a motivator, the social status related to landholding was. The difference between "smallholders," "middling farmers," and "strong farmers" was in the amount of land that they held. The smallholder would raise food mainly for his own family's consumption; the strong farmer was a nineteenth-century version of the modern agribusinessman; and the middling farmer was somewhere in between.[16] The amount of land a farmer owned was not only a status symbol; it was the means by which he moved beyond mere subsistence. In addition the kind of crops that a farmer could raise profitably, or his ability to devote some land to easy and profitable pasturage, was contingent upon the amount of land the farmer owned.[17] So when a character in twentieth- or twenty-first-century fiction or drama is obsessed with land; when he clings to life on the land even when it is no longer possible to make a living from it; or when he lusts over land that is not his own, it is this historical memory that motivates him. The result can be humorous, as in Patrick Boyle's "Pastorale"; exploitive, as in William Trevor's "Kathleen's Field"; or tragic, as in Edna O'Brien's *Wild Decembers*.

"Wisdom of serene old age"?: Patrick Boyle's "Pastorale"

Éamon de Valera's view of rural Ireland as role model for the nation was so idealistic as to be an object of satire and was readily recognizable as such to an Irish audience. Patrick Boyle's (1905–1982) short story "Pastorale" was published in 1972, twenty-nine years after the St. Patrick's Day radio address in which de Valera extolled the virtues of the people he thought of as the backbone of the nation. In Boyle's story, however, the rural farm family, the Bennetts, are depicted as practitioners of a good few of the seven deadly sins. In that peculiar combination of comedy and tragedy common in Irish writing, the story, a comedy, takes place during the final hours of the family's patriarch, "Old James" Bennett. The term *pastoral* is derived from the Latin *pastor,* shepherd; a pastorale in music is "an instrumental or vocal composition having a pastoral theme"; and a literary pastoral idealizes the supposed "innocence and serenity of the simple life" in the countryside (*Merriam-Webster Unabridged Dictionary*). The Bennetts' lives, however, lack either serenity or charm; far from being exemplars of the "right living" desired by de Valera, they are as greedy, vengeful, and corrupt as the stereotypical denizens of the wicked city.

Love of land is the root of all evil. Old James is the longtime owner of a parcel of land adjacent to that of another family, the Gormleys. For years he has been buying up surrounding lands to such an extent that the Bennetts "had gathered together a few hundred acres of the best land hereabouts," an achievement that makes them "big farmers itself," "wealthy ranchers."[18] Two of his sons, Martin and John, remain on the land to assist "the Boss-man," as they call their father, and their mother, Susie; another son, Francie, has emigrated. True to the reputation of elderly property owners, Old James has not relinquished control of his property to one or both of his sons, nor has he made a will, and now he is old and ill. If James were to die intestate, Francie, the emigrant, would be able to come back and claim a share of the land that he has not farmed for all these years. Since neither of the resident Bennett brothers wants to diminish his own holdings for the return of this prodigal son, one of them, Martin, busies himself at his father's bedside with pen and paper, trying to get his "old fellow" to sign the will (350).

A further complication is Old James's rivalry with his immediate neighbor, Peter Gormley, over a piece of land, "the source of contention and doggery" (341), which James wants to buy and Peter refuses to sell. This land is particularly valuable to James in that it carries with it the right for the Bennetts to water their animals in the river. Not only does Gormley continually refuse James's purchase offers, he is extending a "haggard," a structure on the land, "an old timber shed . . . used for storing" (341), from which Gormley conducts second-hand farm-equipment garage sales as a sideline. This exercise in property rights flaunts Gormley's intention to keep the land and inflames James's lust to buy it, even from his deathbed.

To complicate matters even further, rumor has it that three members of the younger generation of these two families, Francie Bennett, Helen Gormley, and Robert Gormley, have emigrated under suspicious circumstances: Francie and Helen to escape the consequences of a nonmarital sexual relationship, and

Robert, a "spoiled priest" (347), after having been ejected from the seminary due to Helen's behavior. Francie's bad reputation in the community provides his brothers with yet another motive, or at least excuse, for attempting to cut him out of his inheritance.

As if this were not enough petty meanness for one story, a further complication involves the viewpoint character. This unnamed man, a neighbor and friend of the family, is the filter through whom the doings of all the other characters are perceived, and he is as mean and petty as any Bennett or Gormley. Despite the fact that "there's been a chair for [him] at their kitchen fire every night for a score or more years" (338), the narrator interprets every action of the family with scorn and contempt. The Bennetts' acquisition of land makes them, in his eyes, "notorious bloody land-grabbers. They've gobbled up every small holding in the townland that went on the market for years past. Even where it was a forced sale" (338). To the narrator the family's progress from "small farmers like the rest of us" to "wealthy ranchers" is a consequence not of wise investments and hard work but of "sweat and skullduggery" (343). His description of "the rest of us" as small farmers is key to his resentment: he has not been as successful as the Bennetts. But the jaundiced eye with which he sees the events he narrates makes him a biased storyteller. It may be true, as he says, that the extended Bennett family was also "a queer broody class of connection" (344) with enough idiosyncrasies for the population of Dublin, much less this little farm village, but because the narrator has never a kind word to say about anyone, he himself is suspect.

To top it off, the Bennetts are Catholics. Old James's spiritual task is to attempt to die well, in what Catholics call the state of grace. To that end the last thing that his sons should be doing is pestering him about his worldly possessions. According to Catholic tradition, the priest comes to give James the last rites and hear his confession. But Father Bourke's evaluation of the situation is naive in the extreme: he believes that James has, as the church prescribes, confessed his sins and set right his spiritual accounts, forgiving his neighbors the Gormleys as he hopes himself to be forgiven for his own "trespasses" (346). The biblical term for sin, quoted from the Lord's Prayer, conveying as it does the additional, and quite temporal, connotation of encroaching on another's land, provides the perfect ironic touch. Father Bourke consoles the equally stereotyped Susie that he "never saw a man better prepared for death" (346), but the surprise ending to the story shows that Old James's idea of preparation for death is not what the priest intended.

"The Ireland that we dreamed of would be the home of a people who valued material wealth only as the basis for right living, of a people who, satisfied with frugal comfort, devoted their leisure to the things of the spirit." De Valera's dream of "frugal comfort," rural style, becomes the nightmare of greed and vengeance that is the life of the Bennett family. Not even true Irishmen, much less true Christians, they covet their neighbors' goods, lust after their neighbors' daughter, speak ill of their neighbors, spread scandal far and wide, rage against the success of others, and even, in the rumored case of Francie, consume alcohol gluttonously. And yet, because it is satire, it is funny. Boyle skewers the idea of rural Ireland as bedrock of spiritual values, showing its residents to be as mean and nasty as people anywhere. Satire requires that one knows the object satirized; and so, with de Valera's radio address in the background, it is possible to see Boyle's story not just as a comic variation on the landholding theme but also as clever political satire.

"Laughter of happy maidens"? William Trevor's "Kathleen's Field"

The darker side of a land transaction in rural Ireland is the subject of a story by William Trevor (b. 1928), of a farmer who, in 1948, wants to buy an additional piece of land but cannot get financing for the purchase. Like many Irish families before and after them, the Hagertys have produced people for export: of the ten children, "seven . . . had emigrated, four to Canada and America, and three others to England."[19] Remaining behind on the land are the son and heir, Con; Biddy, who "wasn't herself" (1246) and will never be independent; and sixteen-year-old Kathleen, just on the verge of making a life choice similar to that of her older siblings. The story of Kathleen's relationship to the field is one of destruction and exploitation; used by her parents as collateral to buy a piece of land, she becomes collateral damage.

The economic situation of the Hagerty family is precarious. Hagerty and Con are cultivating the farm on which Hagerty had himself been "barefoot . . . as a child," but the farm is heavily mortgaged, and Hagerty has an "overdraft . . . with the bank" (1245–46). Now, due to the death of a neighbor, he has the opportunity to buy from the widow a choice piece of land adjacent to his own. This land is desirable because the owner "had spent his lifetime carting the rocks" out of the field, so that for Hagerty "there'd be almost as much profit in that single pasture as there was in all the land he possessed already" (1245). The stakes are high. This field could make the difference between subsistence agriculture and a comfortable old age for him and his wife, a permanent home for the impaired Biddy, and a proper inheritance for Con, enabling him to marry his sweetheart.

But as the story opens, a banker has just turned Hagerty down for a loan due to the fact that there is "a fair bit owing" on Hagerty's debts as it is, without the additional expense of a new loan (1245). Then as now, banks are reluctant to lend money to anyone but those who do not need it, and Hagerty knows that he has little hope of raising more money from a bank at which he has been overdrawn for seventeen years. What are his options? The general economic situation is poor; he has failed to get a good price for his cattle; his emigrant children send home money, but not enough. Clearly he must arrange some creative financing.

He identifies a negotiable asset: his daughter Kathleen. Too young to have carried out plans of her own but old enough to earn money, still a child devoted to her parents but old enough to be desirable, Kathleen is sold into indentured servitude at best, sexual slavery at worst, to the moneylender Shaughnessy, the scorned "gombeen man," or usurer, and his wife. In Ireland in 1948, options were few for a young girl like Kathleen. She has recently left school but with no particular skills. Therefore work as a domestic is one of her few options, whether she stays in Ireland or emigrates like her siblings. Her sister Mary Florence is just beginning the process of getting Kathleen "fixed up" (1247) with a job in England, but her father moves first. Under the guise of keeping her close enough to home to be able to visit once a week on her day off, Hagerty indentures Kathleen to the Shaughnessys for the (uncertain, given Hagerty's poor credit history) duration of the loan: "Twelve years or maybe fourteen, she said to herself, lying awake in her bedroom; as long as that, or longer" (1260). Until she is thirty years old, Kathleen belongs to the Shaughnessys.

Her attempts on her weekly visits home to appeal to her parents for help are unsuccessful. Her father is convinced that the Shaughnessys are "decent people" (1252) and that his plan for his daughter is a good one. Her mother, who should be a natural ally, is no help. An innocent, Kathleen does not even have the vocabulary to tell her mother what is happening between her and Shaughnessy; she blames her discomfort in the Shaughnessys' house on linguistic misunderstandings and on her own loneliness. But even if she were able to tell her mother of Shaughnessy's sexual predation, her mother would be unsympathetic; Mrs. Hagerty is terrified of becoming one of the dispossessed of the earth, people "whose farms failed on them": "They're walking the roads now, no better than tinkers," she says, referring to the itinerant Irish subculture that occupies the lowest rung in the social ladder (1256). The mother's limitations of mind and spirit are apparent in her mulish insistence on a slogan in the face of her daughter's misery: "A bargain had been struck . . . and a bargain was a bargain" (1261). Her parents call the land "Kathleen's field," but it is clear that Kathleen belongs to the field, not the field to her. She will not even inherit the land she has been sold to finance. Con will.

Trevor's story can be read as a metaphor for the inadequacy of Éamon de Valera's vision of Ireland. By setting the story five years after the famous St. Patrick's Day radio address, Trevor stresses how radically wrong de Valera was. It is clear that, for Trevor, living in the country provides no guarantee of Christian virtue or even baseline human decency. Quite the contrary—the rural peasantry is capable of any degree of venality to continue to maintain a doomed lifestyle. Farming is difficult, the rewards few, and options nonexistent. Social inequality is alive and well; the wives of the well-off abuse and exploit their neighbors' daughters for the sake of their own gratification and status, and that is the least of these young girls' misfortunes. If the farm is a metaphor for the Irish past, to be maintained at all costs, then the story suggests that this way of life should be seriously examined, perhaps jettisoned. An overwhelming majority of the country's youth (seven out of ten, in the Hagerty family) had voted with its feet to leave Ireland behind. The few who stay—Con, representing the one of the ten who has a hope of inheriting something, however valueless; the disabled, represented by Biddy; and poor, exploited Kathleen—are, in Trevor's story, the future of Ireland, mortgaged to a false vision of the past.

"Romping of sturdy children"? Edna O'Brien's *Wild Decembers*

"Fields . . . mean more than fields, more than life and more than death too."[20] To men who wrest a living from it, land is not a mere possession but rather a passion. As literary critic Heather Ingman points out, "Edna O'Brien is a writer more often judged as dealing with private passions than the wider world of politics";[21] but O'Brien's (b. 1936) novel *Wild Decembers* deals with both the private world and the public world. It is a tale of forbidden love between members of warring families, an Irish *Romeo and Juliet,* and a lament for Ireland's obsession with the past at the expense of the future. Two opposing but interrelated symbol systems carry the weight of both themes: one pertaining to land and the other to babies.

The first issue in understanding the novel is placing its events in time. Bugler's tractor is "the first tractor on the mountain" (3), which means that the events of the novel must take place after the invention of the gas-powered tractor in 1892; but since the little town of Cloontha is hardly in the forefront of agricultural innovation, it could be much later. No events in the larger world fix a date of the story's action, reinforcing the point that the main characters, Michael Bugler, Joseph Brennan, and Joseph's sister Breege Brennan, are as detached from the larger world as they are obsessed with their smaller world. While there are no references to the specific historical year, there are references to the cyclical liturgical year of the Roman Catholic Church; the plot moves toward its violent conclusion during Advent, the four weeks preceding Christmas, and comes to a climax during the week between Christmas and New Year's Day. As the church celebrates forgiveness for sins and hopeful anticipation of the birth of a child, these Christians move toward vengeance, madness, and death.

While the temporal setting of the novel is ambiguous, it is clear that, writing in the 1990s, O'Brien could assume that a good portion of her reading audience would have seen the film *The Quiet Man.*[22] The film's plot revolves around an Irish character type, a "returning Yank," who, to fulfill the dreams of his late mother, comes back to rural Ireland to settle land he has inherited and undertakes to buy more. The cinematography stresses the pastoral beauty of the Irish countryside; the film represents a vision much like de Valera's, of the rural homestead as image of innocence, to which the hero, Sean Thornton, can escape from the wickedness of his life in the States. Immediately upon his return to Ireland, Thornton meets Mary Kate Danaher, her long red hair and shockingly blue eyes making her the epitome of Irish womanhood. Naturally he falls in love with her, and she with him; but his rivalry with her brother complicates the situation. An all-purpose busybody named Micheleen inserts himself into matters that are none of his business, but innocently; a leprechaun of a man, he smiles benignly upon the lovers. The clergy, always a fixture of rural Ireland, are officious, but comically so and basically harmless. Despite their wee faults, the Irish people in *The Quiet Man* are basically good; all ends happily, with tensions resolved and hope for the future.

Wild Decembers contains many of the same plot elements as *The Quiet Man:* Bugler the returnee, this time from Australia rather than the United States; Breege the country colleen; Joseph the rivalrous brother. But if, while reading the beginning of the novel, the reader is lulled by these parallels to the film into expectations of comedy, those expectations will be foiled. Sweet Micheleen is paralleled in the novel by the Crock, a distortion of all that is human; clergymen have minor, but negative roles; eccentricity is replaced by madness; the legal system is mired in Dickensian absurdities; the psychiatric care system is an instrument of social control, not healing. And the center of all this is the land, repository of the passions of past generations. On such a foundation, no future can be built; because of the obsession of landholders, the land becomes an inhospitable home to the sturdy children sanguinely depicted in de Valera's address. In the conflict between the past and the present, the past wins.

The prologue sounds the key themes of the novel. The land holds the remains of the past, "relics of battles of the long ago . . . the bone babes and the bone mothers, the fathers too" (1). The land preserves history older than the ancient Celts, "the sons of Oisin, the sons of Conn and Connor," extending back to the biblical past, "the sons of Abraham, the sons of Seth, the sons of Ruth, the sons of Delilah, the warring sons of warring sons" (2). Buried deep within the land is the ancestral memory of the first planting of potatoes, prelude to the Great Famine. Land that has been the scene of so much suffering is paradoxically coveted all the more; those who live on the land are "locked in a tribal hunger that bubbles in the blood and hides out on the mountain, an old carcass waiting to rise again, waiting to roar again, to pit neighbor against neighbor and dog against dog in the crazed and phantom lust for a lip of land" (2). Nothing good can come of this. The few contrasting images of life and fecundity in the passage, the "great whooshing belly of the lake" and the "quickening" of the soil in the spring, cannot compete with the "enemy" that is "always there and these people know it" (1): the passions aroused by possession, by the desire to say, "This is mine," with its inevitable corollary, "This is not yours." In the vocabulary of land ownership, the concept of "mine" is paramount and the concept of "enough" is nonexistent. Owning some land inevitably results in a hunger for more.

Hence the boundary issues that plague the relationship between Joseph Brennan and Michael Bugler. At first they behave like good neighbors, but their lust for the land itself, for the goods it can produce, and for the status that ownership of it provides leads to intense rivalry. The earliest bone of contention between them is the noise and general invasiveness of Bugler's tractor. The large machine, with its implications of nontraditional farming methods as well as the sort of brash assertiveness often associated with returnees, aligns Bugler with the future and Brennan with the past. The house Bugler is building for himself and Rosemary, his fiancée, is intended as a base for his new family; their future children will enhance his status in the community, and the road he cuts to the house makes that plan all the more emphatic. For Brennan family equals him and his sister, a relationship that pays tribute to their dead parents but will produce no children. Brennan's possession of the land means obsession with the past.

History, to Brennan, does not merely influence but determines the present. To him the way in which land was acquired in the past determines the morality of land ownership for all time. This is illustrated in Brennan and Bugler's argument about the mountain that both claim to own. As their conflict escalates, Brennan uses history as a weapon. He claims that Bugler's half of the mountain is his "because [his] people worked for the landlords. They were bailiffs. They were hated. That's why most of them emigrated" (91). Brennan clearly believes that he is the more legitimate landholder of the two of them because of Bugler's ancestors' alliance with the Anglo-Irish landlord class. There seems to be in Brennan's mind no morally acceptable method for acquiring land other than inheritance, and even heirs must inherit from people on the right side of history. To him Bugler's modus operandi, taking over a previously unoccupied farm (left to Bugler by an uncle) is illicit. That this is not an unusual opinion is indicated by the fact that the attorney Barry agrees with Brennan, calling Bugler a "grabber" (166), as if he were stealing land that had, by dint of the interruption in Bugler's use of it, somehow reverted to Brennan.

When Bugler outbids Brennan on the use of Lady Harkness's land, Brennan is offended, assuming that his past practice of renting gives him a right to the use of the land. To Lady Harkness land is supposed to produce money, as much of it as possible; so she does not feel bound by her traditional rental deal with

Joseph but accepts the higher bidder. From one point of view, neither man has a right to the use of the land; it belongs to Lady Harkness. From another point of view, her British name means that either she or her husband or both are descendants of the Anglo-Irish landholders whom many besides Brennan regard as unjust occupiers. This theme of morally questionable acquisition of land is the point of a set of minor characters, the "saucy sisters" Reena and Rita (11), who accumulate land through purchase; but their method of doing so involves manipulation at best and prostitution at worst. Owning land appears to be a dirty business all around; but what Joseph Brennan fails to see, in his assumption of his own virtue, that he is the one most corrupted by ownership, not Bugler or even the "saucy sisters."

The farmlands over which Brennan and Bugler compete are less desirable for farming than other more fortuitously situated fields; as Brennan tells the story to Breege, their "forebears . . . had been evicted from the arable lands . . . and [were] constantly being told to move on, move on, just like vermin," finally arriving "up the mountain where no one could find them and hence no one could evict them" (8). The people who live in these isolated areas are referred to as "mountainy men," a derogatory term like *hayseed, hillbilly,* or *bumpkin* in American English, with connotations of low social class and intellectual backwardness. Mountainy men are usually described in Irish literature as strange, isolated sorts, typically unmarried as they were "unable to attract any woman to such a lonely place."[23] Brennan hears a judge refer to the "god-forsaken mountain" and to Brennan and his ilk as "bog-trotters" (111); the secretary of the lawyer O'Shaughnessy describes Brennan as a "mountainy man" (162). Even the Crock, no aristocrat himself, describes someone else as a "poor mountainy yokel" (15). Such people occupy a low echelon of Irish society. The Travellers, nomads with no land at all, are considered lower. Travellers in their turn hold the "settled people," with their preoccupation with a single patch of ground, in contempt.

Still, the mountainy man's mountain and the bog-trotter's bog are, to them, "more than fields" (1). Rivalry over the possession of space, even undesirable space, is colloquially known in the United States as a turf war, but here the war is in fact about turf, pieces of sod cut from the soil and used for fuel. In the time before Brennan and Bugler become enemies, Brennen writes to the newcomer explaining the significance of the bogs from which the turf is cut: they are "sacred places and the storehouse of our past. To dig deep into a blanket bog is to cut through time to unearth history. . . . No one cuts turf now, as they say we do not have the summers anymore to allow it to dry. Laziness. Yet in one sense we are preserving our past" (26). To Brennan the bog is not the equivalent of a disreputable trailer park but the repository of history. The irony that the bog, composed of decaying organisms, represents a dead past escapes both him and Bugler. Bugler claims his piece of history by cutting turf. Via the traditional turf fire, with its strong association with rural life and hence with the presumed ideal Irish character, Bugler too hopes to establish, if only to himself, his authenticity; so turf cutting "appealed to him, a new skill to be learned, to be mastered" (123). This does not mean that Bugler intends to abandon his tractor, the symbol of modernity; rather he asserts his right to pick and choose what elements of the Irish past work for him, and turf does.

Shortly after the turf-cutting incident, Brennan has a dream in which he and Bugler are competitors in a hurley match. Hurley, or hurling, is a traditional Irish game. The dream crystallizes the assumptions that underlie Brennen's increasingly hostile attitude toward his neighbor: one of them must lose for the other to win, and whatever Bugler gets is taken away from Brennan. Since there is clearly not enough turf to go around in this land of limited opportunity, the legal system intervenes, albeit incompetently. Pompous correspondence goes back and forth, but the law seems to be on Bugler's side. In a case similar to Brennan and Bugler's, a judge rules that "moving cattle when you shouldn't and where you shouldn't is an offense. . . . The Brehon laws are out, finished. . . . Adjacent lands, even on a godforsaken mountain, are not your own lands" (106). The Brehon laws of the seventh and eighth century regarded lands occupied by a clan as belonging to a clan; occupation, rather than legal title, was key. But that was in the past. The judge's comment suggests that tradition is all very well, but even the most ancient customs have their day. Brennan should learn from this that his case is hopeless; but he cannot control his land hunger.

Brennan's increasing obsession first with the tractor, then with the mountain, and then with the turf culminates in his obsession with the body of his sister. Given the longstanding identification in song and story of Ireland with a woman, Brennan's patriarchal assumption that he owns his sister's virginity much in the same way as he owns the land is at least partially understandable. If, in a metaphorical sense, the woman is the land, is indeed Ireland, then Breege is Ireland, and Ireland's purity rises and falls with hers. Brennan's assumptions on this matter involve traditional cultural commonplaces. The women of Ireland had long been "associated with both national identity and the moral health of the nation."[24] Women were regarded as "the guardians of public morals and sound family life," especially since the 1937 constitution for the Republic of Ireland embodied Éamon de Valera's "utopian vision of comely maidens dancing at the crossroads preparatory to their destiny as devoted mothers living in frugal comfort in cozy rural homesteads."[25] In historical hindsight this idealization of women as symbols of the nation did actual women little good: "Sexuality . . . became bound up with nationality," and "nationalism in Ireland became the language through which sexual control and repression of women were justified."[26] Hence the overwhelming significance of Breege's virginity to her brother is not just a symptom of his own severe psychological disorder but also a national preoccupation.

As an Irish woman, Breege is a symbol of an uncontaminated Ireland. Living the life of a national symbol, however, means that she must play her role in the Irish homestead by keeping house for her brother. Her possible desire for marriage and a family, or even for a more stimulating environment, is not taken into account. Not much has changed since the late nineteenth century, when "the dullness of country life, when juxtaposed with the attractions of the bright city lights and the exotic 'otherness' of life abroad," drove many women to emigrate.[27] So it was in the case of Brennan's fiancée, Catherine, who left Cloontha for "better chances" in London (23). Brennan's extreme aversion to what he sees as Catherine's betrayal of the Irish ideal of womanhood spills over into his relationship with his sister. Presumably he had intended to have children with Catherine; but her rejection of the Irish way of life, and him with it, makes him all the more rigid a caretaker of his sister's virtue.

Women so pure as to measure up to Brennan's ideal will not produce a new Irish generation. "You won't find a child around here," he says at one point (6). While he is not literally correct, his comment calls the reader's attention to a negative set of associations with babies in the novel. In church a baby "calls loudly in the pushchair," and the narrator imagines two possible reactions in the mother, "one exemplifying worldly selfishness and the other willing to sacrifice herself for her young" (214). Despite the fact that it is the third Sunday of Advent, a season devoted to preparations for the birth of the Christ Child, the priest is intolerant of the children's behavior in church: "with infuriated glances he strove to tell these parents to slap their children to chastise them, to take them outside and give them a good shaking, which they deserved" (215). The priest's disapproval of the children's mothers is explicable given the stereotypical images of women expressed in his sermon, as "the great reconcilers, women made in the likeness of Mary, the mother of Jesus, her sister Mary of Cleophas, and Mary Magdalene, the reformed sinner" (214). What of a woman who fails to reconcile warring men? Why is she and not the men responsible for the conflict? What if she is not a virgin like Mary but not like Mary Magdalene either? Can pregnant women and mothers find a place in a church that does not welcome their children?

In an ideal world, by becoming pregnant with the child of her brother's enemy, Breege would become a sign and symbol of reconciliation. For two farming families on adjacent landholdings, a union such as that of Breege and Bugler would be logical, an asset to both families, especially in the next generation. The whole point of primogeniture is to keep landholdings intact and thus as large as possible. There would be great advantage for the future in that, on the combined land, the child of Breege and Bugler could be a strong farmer rather than a middling one. But Brennan cannot see the possibilities for the future; tormented by the fact that the child was conceived with his enemy and out of wedlock, he sees Breege's pregnancy as "Bugler's bastard seed . . . contaminat[ing] her" (86). Without any right to do so, he sees himself as the moral arbiter of Breege's behavior; imagining himself as a priest, he regards her "confession" to him as essential to ridding her of the sin that created the child (86).

Where characters stand on the issue of children is a litmus test of morality in this novel. Other characters in the novel, especially Reena and Rita, develop the theme of nongenerative sex as a symptom of disordered values. The promiscuous Rita "had had her gearbox taken out a few years earlier" so that she can never have children. She regards her sister, who "from time to time broached the matter of love or, worse, a baby," as suffering from a form of madness or at least mental defect, "not the full shilling" (12). Love that should properly be directed toward progeny is misdirected or distorted. Both sisters behave as if Bugler's tractor were itself a child, "tweaking it as they might a baby" (13), and Reena even wants to baptize it. Brennan displaces paternal love onto his beloved racing greyhound; he "snuggled [Violet Hill] to himself as if she were an infant" (50). The Crock's imagination is littered with dead babies; to him "turnips . . . lay like lopped infants' heads" (144). At the house of the "Dutch woman" whom Breege visits apparently in search of an abortifacient or perhaps an aphrodisiac to make her child's father love her, she sees "tiny medicine bottles, the orange nozzles like the teats of babies' bottles. Everywhere there are reminders" (191). Reminders of what? Of the sturdy children envisioned by de Valera, now never to be born? What Cloontha clearly needs is people committed to life and to the future.

A more ambiguous image is the empty crib in Bugler's house. There Breege sees "a child's cot, painted white, and it was like there was a child already in it. He saw me gasp" (194). It is not clear if Bugler ever knows that Breege is pregnant, but to her it seems that this house, and the cradle in it, are intended for Rosemary. She does not know that Rosemary would like to be pregnant, pretends to be, and in fact once was. Bugler's ambivalence about having a child, at least with Rosemary, is evident in the fact that he has taken measures to prevent pregnancy and left her in Australia when she was pregnant; she subsequently miscarried (227). No one in the novel seems to think of his or her world as sustaining new life for the future. Even Breege is tempted to end the pregnancy, as her visit to the Dutch woman's house suggests.

The fact that she continues the pregnancy may be a failure of means rather than a positive choice. Breege's realization that her pregnancy will indeed continue coincides with her loss of speech, as if there are no words to explain what has befallen her. "Silenced and unable to tell her story,"[28] her actions must express her unspeakable, even unthinkable needs until she "regains her strength and her voice."[29] It is the third of the four Sundays of Advent; the reader is reminded that these people are Christians and are supposed to be thinking of atonement and forgiveness of trespasses (250). But they often fail to act on their professed beliefs, as is exemplified by Mrs. Noonan, the sacristan.

Mrs. Noonan admires her parish church's artistic rendering of the universal church's antisexual bias, "the priceless stained-glass windows . . . virgins and martyrs with infants being born not from lower down, but coming out of their chests in clean and undefiled incarnations" (205). This strikes her as a more decorous plan than God's own for the propagation of the species. With these ideas fresh in her mind, she finds Breege "lying in the straw alongside the donkey, the zebra, the infant Jesus, and the Holy Family" (206). Is Breege asking that her child, and by extension she herself, be seen as valuable, like the baby Jesus? Mrs. Noonan, representing Christian orthodoxy, sees her only as a sinner, a "hussy" who had done "something profane . . . in the House of God," against whom the church building must be defended with metal keys and a broom handle (206). Like Joseph Brennan's beliefs, these are not specific to Mrs. Noonan but are shared by the women who regard Breege as "drunk or drugged or out of her mind . . . 'doing it for attention' . . . 'bold' . . . 'flipped'" (207). Like many Irishwomen before and after her, Breege is punished for what others might call normal sexual expression by being incarcerated in one of Ireland's notoriously harsh mental hospitals. Were Jesus's mother, Mary, to have given birth in Cloontha rather than Bethlehem, she might have met the same fate.

Breege's dismal experience during the Advent and Christmas seasons is contrasted to two episodes that express a more positive attitude toward babies. In the hospital she meets a fellow patient, Ger, who recounts a "funny dream" in which he and his (nonexistent) wife are faced with an unexpected choice: "We're in the city and there's a baby on a step, crying, crying its heart out, and my wife says to me, 'Jesus, we're going to have to do something and we're in this terrible fix looking up and down the street for the mother to come and take this baby and no one comes and the baby keeps crying and screaming and my wife says to me, 'We're going to have to take it, you see it's an orphan,' and . . . I don't even have a wife or child . . . I'm not married" (229). Shortly thereafter a bouquet arrives from Brennan to Breege, who accepts it as if she were "holding an infant" (230). Ger's dream plus the bouquet equal O'Brien's prescription for the wider world. Ger, who like Breege is regarded as mad, has grasped the root of Ireland's problem via that most irrational of vehicles, the dream. His dream means not only must Ireland become much, much less like Mrs. Noonan, abandoning sterile righteousness and lovingly accepting its children, but also it must accept what the baby represents: the future. Not to do so is to ally oneself with the bog, the turf, the "bone babes and the bone mothers, the fathers too"—the dead past, with all that has been rotting underground for millennia.

A second episode strikes the same note. On his way to kill Bugler, Brennan comes upon Bugler's mare in the process of foaling. "Though he hated the man he did not hate the animal," so he continues on his way without interfering with the natural process (239). And in fact the mare does give birth successfully, for which Brennan respects her: "She had done it right" (241). Brennan—whose Christian name reminds the reader attuned to Christian imagery that he, like the biblical Joseph, should stand ready to protect the pregnant woman, no matter the origin of her pregnancy—cannot offer his sister the same respect that he can a mare. And so he continues on his mission, killing Bugler and destroying the future for his victim, for his sister, and for himself.

Breege and Bugler had conceived their baby in a cemetery, suggesting that there might be hope even in the face of death. As the novel ends, Breege has not yet given birth; she is in that characteristic gesture of the pregnant woman "holding her belly" (259). She and Rosemary are now in charge of the land-holdings previously maintained by Bugler and Brennan. O'Brien asks important questions, wondering if these women will continue to fight "the old wars," the "insatiate fight in the name of honour and land and kindred and blood. Will their hearts too turn to treason?" (259). Will they, like others before them, become "relics of battles of the long ago"? The epigraph of the novel announces the theme of memory. But in the novel itself, the most destructive character is the one who remembers too much. Are Joseph Brennan's skewed priorities—land over children, the past over the present and future—part and parcel of being male or of being Irish? Can women do better than men have done? If a sequel to the novel were set in an ideal world, Rosemary and Breege might come together because of their mutual love of the baby's father, the baby at least to some extent a replacement for Rosemary's own lost child. Breege's baby would represent the future, in which the lands would be joined in per-petuity and the continuing battle over small bits of inhospitable geography ended. If this utopian view of a world run by women strikes the reader as hope-lessly naive, so might Ireland's future as one land, no longer divided by warring ideologies.

The physical setting, then, situates characters in terms of what the landscape has meant in Irish history and culture. Who can and does own land, how much of it, where that land is, how they came to own it: all this is conveyed by the setting. When a character moves from one setting to another, that motion in space is also fraught with significance. If a northerner goes south, a city dweller to the country, and above all if anyone leaves this small island and crosses the ocean or even the English Channel, major psychological shifts are implied.

In addition to location in space, setting is also temporal, situating the action at a particular moment in time. One way in which Irish writers often incorporate elements of the past into the present is via storytelling, the narration of long-ago events to contemporary characters. And who is more likely to be a tale-teller than a dweller in the rural areas, especially in the west of Ireland, where the modern world coexists, often uncomfortably, with ancient tradition?

Chapter 2

Just Tell Them the Story

Tradition Bearing

At Blarney Castle in County Cork, tourists queue up to kiss the Blarney Stone; legend has it that doing so will confer the "gift of gab," a facility for fluent speech. As novelist Maeve Binchy points out, the Irish are generally thought to be, and think of themselves as, loquacious people, and verbal ability is a highly valued trait.[1] In Irish fiction and drama, the storytelling episode is a point of connection between speech and writing. A smaller narrative woven into the larger narrative, a story-within-a-story, requires close attention to determine the connections between the two.

Before considering the importance of storytelling in Irish history and culture, it is necessary to look at the storytelling episode from a literary point of view. When the telling of a short tale is included as part of a longer tale, the narrator of the short tale might not be the primary narrator of the long tale. Thus the storytelling episode can involve a shift in narrative viewpoint and a repositioning of the main narrator with respect to the storyteller. When a character other than the main narrator tells a self-contained story that is incorporated into the main narrative, the main narrator steps out of that role to join the listening audience.

This technically complex process adds another dimension to the main narrative. Changing narrators means introducing a different point of view. Once the main narrator becomes a listener, he or she must react to the smaller tale. Listeners play an important role; without them the storytelling situation could not realistically be rendered. Each one of them, including and often especially the narrator, must respond in some way to the story being told. Key questions can be asked about the members of the audience. Why these people? Why do they need to hear this particular story? In what way are they, or should they be, changed by the story? The response of the fictional members of the audience to the story is one of the elements connecting it to the larger narrative.

In addition to adding another layer of meaning, thus rendering the story more complex, storytelling also functions as a highly specialized form of dialogue. Dialogue in drama is all there is. Dialogue in fiction is usually interspersed with narrative and description as both a mode of developing the character of the speaker and an indicator of the nature of the relationship between speaker and listener. As with other kinds of dialogue, what is said or not said depends on who is listening and subtly alters the relationship between speaker and listener. The speaker's motives are always relevant; characters have reasons for saying what they say to particular listeners or not saying what they do not say.

Then there is the issue of truth and falsity. Stories can be true, not true, or partially true. These categories are not, however, absolute; they blend and blur around the edges. Everything said is filtered through the perceptions of a particular speaker, and the speaker is influenced by who is listening. Where the truth lies is often unclear to the listener, in that he or she was not present at the events being narrated (the presence of the listener at the events narrated in the story would render the story redundant). Such considerations affect the meaning of storytelling in fiction and drama.

Irish storytelling in particular, like much else about contemporary Irish culture, involves complex interrelationships between past and present. According to folklorist Clodagh Brennan Harvey, the custom of storytelling grew in Ireland, especially in the rural areas, in response to long winter nights and bad winter weather. Before radio and television encouraged people to stay home in the evening, nighttime entertainment revolved around "the custom of nightly visiting."[2] This provided an audience for the community's storytellers. More than an entertainer, the storyteller or, to use the formal title, *seanchaí* (Anglicized to such forms as *seanachie* or *shanachie*) was the preserver and transmitter of folk wisdom. A primary function of the shanachie was as a "tradition-bearer" linking the present to the past.[3]

The shanachie's tales were, by definition, old. By story type Harvey classifies them as mythological (stories of Ireland's legendary heroes); folkloric (tales of the supernatural); macrohistorical (narratives of Irish history); or microhistorical (community or family history, sometimes with connections to the bigger historical picture). The tales can also be classified by length: the stories of the gods and heroes of the Celtic past tended to be long, while folk tales, family sagas, or local history tales tended to be short. Custom dictated that only men could tell the long mythic tales, but either men or women could narrate the short tales.[4] When the storyteller is incorporated into a larger work of fiction or drama, only short tales can be used, and so the reader finds fictional storytellers of both genders.

The older the tale, the greater its claim to authenticity. The authority of the shanachie similarly increases with age as it places him in closer connection to the events narrated. This latter qualification—the age of the storyteller— threatens the tradition. A performance art that relies on human memory, traditional Irish storytelling depends for its survival not only on the continued respect for the tradition, which provides an audience, but on the survival of the actual storytellers. In the first few decades of the twentieth century, storytelling seemed to be in danger of dying out. In 1935, in an attempt to capture the tradition while its practitioners were still alive, the Irish Folklore Commission was formed, its task to locate, record, and preserve this piece of traditional culture. Harvey describes how the commission members went about their task and how their efforts shed light on the nature of oral tradition itself.

The first step for the Folklore Commission collectors was to identify storytellers. Collectors were led to storytellers by other members of the community and recorded the tale-telling sessions. Recording and preserving, however, influenced the development of the tradition. As every college professor knows, recording a lecture changes the behavior of both the professor and the students, so that what is recorded is not the class as it would have been had there been no recording or if the recording was done without the knowledge of either speaker or audience. So it must have been for the storytellers and their listeners. Another factor is that the collectors' involvement privileged not only specific tellers but also specific versions of their tales, that is, the ones recorded. The honor of having been collected by the Folklore Commission conferred official status, further enhancing both the storytellers' reputations in the community and their own "self-concept of storyteller."[5] The very respect accorded to the collected storytellers may have discouraged the development of new storytellers, ironically accelerating the very process the commission hoped to arrest. In addition the recorded version seemed to be the only official version, whereas in the natural course of events it would be only one of a varying series, versions of the same tale told by the same storyteller but evolving and subtly altering with each retelling.

More significant for the later understanding of the Irish storytelling tradition was the Folklore Commission's decision that collectors would seek out tellers and tales only in the rural parts of Ireland. It would seem logical that the tradition would survive longest in those parts of the country least affected by the technological developments that were threatening its survival elsewhere, and this would justify the rural bias of the commission's activities. But seeking out rural storytellers exclusively had other, perhaps unintended effects. According to historian Richard White, the commission's procedures singled out "rural people [as] the designated keepers of the national memory," defining them and them only as the "repository of true Irishness."[6] Possibly inadvertently the folklore collection process suggested that Dubliners, for example, were somehow less Irish than their country cousins and Dubliners' traditions less worthy of preservation. The Folklore Commission's role was to find and preserve such tales as would be consistent with the then-current belief that the best and truest Ireland could be located in a simple, primitive, peasant culture. The storyteller's function was to preserve that lost paradise.

In Irish life the storyteller's position was one of prestige, power, and authority.[7] In literature the storyteller character stakes a claim to the authority inherent in the role in some fashion, whether it be as an eyewitness to the events being described or as having heard the story from another, older, equally or more authentic storyteller. The listeners may or may not accept the storyteller's authority and may or may not even be content to allow the storytelling to proceed. Claiming the role of storyteller is a power move; the storyteller asserts authority via the tale, presenting his or her experience of the past as more important, more valid, especially more authentically Irish than what the listener characters are experiencing in the present. Sometimes the audience may include a skeptic, who may undercut the authority of teller or tale; this adds a further dimension of ambiguity, as the other members of the audience (and the reader) are invited to take sides with one or the other. Sometimes an interrupter will, as interrupters do in life, make a countering power move to steal the attention of the audience and direct it toward him- or herself. Either of these will disrupt the process of tradition-bearing.

The story has an additional function in developing the character of the storyteller. Especially when the story focuses on episodes of the family history in which the storyteller was also a participant, storytelling is fraught with all the traits of human memory and motivation that make personal narrative unreliable. All stories are told by an individual, so that a given story is "X's story" and no one else's; what X remembers is unique to X, as is what X adds to or subtracts from the story. The story, then, is more reliable as a guide to the character of its teller than it is to the events it purports to recount.

This is a characteristic not just of fictional storytellers but also of oral narratives in general, according to Richard White. Reflecting on the past of his mother's Irish family, he notes how unreliable human memory is as a guide to actual events. While a historian "values most what is least altered," a storyteller "wants to rework not just the story but the very facts themselves."[8] To the professional historian, memories are notoriously fallible. The storytelling medium can itself fail; once a tale is no longer told, memory of the happenings it narrates fades along with it. Forgetting a tale and consciously or unconsciously suppressing it are both principles of selectivity.[9] Unlike the stories told by recognized storytellers and collected by professional folklorists, which are frozen in time at the point of collection, personal stories told informally by unofficial storytellers based on their own memories are seldom recorded; these latter tales continue to develop within the oral traditions from which they emerge. Stories are conflated with other stories; they are subtly altered with each retelling (often depending upon who is listening); details are added, subtracted, emphasized, deemphasized; and tales are told so vividly that the teller as well as the listener can be convinced that things happened as described, whether they did or not.

Another angle from which to look at storytelling in fiction is to consider stories that are not told at all but should be or stories that are told in such a way as to suppress something important. "Whatever you say, say nothing": the paradoxical secretiveness of a loquacious people to which the Ulster proverb refers is often explained by the need of a people long subjected to the rule of others to maintain areas of privacy, while at the same time conciliating the powerful by appearing to be friendly and communicative. In literature "saying nothing" takes the form of telling stories with significant omissions or suppressing stories that cry out to be told. In such cases the motives of the character who is withholding the story or telling the story but withholding something crucial must be examined. Sometimes a story is based on a historical event about which the reader may know, or can discover, more than the listening character does. When the story is about an aspect of the Irish past recoverable in some other way than the oral tale, the reader is invited to learn about it, form his or her own judgment, and analyze the interaction between storyteller and listener on the basis of that judgment. Has the storyteller altered the story in honest error? In an attempt to deceive or manipulate the listener? As a consequence of ignorance or other kinds of limitation? Once the conventions surrounding the storytelling episode in fiction are understood, the episode will be seen to enrich the larger work by providing another layer of meaning.

Saying Nothing: John Millington Synge's "An Autumn Night in the Hills"

To illustrate how the conventions of Irish storytelling work in a particular story, consider John Millington Synge's (1871–1909) "An Autumn Night in the Hills." The setting is an isolated cottage in the Wicklow Mountains, an area not far from Dublin but, in 1903 when the story was published, rural. It is a September afternoon, and the weather is fine after a rainstorm of the previous night. The first-person narrator of the main story is, as is evident by his thought patterns and speech, an educated and sophisticated man, presumably a city-dweller. He is in the Wicklow area to search for a wounded hunting dog; he finds the dog, now recovered, at a cottage. The residents at home at the time are an old woman and a younger one. A "sudden shower" typical of the Irish climate isolates him in the cottage with the two women, where it emerges in casual conversation that no men are around to keep the narrator company because they have all gone to Aughrim, a town in west central Ireland, to bring home the body of a townswoman, Mary Kinsella, for burial.

In response to the narrator's questioning, the old woman describes the deceased as "a fine young woman with two children" who "a year and a half ago . . . went wrong in her head, and they had to send her away. And then up there in the Richmond asylum maybe they thought the sooner they were shut of her the better, for she died two days ago this morning, and now they're bringing her up to have a wake."[10] The reader easily imagines questions that need to be answered. How did it come to pass that so fine a young woman went "wrong in her head"? And what might wrong in the head mean? Who sent her away? What became of the children? Who wanted to be shut of her—the same people who put her in the asylum in the first place or the people in the Richmond asylum? Above all, who or what killed Mary Kinsella? The reader wonders at the narrator's failure to ask the obvious questions. Is he indifferent? Emotionally detached? Respectful of the villagers' privacy with regard to the sad fate of one of their own? In any case Mary Kinsella's story needs to be told.

That, however, does not happen. Having revealed the bare outlines of Mary's story, the old woman drops the subject, and two other tales are told, one by the old woman and one by the young woman. The presence of two storytellers raises the issue of their relationship to each other: competitive, cooperative, or complementary. The girl begins to tell the story of how the dog came to be wounded and rescued but is interrupted by the old woman, her mother. The old woman's tale, a bit of local folklore, is of two encounters with a lake-dwelling spirit. In the first encounter, a fisherman is terrified by the spirit and flees. In the second encounter, a man who has swum in every lake in Ireland wants to swim in the lake in which the spirit lives. The old woman's brother warns him off, but he is determined. Upon the advice of the brother, the swimmer sends his dog into the lake to test the spirit's power; the lake-dwelling spirit destroys the dog, and nothing of the animal remains but "the inside out of him" floating to the top of the haunted lake.[11]

Over a cup of tea, the younger woman resumes her tale, a newer and more realistic narrative that seems destined to become a part of local history. Her tale recounts how the hunting dog being sought by the narrator had been wounded, yet recovered. The hunters thought he might well have been killed, and sent out "two lads . . . with a sack to carry him on if he was alive and a spade to bury him if he was dead" (87). The dog, though injured, jumped on to the sack, as if to opt for survival; he is brought to the cottage and nursed back to health, in the process developing great loyalty to the young woman. Supplementing the young woman's story, the old woman adds a detail to it: when a letter from a gentleman came about the dog, Mike, one of the men (probably the young woman's brother), tells her that the letter contains an inscription for the dog's tombstone. The young girl, apparently illiterate, believes this and has a psychological reaction: she "went down quite simple" until she discovered that she had been "humbugged" about the dog (89).

On the surface, neither of these stories has anything to do with Mary Kinsella. At the end of the story, the narrator sees, through a heavy rain, through a fog that at once distorts his vision and renders the atmosphere grim, "the shadow of a coffin . . . with the body of Mary Kinsella" (90). But he never hears her story. Why is this?

There are at least three possibilities. When the old woman first begins to talk about Mary, the narrator "had been examining a wound in the dog's side near the end of his lung" (85). This body language suggests that the narrator is preoccupied with the dog and indifferent to the story about Mary. The old woman, responding to what she perceives as the lack of an interested audience for Mary's story, stops; then both she and the younger woman respond to the narrator's apparent exclusive interest in the dog by telling two dog stories. Thus, perhaps without intending to do so, the narrator loses his chance to hear what must surely be a more significant story than the ones he does hear: the story of a young woman lost to madness.

Another possibility is that the old woman realizes that, having said what she has said about Mary Kinsella, she has already said too much in a situation in which she should have said nothing; the townspeople's privacy, and that of Mary, would be violated by revealing any more of her story. So the old woman seizes the opportunity presented by the narrator's momentary lapse of attention, which coincides with the younger woman's return to the room, to end the story. After all, if Mary's awful fate—sent away (by whom?) to an asylum in Richmond to die alone—had been any responsibility of the townspeople, it would be best to say nothing.

Yet a third possibility is that Mary's story has indeed been told, but in a symbolic way, via the two dog stories. The two storytellers' vocabulary with which to describe abnormal psychological states is unsophisticated. The old woman describes Mary as "wrong in her head"; the young woman describes herself as grieving for the dog to the extent that she "went down quite simple." It is clear that any understanding of Mary's mental disorder will have to come through interpretation of the stories' symbolism; at the same time, the tale-tellers can both deny that they are speaking of Mary at all, thus preserving Mary's privacy and possibly the community's complicity in her fate. The common element in both stories is a dog. In the first one, the tale of the supernatural related by the old woman, powers stronger than the dog doom him. The old woman's brother regards the dog as expendable compared to the swimmer and so recommends testing the haunted waters with the dog. This dog's fate mirrors Mary's. The dog's situation is hopeless, as was Mary's: sent away by people who wanted to be rid of her, she was no match for their overwhelming power.

The young woman's story, in contrast, is more hopeful; in her tale the dog seems to represent herself, not Mary, and the possibility of life and love. The dog's symbolic resurrection from the dead expresses the woman's hope that she can survive, though Mary did not; the dog's love for her is similarly a sign of hope. But her identification with the dog is so strong—when she thinks it is dead, she is deranged with grief—that it suggests the opposite fear that, without the hope that the dog represents, the young woman herself might meet Mary's fate.

The two dog stories, taken together and factoring in the untold story of Mary Kinsella, carry a message all the stronger for being impossible to articulate in other than symbolic terms: there is something about rural life that drives young women mad. Without an authoritative version of Mary's story, the reader of Synge's tale is invited to re-create it, to consider what might have driven "a fine young woman" with two children to madness and death and to evaluate whether the young woman storyteller runs the same risk. But the narrator clearly misses an opportunity by not responding in such a way as to encourage the telling of Mary's story and by not understanding the stories that are told in its place.

"A Dark and Stormy Night": Conor McPherson, *The Weir*

In Lisa Carey's 1998 novel *The Mermaids Singing*, two characters are discussing a funeral, and one, Clíona, an Irish-born character, explains to Gráinne, her American-born granddaughter, that the Irish practice two religions: "We Irish are devout Catholics, but we're fanatic pagans as well."[12] With the coming of the Christian missionaries in the fourth and fifth centuries, pagan beliefs and practices were gradually absorbed into the new faith.[13] But even in the twentieth century, when Catholicism was recognized in the constitution of the Irish Republic, vestiges of the old faith remained, especially in the rural countryside. Old beliefs survived even in the face of modern rationalism. Carey's Clíona might also have said, "We Irish are devout Catholics, fanatic pagans, and secular rationalists as well.'" The tension between these incompatible belief systems is in the background of the storytelling episodes in Conor McPherson's play *The Weir*.

McPherson (b. 1971) "began his theatrical career by scripting monologues,"[14] and this play is essentially a set of stories in the form of monologues, connected by the "funny banter" of the five men in the pub.[15] McPherson's childhood visits to the rural Irish countryside included storytelling episodes. In his author's note prefacing the play, he tells the story of his "visits to Leitrim to see my granddad. He lived on his own on a country road in a small house beside the Shannon. I remember him telling me once that it was very important to have the radio on because it gave him the illusion of company. We'd have a drink and sit by the fire. And he'd tell me stories. When you're lying in bed in the pitch black silence of the Irish countryside it's easy for the imagination to run riot."[16] McPherson's grandfather, living in what many think of as the authentic Irish manner (in a cottage near a body of water down a lonely country road in a sparsely populated area in the rural northwest), is in touch with the ancient storytelling tradition and bears it to his grandson. The pagan beliefs that antedated Christianity never entirely died out in the Irish countryside, and in writing *The Weir*, McPherson becomes himself a tradition-bearer, a link between the ancient tales and the modern theatergoer.

The ancient beliefs reflected, albeit skeptically, in the play involve not the myths of gods and heroes but those of the fairy faith, a folkloric tradition featuring a "community of spirits or supernatural beings who are living beside human beings but are normally concealed from them."[17] Their territory includes the hills, mounds, and forts, the fairy paths along which they traveled, and other sacred spaces, especially "springs and streams."[18] These beings of the other world (the leprechaun being the most familiar outside of Ireland) are not necessarily friendly to humans—quite the contrary. The fairy otherworld can be a frightening place, and tales of human encounters with it are often tales of terror.

The fairy faith is not a codified religion with a set of rules or a theology or a hierarchy but rather a set of beliefs captured in an oral tradition. Were it not for the activities of folklore collectors, these traditions would have been lost. A key figure in the history of Irish folklore collecting is Lady Augusta Gregory (1852–1932). A member of the Protestant Anglo-Irish aristocracy by birth, Augusta Persse married Sir William Gregory in 1880 and thus became the mistress of Coole Park in County Galway, one of the so-called Big Houses of the Protestant Ascendancy. Unlike many of her social peers and coreligionists, however, Gregory was a Nationalist, and she played many roles in encouraging her fellow Irish to think of themselves as a nation apart from the British Empire. Especially after Sir William's death in 1892, she became the center of the movement that would come to be known as the Irish Literary Revival.

Gregory's role with respect to other like-minded writers such as John Millington Synge and especially William Butler Yeats (1865–1929) was multifaceted. She made Coole Park into a writers' colony; she critiqued, edited, reviewed, and cowrote; and she cofounded, raised money for, and publicized the Irish National Theater and the Abbey Theater. By modern standards she was slow to recognize her own creativity in her commitment to supporting the men in her life, not just her husband and son but most of the greatest writers of her time (again, especially Yeats). The extent of her collaboration has been recognized lately in that in more recent editions of some of Yeats's works, her name appears as coauthor.

Of Gregory's activities, the one most relevant to the modern audience's appreciation of *The Weir* is her folklore collecting. One of the key issues for the writers of this cultural revival was the search for a set of traditions in the Irish past that were not influenced by England. The storytelling of the Irish peasantry filled this need in many ways. For one thing, in that it was a small-group tradition shared among members of a local community, it did not have to meet any standards but Irish ones, as opposed to written works that would need to be vetted by British publishers. Second, because storytelling was connected with the rural peasantry and with the past, it met the criteria of authenticity. Third, because many of the storytellers were Irish-speaking, they could not be accused of pandering to the literary tastes of the British. Thus the storytellers were in effect able to fly under the literary radar, which was the good news; but the bad news was that, if not collected, the tales would die when the tellers did.

Gregory was the right person at the right time to collect these stories. She was born in and lived her adult life in the west, in County Galway, in close proximity to the Irish-speaking part of the country, the Gaeltacht; she was willing and able to learn Irish; and she had an excellent relationship with the peasantry in the area surrounding Coole Park. One of the results of this folklore project is her collection *Visions and Beliefs in the West of Ireland* (1920). Still in print, *Visions* divides the stories collected by Gregory into a variety of tale types according to the particular belief they record. Four of her twenty-seven chapters are relevant for understanding McPherson's play: "Seers and Healers," "In the Way," "Banshees and Warnings," and "The Unquiet Dead." Five tales are told in the play; four are of experiences of the supernatural, and one is not. The four supernatural stories form the point of connection between Gregory's folklore and McPherson's play, while the fifth takes a contrasting path. In each of the four supernatural tales, the fairy faith, Christianity, and secular rationalism interact in a way that simultaneously affirms and denies the old-time fairy faith.

The setting of McPherson's play is ideal for the storytelling situation. The pub is located in an isolated rural area, northwest Leitrim or Sligo; the high summer season, when the tourists, lumped together by the pub-goers under the label "Germans," have not yet arrived, and the loneliness of the area is stressed as the characters arrive "at staggered intervals, slightly blown and bedraggled."[19] In this pub Brendan has acquired modern communication devices, but "the fact that he has not turned on the television or the radio suggests a continued preference for storytelling"[20] over passive consumption of electronic media. All this sets the stage for the storytelling sequences in the play.

McPherson takes the risk of using the "standard Gothic equipment" by setting his play on a literal "dark and stormy night."[21] Similarly conventional is the arrival of "a stranger . . . someone whose very presence will change the course of the men's habitual conversation."[22] This is Valerie, who has moved to the town from Dublin. In the process of introducing her to the customs and culture of the area, four of the five characters, all but Brendan the pub owner, tell "half-disbelieved folk-stories" with the newcomer as audience.[23]

If the west of Ireland functions as metaphor for the past, Dublin, the Republic's most sophisticated city, home to major centers of learning, government, the arts, and entertainment, represents the modern world. It becomes clear that Valerie has traveled westward not to get in touch with the past, as might be expected, but to come to terms with an experience that cannot be explained rationally. In Dublin her experience was viewed as psychiatric disorder. In the west Valerie finds people who will listen to stories like hers, stories about an opening between the physical and spiritual worlds. This may be no coincidence: "Perhaps she has come precisely because instinct tells her that such communication will not be so readily dismissed in this community."[24]

That the setting is charged with supernatural power is suggested in the title of the play. A weir is a structure that dams up water "for generating power for the area," as Finbar, the local real estate broker, explains.[25] In the pagan world view, water is a prime source of spiritual energy, so electricity is not all that is generated. Pent-up spiritual energy is ready to be released, and the storytelling situation releases it. Not everyone will experience the spiritual energy, however, even in that place; Brendan, the pub owner, for example, listens respectfully but has no tale of the supernatural to share with the others. Those who do make contact with the otherworld through direct experience can be termed "seers"; this is the term Gregory uses in her folklore collection. In her chapter "Seers and Healers," she collects the stories of men and women who are able to connect with the fairy world, for all that such contact is contrary to Catholic doctrine. In the words of one storyteller who was clearly Catholic, "some see these things, and some can't. It's against our creed to believe in them."[26]

One of those who see, Biddy Early, acts as a combination of folk healer, prophet, and life coach. When presented with a man who was "losing his health," she advises him to "give over drinking so much whiskey"; he does and begins drinking only gin (46). But above and beyond her medical knowledge and common sense, she is regarded as having psychic superpowers, including preternatural hearing ability; as one storyteller says, "although it's against our creed to believe it, she could hear any earthly thing that was said in any part, miles off" (35–36). Not surprisingly the priests, her rivals, "were against her," as were the doctors (37). To facilitate her fortune-telling, she had a bottle in which she could see the future, but in order for her to receive the last rites of the church on her deathbed, some said she had to break it, and others said that she had to turn it over to the priests, who "found black things in it" (41). Many said that she had been away, taken to live with the fairies, and so became expert in what would and would not be acceptable to them. The fairies can apparently be very particular. Biddy Early tells a woman that "if you have a bowl broke or a plate throw it out of the door, and don't make any attempt to mend it, it vexes *them*" (40; italics in original). As ambassador to the fairies who were regarded as "her *people*," Biddy Early was a conduit to the spirit world (45).

Each of the four tellers of supernatural tales is, at least for the moment in time recounted in the tale, a seer like Biddy Early. Like Biddy they seem also to be Catholics, so they occasionally add a proviso, similar to hers, that the stories are "against our creed" but proceed to tell them anyway. Unlike Biddy they are modern people, and so they also attempt to deal with their experience through the lens of scientific rationalism. In three of the four supernatural tales, a member of the clergy is involved, working his own "magic"; physicians are mentioned as possible resources in three; and medical/psychological explanations such as alcohol- or fever-induced hallucination and mental illness are offered. In each the tale-teller includes some form of denial of the supernatural elements of the narrative or simply resorts to mockery ("old shit," "old cod") of the supposedly outmoded beliefs recounted in the tale.[27] For once religion and science are allies; both cast doubt upon the validity of these otherworldly experiences.

The first story, Jack's tale of the fairy road, relates the events that took place eighty or so years earlier—"back in about 1910 or 1911" (31)—in Maura Nealon's house, which Valerie is currently occupying; the source of the story is Maura herself, an eye- and earwitness. The relatively benign nature of the occurrences—unexplained knocking at a place low on the door, "not where you'd expect a grown man or a woman to be knocking"(32)—allows mild dramatic tension to build up, to culminate in the much greater tension of Valerie's tale. The powers of Christianity are called in and, in this tale, are effective; once "the priest came and blessed the doors and the windows . . . there was no more knocking then" (32). Years later Maura found out that "the house had been built on what they call a fairy road. . . . legend would be that the fairies would come down that way to bathe" (33), and they resented the house in their way. Hence their noisy demands to revert to their usual habits. Maura, the seer character, lives to a ripe age and retains her ability to sense invisible presences: "She was always saying, There's someone at the back door or there's someone coming up the path. . . . And there'd never be, anyone there" (31). An eccentric and a drinker as well as a visionary, Maura is the connection between the old fairy-faith tradition and the pub audience via the tradition bearer, Jack.

The type of tale Jack tells is consonant with the ones collected by Lady Gregory and presented in the chapter of *Visions and Beliefs* titled "In the Way": "There's some places of their own we should never touch such as the forths;

and if ever we cross their pathways we're like to know it soon enough, for some ill turn they'll do us, and then we must draw back out of their way" (180). Numerous pieces of testimony are collected on the ill fortune experienced by those who do cross the fairies' pathways, getting "in the way of their coming and going" (180). Most of the narrators recount auditory phenomena: sounds of a "barrel rolling outside the door" (180); "music playing" (181); "feet . . . clapping, clapping on the floor" (182). Some of those who live in such houses are, like Maura, none the worse for the experience, but others suffer misfortunes ranging from poor crops to dead children. It is clear that the tale-tellers attribute all forms of bad luck to being "in the way"; one afflicted man, who emerged from the ill-placed house "walking crooked, with his face drawn up on one side; and so he is since, and a neighbour taking care of him" (184), seems to the modern reader to have had a stroke rather than an encounter with the fairies. But the consensus of Gregory's sources is the same as Jack's: no good can come of living in a house built on a fairy road. Valerie senses immediately that this will have consequences for her. Finbar, who brokered the rental deal, naturally scoffs at this notion: "it's only an old cod. . . . You hear all these around, up and down the country" (33).

Having mocked Jack's tale of the supernatural, however, Finbar proceeds to recount his own "little run in with the fairies" (35). This story is a bit more complex than Jack's, having a double plot involving a supernatural experience that happened to an acquaintance of Finbar's and a related one that happened to Finbar himself. A young woman, Niamh Walsh, has been attempting to make contact with the spirit world via the Ouija board and, to her horror, sees "something on the stairs. Like, no one else could see it. But she could, and it was a woman, looking at her" (38). Niamh's anxiety causes the people around her, including Finbar, to summon help both secular and religious: the local doctor and the parish priest. The former gives her a sedative. The latter, being "more Vatican Two," that is, relatively modern compared to other priests, is skeptical of "the demons or that kind of carryon" and does a perfunctory exorcism, "sort of blessed the place a little bit" (39). Immediately thereafter the phone rings, announcing the accidental death of a neighbor. Niamh's woman on the stairs thus appears to be a common figure of folklore, the death messenger.

Niamh's woman on the stairs is not the banshee, however, as described by Gregory in the *Visions and Beliefs* chapter "Banshees and Warnings." The woman on the stairs is silent, while the banshee, notoriously, wails. The banshee in Gregory's tales and elsewhere in folklore is defined by the sound she makes; she is a "keening woman," uttering loud, unearthly cries, "the most mournful thing you ever heard" (172)—not lamentations for the dead but a warning that someone is about to die. The woman on the stairs does not resemble the physical description of the banshee or engage in her other characteristic activities, either: the banshee is female, "young . . . thin and white-skinned and having yellow hair, washing and ever washing, and wringing out clothing that was stained crimson red, and she crying and keening all the time" (170). Niamh's woman, then, is not the banshee, but death messengers can be various, ranging from bright lights to fire to "a shadow . . . or a noise of knocking or a dream" (171). In fact in Gregory's tales anything even mildly strange happening immediately before a death can be elevated to the status of supernatural death messenger in retrospect; and it is through this lens that Niamh sees her vision and those around her, including Finbar, interpret it.

In Finbar's episode dramatic tension rises but is also deflated, as his experience results in something positive rather than negative: quitting smoking. At home later that night, having his last cigarette of the evening, Finbar, like Niamh Walsh, senses something on the stairs, a presence so powerful that it not only renders him physically unable to turn around but also ends the cigarette habit with which he associates the presence. He discounts the connection between the presence and his instant, and permanent, aversion to smoking—"Obviously there was nothing there and everything" (40)—but he would not have told the tale as a sequel to Jack's if he thought there was no connection between Jack's tale and his own. He had called his own tale "not even a real one" and the people involved in it a "crowd of headbangers," thus undercutting the truth of his own tale via humor: "Yous all think I'm a loolah now. . . . I'm the header, says you, ha?" (38, 40). A person who is mentally ill—a "loolah," "header," or "headbanger"—might have visions too, but they are scarcely to be believed by others. They all laugh as if to reassure him, but Valerie's response is the most telling: "I'd imagine, though, it can get very quiet" (40). Valerie is testing the waters to judge how her own story will be received.

The dramatic tension increases with the third story, Jim's, of a dead pedophile and murderer seeking to be buried in his apparent victim's grave. In Irish funerary practice, the body of the deceased reposes in church before the "removal," in which the coffin is brought to the cemetery for burial. Jim and a friend have been asked by the priest of a parish other than their own to come to dig the grave. This request strikes Jim as odd in that parishioners would typically do this; when Jim's friend, Declan, asks the priest about this violation of custom, the priest "[gets] a bit cagey" and answers evasively (45). The atmosphere is dismal; it is again a dark and stormy night. As the playwright noted in his prefatory comments, this environment stimulates the imagination. Adding further ambiguity to the narrative, Jim is sick with the flu and running a high fever, perhaps high enough to cause hallucinations. And then there is the *poitín*, a potent homemade alcoholic beverage, consumed by both young men. Paradoxically all this evidence that the story is the product of a fevered imagination gives it more, not less, impact. Because the audience is "desperate to disbelieve it, [Jack's story] carries the more credibility."[28] The dead man's violent and un-natural desires persisting beyond the grave transform the narrative "from fairy story to horror story."[29]

Such beings as the one Jim sees appear in Gregory's chapter "The Unquiet Dead." As many of her storytellers note, the restless dead have no place in Catholic concepts of the afterlife. According to the branch of Roman Catholic theology known as eschatology, after death the soul is judged by God and as-signed to eternal reward in heaven, punishment in hell, or a term in purgatory, a temporary state of preparation for heaven. Some of Gregory's folklore sources have visions informed by this Christian view of the afterlife. Others, however, make a distinction between what "those that mind the teaching of the clergy say" and "what the old people say" (191). The "old people," traditionalists in touch with the pagan past, recount visionary experiences that cannot be recon-ciled with Catholic orthodoxy.

In their stories the dead are unquiet because of unfinished business. They may mourn the living as much as the living mourn them, and so a tale is told of "a father and mother who had died but . . . often came to look after the chil-dren" (194). The dead are often concerned about unpaid debts and unrepented sins but can also interest themselves in more mundane matters. One sports-minded deceased in Gregory's tales breached the gap between heaven and earth to offer his father staffing advice for their favorite hurley team (198–99). Gregory sees these visions as a manifestation of the strong faith of the people of Connaught: "Here in Connaught there is no doubt as to the continuance of life after death. The spirit wanders for a while in that intermediate region to which mystics and theologians have given various names, and should it return and become visible those who loved it will not be afraid, but will . . . put a light in the window to guide the mother home to her child, or go out into the barley gardens in the hope of meeting a son" (190). Gregory espouses this sanguine view despite the fact that some of the stories she collected express great fear. One attributes to a priest the belief that "ghosts . . . are souls that are in trou-ble" (192). Another describes an apparition in Cloughballymore that caused children to die of fright (197). Many of these "poor souls traveling" (198) come back from the dead to the living. Surely these souls cannot be those of the saved. And surely it is one of those whom Jim sees, "unquiet" even in death because of his desire to be united with his victim post mortem.

While Jim's story builds dramatic tension, the spirit in the graveyard is not one to win the audience's sympathy. If he is suffering in the afterlife, he deserves it. But Catholics believe that the spirits of children in the afterlife are welcomed by a loving God. In this context Valerie's story of the phone call from her dead daughter is almost unbearably painful. McPherson describes how, in previews, the scene caused unexpected reactions in the audience: "every night, people in the audience fainted. For some reason people kept having to be carried out. It was awful."[30] Valerie and her husband, both employees of Dublin City University, are urban professionals, far removed from the banshees and fairies of the west, and so Valerie is an unusual practitioner of the predominantly rural art form of storytelling. When their five-year-old daughter dies in a swimming accident, she and her husband grow apart in their different ways of grieving. While her husband immerses himself ever more deeply in his work, Valerie's grief borders on obsession, leading to her being regarded, even by herself, as "crazy" and needing treatment (57–58). The child, named Niamh like the young woman in Finbar's story, had been in life an anxious child, experiencing mysterious presences: "people in the window . . . people in the attic . . . coming up the stairs . . . children knocking, in the wall . . . a man standing across the road" (54). The child's visions mark her as a seer, one with a closer connection to the supernatural in life. But in death the child is as troubled and anxious as ever, calling for her mother as she did in life.

This is a horrifying theatrical moment both for the small audience composed of the pubgoers and for the larger one in the theater. Throughout the play the stories have sowed the seed of belief in a pagan supernatural, not only in the listening audience within the play but in the theatrical audience as well. Whatever the audience members' beliefs, or lack thereof, with regard to the afterlife, the idea of a child suffering for all eternity, fearful and deprived of the mother who wants nothing more than to be with her and to console her, is a glimpse into the heart of darkness.

There is no place in Catholic eschatology for the concept of a dead child in an afterlife of torment. One of Gregory's storytellers describes an orthodox religious path to accepting the loss of a child: "When my own poor little girl was drowned in the well, I never could sleep but fretting, fretting, fretting. But one day when one of my little boys was taking his turn to serve the Mass he stopped on his knees without getting up. And Father Boyle asked him what did he see and he looking up. And he told him that he could see his little sister in the presence of God, and she shining like the sun. Sure enough that was a vision He had sent to comfort us. So from that day I never cried nor fretted any more" (191). This same theology is echoed, with sincerity and genuine concern, by Jim: "I'm very sorry about what's happened to you. And I'm sure your girl is quite safe and comfortable wherever she is, and I'm going to say a little prayer for her, but I'm sure she doesn't need it. She's a saint. She's a little innocent" (60–61). In voicing these sentiments, Jim expresses himself both with empathy and with accuracy regarding Catholic beliefs. A child, a "little innocent," would be incapable of serious sin and would thus be in heaven with God, safe and comfortable. She would not need prayers as she could not be in purgatory;

she is a saint, among the saved in heaven, all of whom are saints even though only some of them have been declared so via the formal canonization process of the church. So when Jim prays *for* her, he would technically be praying *to* her. She does not need prayer, but the benefit of it would be to Jim himself and to Valerie. He acts as a good Catholic should, as a minister of God's love and comfort to the afflicted mother.

The empathetic reactions of the four men explain why it is that Valerie sought understanding in the west. Away from the superficial rationality of Dublin, which would trivialize her grief by defining it as a mental health issue to be treated, she finds an empathetic audience for her story of her encounter with the supernatural. In the west, in the lonely countryside, she finds a weir, a source of spiritual energy that builds up and is released in the storytelling experience. She finds an opening between the natural world and the spirit world such that her encounter with her daughter across the boundary between life and death can be better appreciated. Catholicism emerges in Jim's speech as the kinder view of human destiny than that of the "unquiet dead" of Celtic paganism.

The discussion of the fate of the child in the afterlife is not the end of the play, however. The fourth tale-telling episode is that of Jack, telling Valerie about his lost love, she who wanted to "go up to Dublin" (64) for a better life. At first glance this final story seems unconnected to the other four. But if the play is about "the loss and loneliness that eventually haunt every life,"[31] Jack's story is a tragedy of lost opportunities on the purely human level. For reasons that he himself does not understand, he was unable to leave the west of Ireland for what he perceived as a hostile environment. Thus he has doomed himself to a life of routine and desperate loneliness. Is there a suggestion that he and Valerie, both survivors of human tragedy, can somehow console each other? If so the play ends on a note of hope. But if they cannot, then the natural world holds as much sorrow as that other world depicted by the tellers of tales.

In Synge and in McPherson, the journey of the city dweller to the western regions means approaching the Irish past in a way that is not possible elsewhere. The storyteller transmits tradition to his or her immediate audience and, through them, to the audience of readers or playgoers. This tradition bearing, however, often sends an ambiguous message. Facts are filtered through the subjectivity of the tale-teller. Crucial elements are unknown or withheld or distorted; even when the tale-teller intends to be accurate, the slippery meanings of words make language an imperfect medium to bridge the gap between the past and the present or even between one person and another.

Speaking the same language is a metaphor for understanding. When a country's original language is suppressed or abandoned or survives only as an antiquarian interest, something crucial to the common heritage is lost. Contemporary writers such as Brian Friel and Roddy Doyle explore the issue not just of the Irish language—so long threatened by the political and military hegemony of the British Empire, now challenged by the cultural dominance of the United States—but also of language itself as a vehicle of self-definition.

Chapter 3

"The abuse of language"

Irish, English, American

Secondary school students in Ireland who are following a college preparatory program study for their leaving certificates, a set of at least five examinations administered at the end of high school, the scores of which will determine their eligibility for the next level of education. Among the five is an examination in the Irish language, required of all but a few students. English is their dominant language and Irish is a second or "school" language, but for none will Irish be their only language. The story of these two languages and their role in Irish history forms the background to Brian Friel's *Translations*, and Roddy Doyle mined similar territory when he used Dublin slang, American song lyrics, and vulgarisms to illustrate the use and abuse of language in his novel *The Commitments*.

Edmund Spenser (1552–99), better known as author of *The Faerie Queene*, also wrote *A View of the Present State of Ireland* (1596), in which he criticized what he termed "the abuse of language, that is, for the speaking of Irishe among the English, which is as unnaturall that any people should love another language more then ther owne, soe it is very inconvenient, and the cause of many other evills. . . . for it hath always bene the use of the conqueror to dispose the language of the conquered, and to force him by all meanes to learne his."[1] Ireland was the conquered and England the conqueror when Spenser castigated the group of Britons known to history as "Planters," a group to which he himself belonged, for their linguistic perfidy. The Tudor monarchs had been making grants of land in Ireland ("plantations") to English colonists for the preceding half century; the descendants of the original grantees would be known as Anglo-Irish to distinguish them in perpetuity from the native Celts. In return for their lands, the Planters were supposed to acculturate the native Celtic population and transform them into proper citizens of the British Empire. But as Spenser sees it, the opposite was taking place. Some Planters assimilated all too readily, chiefly by intermarriage, into the culture that they had been sent to subdue, to the point that they became "much more lawlesse and lycencious then the very wild Irish." One of the worst of the "ould badd Irish Customes" that Spenser felt should be replaced by the "more cyvill fashions" of the English was speaking Irish, since, as seemed to Spenser self-evident, the Irish were supposed to adopt the language of the conqueror. For several hundred years before (and after) Spenser, the British government made a concerted effort to force the Irish do just that.

The effort to stamp out the Irish language proceeded through a series of laws enforced and battles lost. One example of the former is the Statute of Kilkenny of 1367,[2] which, 229 years before Spenser's essay, addressed the perceived problem of Celticizing among the English. As the statute notes, at first the English in Ireland behaved well, observing British law and custom and speaking English. But as time passed, says the statute, they increasingly "live and govern themselves according to the manners, fashion, and language of the Irish enemies." To stop this dangerous trend, the law provides, among many other restrictions, that "every Englishman do use the English language, and be named by an English name, leaving off entirely the manner of naming used by the Irish . . . and if any English, or Irish living amongst the English, use the Irish language amongst themselves, contrary to the ordinance . . . his lands and tenements, if he have any, shall be seized into the hands of his immediate lord."[3] Spenser's thoughts on language, then, were far from new when he wrote them in 1596. For the Irish, long punished under these and similar laws for speaking their own language, the use of English equaled capitulation.

Another turning point in the fate of the Irish language was the Battle of Kinsale in 1601, at which the Irish earls were decisively defeated by the British. Irish president Mary McAleese described this battle in a 2001 ceremony commemorating its four hundredth anniversary: "The Battle of Kinsale was the last battle fought by the Irish Chieftains. As battles go it was little more than a rout, but with defeat came decimation of the Gaelic way of life. Government, systems of control, language, customs, religion and ownership of land all changed in Ireland."[4] The decline of the Irish language paralleled the decline in the political, religious, and economic power of the Celts compared to their British occupiers. From 1601 to the time in which Friel's *Translations* is set, 1833, the Irish language was under attack.

Like many other elements of Irish life, the language represents the political, social, and cultural divisions in the country. Because in the past speaking English meant aligning oneself with England, speaking Irish, especially in the North, connotes a separate Irish identity and protests Northern Ireland's continuing relationship with England.[5] In the past the English-speaking British were primarily Protestant and the Irish-speaking population largely (though not totally) Catholic. The speaking of Irish, then, also connotes Celticism, Catholicism, and Republicanism. Those who advocate the use of the Irish language in all areas of Irish life act as if they believe that Spenser, though for the wrong reasons, was right: "the speache being Irish, the hart must needes be Irishe."

"Interpreting between Privacies": Brian Friel's *Translations*

One of the many linguistic ironies in Brian Friel's *Translations* is that this play about the Irish language was written in, and must be played in, English. While there are Irish-only authors writing today, to reach the widest possible audience even in Ireland, much less worldwide, one must write in English. The language of the play is thus a symptom of the problem: "all the Irish characters are obliged to speak in English to be understood by an audience, including an Irish one."[6] This linguistic confusion sets the tone for the play. Furthermore Friel (1929–2015) tacitly acknowledges that not many members of the reading audience will have Latin and Greek at their command as does Jimmy Jack Cassie, the "Infant Prodigy," and so he appends a translation (into English). Jimmy's facility with regard to ancient languages, which he prefers to either English or Irish, opens another dimension in the play. *Translations* is not about the Irish/English controversy only, but also about language itself as an imperfect vehicle of human communication.

To consider the more universal level of meaning in the play, it is first necessary to sketch in the background to the events of 1833. One of the many unsuccessful attempts to throw off the yoke of British sovereignty is known to historians as the United Irish Rebellion of 1798. The connection between this failed military action and the events of the play is that the schoolmaster Hugh and his classics scholar, Jimmy, are reputed to have taken part in the uprising. Reminiscing, Hugh identifies himself and Jimmy with the gods and heroes of ancient times; yet it emerges that they did not actually participate in the battle but only got as far as the pub in Glenties. These two would-be patriots, who marched bravely off to war with "the *Aeneid* in their pockets"[7] and then promptly marched back again, paradoxically identify with the ancient Greek and Roman heroes and with their ancient languages instead of with Irish heroes and *their* language. Since then the two have focused their attention not on the survival of the Irish nation or even the language but on the survival of Greek and Latin.

For the intervening years between the United Irish Rebellion in 1798 and the dramatic present, 1833, it was becoming ever clearer that English was the language of the future. When another language opens doors of opportunity, the native language becomes a hindrance. Maire, who is determined to learn English, quotes the nineteenth-century Nationalist leader Daniel O'Connell

(1775–1847) to the effect that "the old language is a barrier to modern progress" (270). She is right; O'Connell, so prominent in Irish and particularly Catholic emancipation that he earned the sobriquet "The Liberator," was willing to detach Irish progress from the Irish language. In a letter to a friend, O'Connell stated his case succinctly: "although the Irish language is connected with many recollections that twine around the hearts of Irishmen, yet the superior utility of the English tongue, as the medium of all modern communications, is so great that I can witness without a sigh the gradual disuse of Irish."[8] Maire is interested in progress and modern communications not because she is fond of the British or of their language but rather because she wants to immigrate to that other, better English-speaking country: America. O'Connell was ahead of his time in anticipating that "by the middle of the nineteenth century, English [would] become not only the language of prestige but also of economic progress."[9] The Great Famine and the wave of immigration it triggered is twelve years in the future, yet America already beckons the adventurous and ambitious. For them the question of language is primarily a pragmatic one, and as a scholar of language, Hugh supports such people's learning English on the grounds that "words are signals, counters. They are not immortal. And it can happen—to use an image you'll understand—it can happen that a civilization can be imprisoned in a linguistic contour which no longer matches the landscape of . . . fact" (286). Without English the Irish are confined to a historical as well as linguistic backwater.

The "landscape of fact" in 1833 included two historical events impacting the language issue: a military survey of Ireland and the recent creation of the National School System. With regard to the survey, the purpose was to construct an accurate map of Ireland that would give Britain a military advantage over the conquered population. The fact that it is the military who are in charge of this makes it a colonialist power play. The mapmaking process, and the actual maps in the hands of the soldiers, are constant reminders of Ireland's subordinate status. Similarly the map of the United States that Maire carries is a sign of the cultural dominance of this other Anglophone people.

The mapmakers are also in charge of renaming geographical landmarks, thus "Anglicizing" the countryside in an act of "linguistic imperialism."[10] After the establishment of the Republic of Ireland in 1922, some, but not all, of the place names thus Anglicized were re-Celticized; the town of Cobh, for example, was renamed Queenstown in 1849 in honor of a visit by Queen Victoria, then returned to its original name in 1922. A quick glance at a modern map of Ireland will, however, demonstrate that this re-renaming is far from universal; vestiges of British rule survive in the names of many towns. In County Donegal, for example, where the play is set, English-sounding town names such as Castlefin, Burtonport, and Greencastle exist alongside Irish-sounding ones

such as Ballyshannon, Dunfanaghy, and Dungloe. Friel acknowledges this linguistic anomaly by giving the town in which the play is set both Irish and English names: Baile Beag/Ballybeg.

The other major historical event in the background of the play is the establishment of the National School System, which was intended to, and would
in fact, stamp out the informal "hedge school" system in which teachers like
Hugh and his son and assistant, Manus, took private students and were paid
privately. While historians disagree about the extent to which the hedge schools
either taught Irish or used it as the language of instruction, there is no doubt
that Bridget, a young townswoman of Ballybeg, is right about the National
School System: "from the very first day you go, you'll not hear one word of
Irish spoken. You'll be taught to speak English and every subject will be taught
through English" (266–67). Thus the language caused English-speaking Irish
children to identify as English. The effect of this over time would be the association of the English language with progress and power and the Irish language
with backwardness and poverty.

The events of 1833, however, neither exhaust nor fully explain the theme
of language in *Translations*. First note the play's title: plural, to suggest that
there is no one flawless way of transmitting thought from one language system
to another. Language use and abuse is much more complex than making an
either/or choice between Irish and English, and this is the point at which the
play acquires universal appeal even for those not politically invested in the language issue in Ireland. If the speech act is, as Hugh says, an effort to "interpret
between privacies" (308), it is an imprecise business at best, rife with possibilities for misinterpretation. The key issue is the "personal existential crisis in
which the privacy of the individual is never fully expressed by language"[11] even
when speakers share a common language. Monolingualism therefore cannot be
the answer, because even within one language system, words signify differently
to different people. Toward the end of the play, Hugh expresses the insight that
"confusion is not an ignoble condition" (307). The character must speak for
the playwright here, as the various speech acts in the play are full of unresolved
contradictions, raising more questions than they answer about the nature of
language.

On the most basic level, the process of naming is an attempt to capture the
essence of a person, place, or object. As the play opens, Hugh is attending the
christening (the giving of a Christian name, ordinarily a saint's name) of Nellie Ruadh's baby. It becomes clear as the characters discuss this that the community does not know the name of the child's father. The community suspects
that Nellie will hint at his identity via the child's name, since typically a child's
formal legal name identifies him or her as a member of his father's family. In
the play this is true of informal as well as formal names. Jimmy's full name

signifies that he is the son of Jack and Cassie, not to be confused with any other Jimmy in the locale. Naming, then, indicates individual identity plus connection with others: the parents, the Catholic Church, and other members of the clan.

Place-names connect an area with its history, and it is this connection with the Irish past that the mapmakers are trying to break. But instead of doing his job and substituting English place-names for Irish ones, Yolland, sent to Ireland as a military mapmaker, falls in love with the Irish names because of their sound as spoken by Maire. Irish place-names connect the place to its history, to its physical features, possibly to current or former residents. Yolland is subconsciously responding to an ancient Irish tradition called *dinnseanchas,* which involves "a uniting of place-names and events into a sort of 'mythical etymology.'"[12] Like Yolland, Owen, Hugh's son, newly returned to Ballybeg as an interpreter for the English mapmakers, comes to question the process that they came to Baile Beag to effect. Discussing the name of the crossroads, he also refers to *dinnseanchas:* "I know the story because by grandfather told it to me. . . . What do we do with a name like that? Do we scrap Tobair Vree altogether and call it—what?—the Cross? Crossroads? Or do we keep piety with a man long dead, long forgotten, his name 'eroded' beyond recognition, whose trivial little story nobody in the parish remembers?" (287). This is the crux of the renaming issue: renaming equals redefining the essence of the thing, and who has a right to do that?

Discussing their mutual project, Owen and Yolland, partially seriously, partially in jest, compare themselves to God in Eden. The toponymic survey has given them godlike powers; as Owen says, "We name a thing and—bang!—it leaps into existence." And being godlike, they cannot make a mistake; they echo each other's words.

> Yolland: Each name a perfect equation with its roots.
> Owen: A perfect congruence with its reality. (288)

But their brief dialogue contains its own contradiction. The term *roots* connotes heritage, which often includes language; so how can Yolland, who cannot speak Irish, equate the word with the essence of the thing? As Hugh's frequent quizzing of his students also reminds the audience, English is itself derived from Latin roots; the boundaries of language overlap at those points.

Owen himself has been in effect renamed Roland by the English, due to their mispronunciation of his name. The fact that his "name is as unstable as the home and homeland from which he comes"[13] and that, for a while at least, this "Anglicization" is acceptable to him indicate his willingness to adapt to the ways of the conqueror. This earns his brother Manus's contempt: "there are always the Rolands, aren't there?" (280), always those who collaborate (work together with, as Hugh would say, from the Latin *laborare*, to work, and *com*, together). But as he works with Yolland, it becomes important to Owen that his coworker know his real name. Even this tiny bit of information is hard to convey in words, as Yolland does not pay attention; but once he does, a moment of real communication occurs. Owen's revelation of his real name to Yolland means that Yolland, at least, has learned something via language.

Language learning is another key theme in the play. Manus is teaching Sarah to speak a first language. Hugh is teaching his students second, third, and fourth languages. If learning to speak any language is good, learning several must be better. Hugh thinks having only one language is clearly a pitiful state, scorning anyone who, like Captain Lancey, "speaks—on his own admission—only English" (269). Yet language learning and teaching are both severely flawed and seem to lead nowhere. Both Jimmy and the schoolmaster Hugh know English, Irish, Latin, and Greek. Historically, at least since the Middle Ages, Latin and Greek study has been an intellectual status symbol. Latin in particular has the cachet of having been the universal language of teaching and learning in the medieval past, plus being the official language of the Roman Catholic Church in the present. Fluency in the classical languages thus places both Hugh and Jimmy at the high end of educational achievement. But Jimmy is sixty years old, shabby, poor, the village eccentric. His obsession with the people in the books, people made out of words, leads him to believe that he can end his dreary bachelorhood by marrying the goddess Athena. And Hugh, for all his fluency in the ancient languages, is rejected as a teacher in the National School System. Further, much as Hugh values the ancient languages, he seems to indicate by his teaching strategies that the main importance of Greek and Latin is their impact on English, as roots for the "real" words—the English ones.

The foolish linguistic constructs that beginning students of language are forced to learn, sentences that have no application to real life, are satirized in the one English sentence that Maire knows: "In Norfolk we besport ourselves around the maypoll" (293). This useless set of words is further flawed by the fact that *besport* sounds overly formal even in 1833 and *maypoll*, presumably *maypole*, is mispronounced. When Maire realizes how little she understands what she has said, she worries about inadvertently saying "something dirty" to Yolland (293)—yet another example of words failing to convey their intended meaning from speaker to hearer.

Translation, like language learning, is a flawed process. There is a problem even with the definition of the term *translation*—from the Latin, *latus*, to bear or carry, and *trans*, across. The bearer-across is the translator, who will choose words to suit his perception of meaning and his own agenda. For example Captain Lancey's professional jargon, his "technolanguage,"[14] preserves emotional distance between himself and the Irish. When Owen translates him, he softens

Lancey's language, humanizing it, to place the best possible construction on the toponymic project and to keep the peace. Manus knows that by doing this Owen is not really "saying what Lancey is saying" (277). Later, when Lancey is threatening to destroy the town if its inhabitants fail to provide information about Yolland's whereabouts, Owen's translations are closer to his language. This suggests that in this instance Owen wants the harshness of Lancey's words to be transmitted without any mitigation. The difference between the two translations highlights the ambiguities inherent in the process itself.

As if the subjectivity of the translation process were not enough, even characters sharing a language do not always agree on the meaning of specific words. The mapmaking project means that place-names will be "standard-ized," which, Owen admits, means that "where there's ambiguity, they'll be Anglicized" (277). But when is there not ambiguity in language? And why is Anglicization seen as the standard? Some—Manus, for example—see Irish as the standard. Owen and Manus's disagreement on this issue resurfaces when Owen, becoming aware of Yolland's presence, urges Manus to speak English lest he offend the monolingual Yolland. Manus regards this as surrender: "For the benefit of the colonist?" Manus's label "colonist" dehumanizes Yolland. Owen restores Yolland's humanity by responding, "He's a decent man." But Manus refuses to accept even this weak term of approval: "Aren't they all at some level?" (288). To Manus, Yolland will forever be subsumed in the category "they," and they will never be "us" no matter how decent they may be.

The they/us categories remind the audience that language is a principle of inclusion and exclusion. The idiom "to speak the same language" is, in English, an expression of like-mindedness. Who can or cannot understand a particular language is a continuing theme throughout the play. To speak a language in the presence of one who does not understand it is to exclude him. Jimmy, quoting Ovid's *Tristia Ex Ponto* (circa 8 A.D.), expresses the feelings of the linguistic outsider: "I am a barbarian in this place because I am not understood by any-one" (305). Lancey, an outsider although he seems unaware of it, tries to com-municate in English to Irish-speaking people by using the slow, oversimplified speech with which one might speak to an intellectually limited inferior; rather than increasing comprehension, this communicates condescension. Everyone in the audience is expected to pretend that the characters are speaking in Irish and that they themselves can understand Irish and are thus not themselves bar-barians but instead part of the play's in-group. Similarly, with the Latin and Greek in the play, the audience must also seem to understand what they do not, thereby claiming membership in the same linguistically agile group to which Hugh and Jimmy belong.

By the end of the play, it seems that the language issues are far from re-solved; in fact they are intensified. In his love for both Maire and Ireland,

Yolland hopes to learn to speak Irish. Yet he comes to realize, as he says to Owen, that this will not entirely solve his communication problem: "Even if I did speak Irish I'd always be an outsider here, wouldn't I? I may learn the password but the language of the tribe will always elude me, won't it?" (283–84). Learning vocabulary, the "passwords," does not ensure admission to the "tribe"; to speak its language, one must have always spoken it, always have been a part of the group that speaks it. Such a love affair as his and Maire's confronts the tribal issue. Worried about his own marriage plans (to the goddess Athena), Jimmy cautions Maire to consider Greek vocabulary: "Do you know the Greek word *endogamein*? It means to marry within the tribe. And the word *exogamein* means to marry outside the tribe. And you don't cross those borders casually—both sides get very angry" (308). Both tribes and languages have a history, and history, says Hugh, is not objective, "not the literal past, the 'facts' of history . . . but images of the past embodied in language" (306). There is too much history between the two tribes, the Irish and the English, for such a love as Maire and Yolland's to flourish. Hugh, though agreeing to teach Maire English, is similarly pessimistic, cautioning her not to "expect too much. I will provide you with the available words and the available grammar. But will that help you to interpret between privacies? I have no idea. But it's all we have" (307–8).

Words, passwords, grammar, none of these compensate for the unspoken knowledge, the "language of the tribe." Some former students of Irish—writer Roddy Doyle being one of them—may well resent what they see as the effort to define the Irish language as the sine qua non of true Irishness, membership in the tribe. For Doyle the Irish language today, at least in Barrytown, is a nonstandard dialect of American English.

Dublin Soul: Roddy Doyle's *The Commitments*

Readers of *The Commitments*, the first novel of the Barrytown Trilogy by Roddy Doyle (b. 1958), and viewers of the 1991 film adaptation[15] understand that Jimmy Rabbitte Jr., founder and manager of the Commitments, finds in soul music a bond with American popular culture in general and African American culture in particular.[16] As the group's self-appointed guiding spirit, Jimmy tries to convince his fellow musicians that they should be "black an' . . . proud."[17] But blackness is only one of several important tropes in the novel. Immature, ill-educated, and inarticulate as they are, they are stumbling along behind Jimmy toward a social theory of the Irish underclass. The vehicle of their thought processes, a dialect of English that marks them as members of that underclass, is only marginally capable of expressing complex ideas. For these Barrytowners there is no question of speaking Irish; that debate has been settled long ago. Yet they do not exactly speak English either, or at least not in a way that is immediately comprehensible to other English speakers. Their dialect marks them as not only urbanite Dubliners but also members of a linguistic subculture that they believe has more in common with African Americans than with other Irish people. Most critical writing on the novel has focused on this "black an' . . . proud" theme, and it is true that this is a key element in the novel. Paradoxically, however, Jimmy rejects the one Irish musician mentioned in the novel, Phil Lynott (1949–86), who was both Irish and black. Lynott, front man for the rock group Thin Lizzy, born in England to an Irish mother and an African father, would seem to combine most of what the Commitments would want in a musical influence; but to Jimmy, Lynott "wasn't soul." He cannot explain why he makes this judgment: "Ah, fuck off an' don't annoy me," he retorts when asked (67). The problem lies in his unspoken definition of "soul." No mere manager, he is the Commitments' theoretician and its semanticist, in charge of defining the concepts by which they shape their sense of themselves. Jimmy specifically, albeit nonverbally, defines soul in such a way as to exclude Lynott; and although he cannot explain it to the other Commitments, his reasons for doing so have to do with Jimmy's—but not Lynott's—rejection of Irish identity.

In a 1990 interview, Doyle describes his own writing style thus: "An awful lot of dialogue, and an awful lot of gaps."[18] Jimmy and the band members share a common language, which reinforces their sense of community, but they also share the "gaps," the unspoken assumptions. Lorraine Piroux calls *The Commitments* "a hybrid genre that looks more like a movie script than a novel."[19] In the film the gaps are filled in visually, as in the scene in which Jimmy's "black an' . . . proud" mandate is received by baffled white faces. In the novel the gaps must be filled in by readers by ferreting out the Barrytowners' shared assumptions. Their total communication system consists of what they do not say as well as what they say. Their brief, apparently abortive discussion of the Irish rock scene, as personified by Lynott, is an example of one of these gaps that needs to be filled in.

Barrytown language is first and foremost an urban dialect that identifies its speakers as city people and distinguishes them from their rural counterparts, whom they call, pejoratively, "culchies." As has been discussed earlier, Ireland has long seen its rural population as somehow more truly Irish than their urban counterparts. From the time of Éamon de Valera's radio address in 1943, the idealization of rural Ireland as the essence of Irishness became a key part of the country's perception of itself. Doyle says that the prevailing belief was as follows: "The real Ireland was west of the Shannon and if you wanted to write, to paint or to create music that was the source to draw on. Rural Ireland was the real place."[20] Doyle's Barrytowners, like their creator, reject the identification of true Irishness with rural life. Jimmy resents that "the culchies have fuckin' everythin'" (13) and are as socially and culturally dominant in Ireland as white Americans are vis-à-vis black Americans.

So strong is their rejection of all things "culchie" that it causes a conflict between two of the Commitments, Billy and Deco. Billy objects to Deco's Dublin-centric adaptation of the lyrics to "Night Train" by mentioning Clery's clock, a popular meeting spot. Clery's Department Store, on Lower O'Connell Street in central Dublin, is, according to Billy, unacceptably nonsoul, a store in which "only culchies shop" (51). After a bit of discussion, the group decides that, while Clery's itself is unworthy, the clock, being "outside o' the shop. On the street" (51), is sufficiently nonculchie. Gaelic football is to them also culchie-related and so an object of contempt: "The gaelic mas would all be culchies, said Dean—They're always washin' clothes" (78). These footballers would be less sweaty-smelling than the soccer players but no more acceptable than Clery's because of their laundry-mad "gaelic mas." First and foremost the Commitments identify with their urban origins, which clearly distinguish them from their rural compatriots. This means that they also reject the definition of Irishness as embodied in de Valera's pastoral myth.

With all this opprobrium attached to rural people, it would naturally follow that the Barrytowners' speech patterns would be as different as possible from those of the country folk. Even if Doyle's characters had been the sort of students inclined to worry about their scores on the leaving certs, they would no doubt share Doyle's own contempt for studying the Irish language, a task foisted on them by a Celticizing educational system. Similarly contemptible would be the Hiberno-English of classic writers of the Irish Literary Revival such as Lady August Gregory and John Millington Synge. One of the goals of the revival was to create art that reflected the true Irish character. While both Gregory and Synge studied the Irish language, both were writing for English-speaking audiences. In a kind of linguistic compromise, both, in their different ways, attempted to capture the Irish-influenced speech patterns of the Irish peasantry in English.

In her prefatory remarks to *Visions and Beliefs in the West of Ireland*, Gregory explains the linguistic origins of her interest in collecting folklore, for the stories but even more so "for the beautiful rhythmic sentences in which they were told. . . . I tried not to change or alter anything, but to write down the very words in which the story had been told" (15). In the following example, one long, flowing sentence tells a story that combines pagan and Christian references in explaining the westerners' folk belief in the "evil eye": "Some say the evil eye is in those who were baptized wrong, but I believe it's not that, but if, when a woman is carrying, some one that meets her says, 'So you're in that way,' and she says, 'The devil a fear of me,' as even a married woman might say for sport or not to let on, the devil gets possession of the child at that moment, and when it is born it has the evil eye" (81).

In another, grammatical inversions, combined with other Irish-language-based expressions, convey the sense of an Irish voice speaking, albeit in English: "A great pity it was about Mrs. Hehir and she leaving three young orphans. But sure they do be saying a great big black bird flew into the house and around about the kitchen—and it was the next day the sickness took her" (84). Grammatical inversions ("A great pity it was" instead of "It was a great pity"), the "habitual be" verb form ("they do be saying" in place of "they always say"),[21] and idiomatic expressions ("and she leaving," for "especially because she is leaving") are likewise characteristic of the speech recorded by Gregory, which came to be termed "Kiltartanese" after the area surrounding her home at Coole Park.

Like Gregory, John Millington Synge was interested in what he perceived to be peasant speech. Synge's characteristic language is seen in the following passage from *The Playboy of the Western World:*

PEGEEN [*with real tenderness*] And what is it I have, Christy Mahon, to make me fitting entertainment for the like of you, that has such poet's talking, and such bravery of heart?

CHRISTY [*in a low voice*] Isn't there the light of seven heavens in your heart alone, the way you'd be an angel's lamp to me from this out, and I abroad in the darkness, spearing salmons in the Owen, or the Carrowmore?[22]

Synge maintained that the language of the play was authentic: "I have used one or two words only that I have not heard among the country people of Ireland."[23] Synge may have used the same vocabulary that he heard in the Aran Islands, but it is hard to believe that the combinations of words that constitute his unique style came from the mouths of uneducated peasants. Fintan O'Toole, an Irish journalist, points to the irony that a Dublin theater group, the Abbey Company, with whom both Synge and Gregory were connected, created plays "made in Dublin, for Dubliners," but glorifying an artificial "image of the countryside."[24] What Synge calls the "exuberant language" of the peasantry in the drama of the Irish Literary Revival was, says O'Toole, intended to establish the following equation: "Irish life equals the peasant, and the peasant equals the landscape."[25]

Dubliners, then, equal neither peasant nor landscape, and their language, while also exuberant, is so in a way that does not speak of Ireland. In contrast to Synge's melodious dialogue, the language of Doyle's Barrytowners is characterized by harsh, short, fragmentary sentences; elisions of final letters;

hesitations, self-corrections, and approval-seeking tags; the requisite vulgar-isms; and a special vocabulary unique to their dialect. On the same subject as Synge's Pegeen and Christy, romantic love, the contrast is evident:

> All tha' mushy shite abou' love an' fields an' meetin' mots in super-markets an' McDonald's is gone, ou' the fuckin' window. It's dishonest, said Jimmy.—It's bourgeois.
> Fuckin' hell!
> Tha' shite's ou'. Thank Jaysis.
> What's in then? Outspan asked him.
> I'll tell yeh, said Jimmy.—Sex an' politics.
> WHA'?
> Real sex. Not mush I'll hold your hand till the end o' time stuff.—Ridin'. Fuckin'.
> D'yeh know wha' I mean?
> I think so.
> Yeh couldn't say Fuckin' in a song, said Derek. (12)

Pegeen Mike might find "bravery of heart" here, but the "poet's talking" is gone. Love is only "mushy shite. . . . I'll hold your hand till the end o' time stuff'"; women are "mots" met in fast-food restaurants, with no "light of seven heavens" in their hearts. Music does not convey romance, but rather "real sex. . . . Ridin'. Fuckin'."

The band's language, then, "connotes both their working-class belonging and the vernacular of their generation"; their way of talking is "their mother tongue," just as Irish, or Hiberno-English, once was to the rural peasantry.[26] The band members are concerned to prove themselves as something other than "tossers," or losers; the most obvious symbol of their current tosser state is their on-the-dole or marginally employed status. But on another level, they are also asserting the importance of "working-class Dubliners . . . a group tradi-tionally silenced by an imagined Ireland which prioritised and fetishised the rural."[27]

Jimmy's use of the term *bourgeois* suggests that he is capable of speaking a language other than the dialect of the Barrytown tribe. The film includes brief scenes in which he is role-playing a radio interview, taking the parts of the interviewer as well as himself. The band's mother tongue is "Dublinese, a Northside dialect."[28] But in his imagined interviews, Jimmy practices what broadcaster Joe Duffy calls the "DART accent,"[29] to be more believable as a ra-dio announcer. The DART accent is a variant of English believed to be spoken by upper-middle-class residents of the affluent neighborhoods served by the Dublin Area Rapid Transit rail system. In Doyle's novel *The Snapper* Jimmy attempts to do this while pretending to be a DJ, and in the film version of *The Commitments,* he imitates what novelist Joseph O'Connor calls "the odd pseudo-English accent that Southside Dubliners have."[30] In the imagined interviews, Jimmy also speaks in longer and more complex sentences, with fewer hesitations and elisions and fewer vulgarisms. Interpreted positively, this means that he is looking to a future in the larger world of Dublin broadcasting; interpreted negatively, it shows that his contempt for "southsiders" (15) is feigned and that he would love to be accepted as one of them. Jimmy does indeed espouse a "class-based politics,"[31] but his linguistic experimentation here shows that he is willing to compromise his principles for his hoped-for broadcasting career.

In his music, however, Jimmy is committed to the music of black America. "Rednecks and southsiders need not apply" (15): neither rural peasantry nor upscale urbanites are relevant. But why does this exclude Lynott? True, he did not perform soul music; he was, as the film of his life and his biography call him, a "rocker."[32] His career parallels that of the members of the Commitments in that he sang with similar short-lived bands for the early part of his career, bands that sound eerily like And And! And. Like the Commitments, these bands had no original material of their own at the beginning and so had to rely on covering songs already popularized by others (such as "Chain Gang" and "Night Train"). The Commitments never get to the point at which they develop their own original material, while Thin Lizzy did. But the centripetal forces that fragment real and fictitious rock bands led to Lynott's launching a solo career and the dissolution of Thin Lizzy.

The main characteristic that makes Lynott an inadequate role model for Jimmy is that he identified with being Irish and used his Irish heritage in his music. Under Jimmy's leadership, the Commitments reject these influences; so "tradition is supplanted by discontinuity and Americanization."[33] Irish readers of *The Commitments,* especially Dubliners, would be likely to know that the breakthrough hit for Thin Lizzy was a rock version of the traditional "Whiskey in the Jar."[34] It is hard to find an Irish band that has not covered this popular song; but as performed by Thin Lizzy, it combines the rock beat Jimmy associates with "ridin'" with Lynott's sexually charged delivery. The fact that the song is a cover of a "trad" piece, though, means to the Commitments that the band was associating itself with the rural past, with Irishness. The song begins "As I was going over the Cork and Kerry mountains" in the rural west. Lynott himself identified strongly with being Irish; he was raised in Dublin, and a statue in his honor was erected there, on Harry Street off Grafton Street, in 2005. This statue's huge Afro represents the style of the times and Lynott's pride in his African heritage; but his live audiences responded enthusiastically to his trademark question, "Is there anybody out there with any Irish in them?"[35] The sort of anomaly represented by this man—for whom being black did not override being Irish—is too much for Jimmy to process.

In addition to his acceptance of Irish music and adaptation of the Irish past, Lynott is also not particularly associated with the urban underclass. Judging from recorded interviews, he did not speak an underclass dialect; his speech, at least to the American listener, is barely distinguishable from that of his interviewer and does not resemble that of any Commitment in the film. Lynott is also associated with Sutton, which in the Dublinizing lyrics that the Commitments devise is a place "WHERE THE RICH FOLKS LIVE" (92), later downgraded to "WHERE THE SNOBBY BASTARDS LIVE" (126). A photograph exists of Lynott on the beach in Sutton,[36] but he was raised in Crumlin, which makes him a "south-sider," one of those who need not apply, according to Jimmy. And the Lynott family was not rich. His unmarried mother, eighteen years old at the time of his birth, struggled to raise him with the help of family members in Crumlin. But with the passage of time, Sutton became an upscale neighborhood, thus, by the time in which the novel is set, reeking of class distinctions that set it apart from Barrytown. To Jimmy Lynott cannot be soul because his associations with Irish traditional music and with southsiders seem to override his African roots.

Deco is the one who mentions Lynott, as is appropriate in that he is to the Commitments as Lynott was to Thin Lizzy: the front man. Deco suggests that being black equals being soul. Jimmy disagrees but cannot explain why. The discussion comes up in reference to American soul singers who died young and tragically from drug-related causes, as did Lynott in 1986 at age thirty-six. Joey the Lips's proclamation that "real Soul Brothers say No to the weed. All drugs.—Soul says No" (67) is as historically inaccurate as Joey's claims to musical experience. But the Commitments are glad to accept his opinion, as they are, whatever their musical ambitions, cautious young men anxious to avoid Lynott's fate. While they scorn traditional music, they hold a good many traditional values. Jimmy disapproves of the intraband flirtations and sexual encounters; Outspan is intimidated by his mother; Derek thinks one cannot say "fuckin'" in a song. And all of them know that "heroin kills" (67).

In the film version of *The Commitments,* the reference to Lynott is omitted. The filmmakers may not have thought that his name was internationally recognizable by 1991. But the fact that Doyle returns in future works to this story of a rocker dying young is evidence that the passing reference is important in *The Commitments.* In *Paula Spencer* (2006), the title character has spent so much time drunk that she does not realize how long it had been since Lynott died. A stranger to the Internet, she is amazed as her son Jack finds a website devoted solely to Thin Lizzy memorabilia. She is impressed by "a photograph of Phil Lynott playing chess. She'd never seen this one before. It was a long time since she'd seen any photo of Phil Lynott. It appeared gradually, scrolled down. He

looked great. Philip Parris Lynott, August 20, 1949–January 4, 1986. . . . There
was no one like him, she said."[37] In "Guess Who's Coming for the Dinner," a
short story in *The Deportees* (2008), the title alludes to the 1967 Sidney Poitier
film *Guess Who's Coming to Dinner,* daring for its time in that the plot revolved
around interracial dating. The Doyle story features a forty-five-year-old Irishman named Larry Linnane, whose daughter Stephanie is dating a man from
Nigeria. Larry's wife, Mona, notices Larry's shocked reaction to the news that
a black man, indeed an actual African, is coming for the dinner:

> Is it because he's black? Said Mona.
> Larry didn't let himself nod. He never thought he'd be a man who'd
> nod: yes, I object to another man's color. Shame was rubbing now
> against his anger.
> Phil Lynott was black, love, Mona reminded him.
> Phil Lynott had been singing "Whiskey in the Jar" when Larry and
> Mona had stopped dancing and kissed for the first time.
> And now he could talk.
> Phil Lynott was Irish! he said.—He was from Crumlin. He was
> fuckin' civilised![38]

As Larry's comment indicates, not only did Lynott think of himself as Irish,
but other Irish people thought of him as such, as not only an Irishman but also
a Crumliner, therefore a Dubliner, therefore "civilised.'" Larry counts him as
among the great musicians—"Phil Lynott, absolutely brilliant"—and moreover counts his respect for Lynott, among other great black people in the public
eye, as evidence that "there wasn't a racist bone or muscle in his body."[39] Yet he
has just pronounced Lynott civilized not because he was black but because he
was Irish. The conundrum that Lynott presented in his lifetime by transcending
and blurring traditional definitions continues to puzzle Doyle's characters after
Lynott's death. If Larry and Paula, each about twenty-five years older than
Jimmy Rabbitte, cannot unravel this puzzle, it is no wonder that Jimmy cannot.
And so he dismisses Phil as not soul, not fulfilling Jimmy's own definition of
the term, but cannot explain why. Language fails him, and so he resorts to the
all-purpose expletive: "Ah, fuck off an' don't annoy me."

In Doyle's Barrytown novels, the issue of language has detached itself completely from Ireland's tortured history with England; indeed the Barrytowners
seem barely to be aware of England. The English language and England itself
is mentioned only in passing in *The Commitments,* the language as a school
course and the country as a place where one might indeed say "fuckin'" in a
song. The pendulum of cultural influence has swung west, to the United States;
the Commitments sing the words of American lyricists. A cover band, they

have no songs of their own, as Outspan laments (73); but this is a true reflection of the fact that, unformed and young, they have few thoughts of their own.

In *A View of the Present State of Ireland,* Edmund Spenser observed that "the speache being Irish, the hart must needes be Irishe," and therefore he urged his fellow British immigrants to Ireland to continue to speak English. If by some miracle of time travel Spenser could read Doyle's work, he would be concerned that the Irish were too influenced by the speech of United States, too little influenced by that of either England or Ireland. Spenser could not have known that a tremendous blow to the Irish language would be dealt by the Great Famine, which decimated the Irish-speaking population and began a great wave of emigration that guaranteed that the Irish would need English not just for their hearts but for their very survival.

Chapter 4

An Gorta Mór

Hunger as Reality and Metaphor

Readers of Irish history and literature soon discover that the Great Famine, beginning with the blighted potato crop of 1845, is the pivotal event in Irish history. Vast bodies of research exist on the subject; an area of academic specialization, famine studies, has evolved. Interpretations of the Famine remain controversial more than 150 years later, but the key facts are simple and stark. In the years before 1845, the population of Ireland, for a variety of interrelated political, social, and economic reasons, grew increasingly dependent upon the potato. It could be grown on small plots of land, and small plots were all that the native Irish had in the mid-nineteenth century. Much of the land was in the possession of the Anglo-Irish descendants of the Planters. What remained to the Irish had for generations been divided up into increasingly smaller plots to support all the sons of a family, rather than preserving a landholding intact as in a primogeniture system wherein one son inherits. On their ever-smaller plots of land, generations married and procreated. The potato was the staple of their monotonous, yet nourishing, diet. Good health plus a tradition of marrying young led to rapid population growth, to an estimated level of 8.5 million on the eve of the Great Famine.[1]

The Great Famine, so named to distinguish it from the smaller famines preceding it, was caused, in the biological sense, by a fungus that destroyed the 1845 potato crop and recurred for the following five years. Famine deaths included those directly caused by starvation as well as those from the opportunistic infections that plague a hunger-weakened population. While the number killed in the Famine cannot be determined exactly, most historians accept a figure for population loss for Ireland in the range of 2.5 million: half of them to death, half to emigration, and of the latter half, many, perhaps most, dying on the journey across the ocean.

Readers of Famine history will find that the single historical work that can be regarded as seminal is Cecil Woodham-Smith's *The Great Hunger: Ireland 1845–49*, published in 1962. Later historians have debated many of Woodham-Smith's interpretations, but the book is required reading nevertheless. Woodham-Smith quotes Famine-era accounts of the suffering of the Irish people in scenes of almost unbearable horror. Typical is that of a British official, Nicholas Cummins, the magistrate of Cork, writing to his superior in 1846 to beg help for the starving population:

> the scenes which presented themselves were such as no tongue or pen can convey the slightest idea of. In the first [cottage], six famished and ghastly skeletons, to all appearances dead, were huddled in a corner on some filthy straw, their sole covering what seemed a ragged horse-cloth. . . . I approached with horror, and found by a low moaning that they were alive—they were in fever, four children, a woman and what had once been a man. It is impossible to go through the detail. Suffice it to say, that in a few minutes I was surrounded by at least 200 such phantoms, such frightful specters as no words can describe, either from famine or from fever.[2]

Any historical work on the Famine contains such scenes, as does fiction and drama set during the period.

Historians take on the task of evaluating documentary evidence of the period in the context of what Famine historian Christine Kinealy calls "folk memory,"[3] the story of a nation's past as told by nonprofessionals who are not trained as historians. Such folk memory, transmitted via formal and informal storytelling as well as through fiction and drama, is not necessarily inaccurate, but it is usually incomplete. Storytelling subordinates such mundane but often crucial matters as taxation, legislation, technology, economics, and ecological conditions to the demands of narrative art. Historians test folk memory against all available documentary evidence, weighing the multiplicity of factors that may not find their way into art. For example they try either to substantiate or disprove the most damning allegation of all, that "huge quantities of food were exported from Ireland to England throughout the period when the people of Ireland were dying of starvation."[4] The excruciating image of hungry people dressed in rags, watching from the shore while the food that could have saved them leaves their ports, is burned into the folk memory. Surviving records on food imports and exports can document to what extent this happened. Why it happened might admit of various explanations. The apparent heartlessness of this policy suggests that those in charge of famine relief in London used a natural disaster to reduce what they regarded as surplus population in Ireland, thus rendering this unruly portion of the empire more tractable. This may well be true; but Kinealy explains that it was also true that "the government's decision to allow merchants to continue exporting food from Ireland, and not to import food itself [was] a move made largely to appease grain merchants in both England and Ireland, a powerful political lobby."[5] So grain merchants—some of whom seem to have been Irish themselves, or at least residents of Ireland—may not have found their way into song and story but did play a part in the tragedy, along with callous bureaucrats.

Another basic assumption underlying the folk memory is that the Great Famine is to the Irish as the Holocaust is to the Jews. The description of the Famine as a *holocaust* originates in the nineteenth century,[6] but to twentieth- and twenty-first-century readers the term would be even more resonant after the horrors of the Nazi era. Journalist and author John Waters's harsh judgment captures this emotion: "the Famine was an act of genocide, driven by racism and justified by ideology."[7] The analogy between the Famine and the Holocaust or other instances of genocide must be considered with the major proviso that the Famine was caused by a fungus, not by any human action. That said, it is clear that the response to it on the part of the British government was so inept as to appear deliberate. Exportation of food from Ireland proved that the British had the ability to ship food in the other direction had they so desired, which, for a time, they did.

The decision to stop providing food for Ireland was made in 1846 by Sir Charles Trevelyan (1807–1886), the assistant secretary of the Treasury and the official in charge of famine relief. The act of discontinuing the shipment of food, with its "enormous symbolic significance,"[8] made it inevitable that this one man would be perceived as the archvillain of the Famine drama. In ballads such as Pete St. John's "The Fields of Athenry" and Nationalist anthems such as the rock group Black 47's song "Black 47,"[9] Trevelyan symbolizes all that was destructive in the British-Irish political relationship. When the name Trevelyan appears in a work of Irish drama or fiction, it reeks of a hatred that the passage of time has not ameliorated. Journalist Laura Trevelyan, Sir Charles's great-great-great-granddaughter, reported an incident in 1994 when an Irish politician, hearing her name, commented bitterly: "To think you're driving around South Armagh, as casual as can be, while the hills of Ireland are drenched in the blood of Charles Trevelyan."[10]

The modern reader can evaluate Trevelyan on his own terms via his 1848 monograph *The Irish Crisis,* "the only written account of the Famine produced by a senior relief official."[11] Trevelyan came to his governmental task with harsh anti-Irish prejudices. His oft-quoted statement, written in an 1846 letter, sums it up neatly: "The present evil with which we have to contend is not the physical evil of the famine, but the moral evil of the selfish, perverse, and turbulent character of the people."[12] That a man with such contempt for the Irish people should come to be in charge of saving them from the Famine's horrors is one of Irish history's chief ironies.

Trevelyan's language is milder in *The Irish Crisis* than in his personal correspondence, but it is clear that he sees the Irish as lesser beings, untrustworthy and radically flawed. Their perceptions of their own perilous condition cannot be trusted, Trevelyan asserts, as complaining, especially about money, has always been characteristic of the Irish: "All classes 'make a poor mouth,' as it is expressively called in Ireland. They conceal their advantages, exaggerate their difficulties, and relax their exertions."[13] Relaxing their exertions is a habit to which Trevelyan believes the Irish to be particularly prone. Thus, he reasons, if the poor are supported at all, it should not be too generously, lest they lose their "motive for exertion" (94). In addition to lapsing into sloth, the Irish evade fiscal responsibility. Trevelyan often expresses concern that the government was not getting its money's worth for what it spent in Ireland due to the likelihood of Irish deception. He provides an example of loans made to fishermen in an effort to subsidize the fishing trade. Far from resolving the problem, what Trevelyan sees as the government's generosity "proved that the fishermen are induced by it to rely upon others, instead of themselves, and that they acquire habits of chicanery and bad faith in their prolonged struggle to evade the payment of the loans" (94). The reader can also see in Trevelyan's writing the assumption that a baseline level of Irish suffering was acceptable. Several times he mentions "unusual" or "permanent" or "real" distress as being worthy of government intervention, presumably as opposed to commonplace or temporary or even imaginary distress, which he regards as normal in Ireland.

Trevelyan did not act as he did only out of contempt for the Irish, however. He possessed a set of beliefs and intellectual influences from which he drew theoretical underpinnings to justify his actions and inactions. His religious convictions included providentialism, that is, the belief that events as they worked themselves out in history were all part of God's eternal plan and thus not to be tampered with by mere mortals such as assistant secretaries of the Treasury. He seems confident that God's plan included dramatic changes in Irish behavior. On the first page of *The Irish Crisis*, he sanguinely predicts that "posterity will trace up to that famine the commencement of a salutary revolution in the habits of a nation long singularly unfortunate, and will acknowledge that on this, as on many other occasions, Supreme Wisdom has educed permanent good out of transient evil" (1).

And what action, if any, was the government in London supposed to take to facilitate this divinely ordained process? Further support for providentialism in theology was found in the laissez-faire theory of economics prevalent at the time throughout Europe, which discouraged governments from attempting

to influence what were believed to be natural economic forces. Trevelyan repeatedly uses the term *interference* when he writes of government activity, de-
ploring, for example, the government's "leaving its province to interfere in the
ordinary business of private life" (97). For a believer in limited government such
as Trevelyan, being in charge of gearing up a large bureaucracy to deal with the
situation in Ireland must have been especially onerous. This bureaucracy cost
the British taxpayer money, as "it was impossible to avoid creating an extensive
staff for the superintendence and payment of the labouring poor" (105). There
is also the vexed question of whether the government should be footing the bill
at all rather than local landowners or private charities. Trevelyan argues against
those who believe that the government should pay the full cost: although "the
deplorable consequences of this great calamity extended to the empire at large
. . . the disease was strictly local, and the cure was to be obtained only by the
application of local remedies" (108). But he did not trust local landlords not to
take advantage of the situation to benefit themselves. That left private charities.
Trevelyan is detailed and effusive in his acknowledgment of the work of charities, especially the universally praised Society of Friends, as he clearly hoped to
shift the financial burden even further in their direction.

These belief systems blended with Trevelyan's fervent desire for the Irish to
be self-sufficient. Habits of dependency on the government seemed to count
for him as, literally, a fate worse than death. Policies designed to withhold
aid and thus encourage self-sufficiency were designed to be as unpleasant for
the Irish recipient as they were economical for the British taxpayer. The Poor
Law Amendment Act enacted eleven years before the Famine, for example,
"ensure[d] that dependency on poor relief was less attractive and materially
less comfortable than the life of even the poorest independent labourer."[14] Trevelyan too observed that "relief ought to be on the lowest scale necessary for
subsistence. . . . Relief should be made so unattractive as to furnish no motive to ask for it, except in the absence of every other means of subsistence"
(186–87). Maintenance at the bare subsistence level would, Trevelyan believed,
encourage the Irish to increase their "exertions" in such a way as to become
independent of government support.

The result was minimal and ineffective assistance to the Irish, who, in Trevelyan's mind, were quite justifiably suffering a regrettable but natural and inevitable corrective to their own improvidence. Had the government in London
thought otherwise, the potato crop would still have failed, but widespread
famine might not have followed. Small wonder, then, that Trevelyan and his
fellow officials bear the weight of history's harsh judgment. It is a rare account
of the Famine that does not include the words of Nationalist John Mitchel
(1815–1875): "The Almighty, indeed, sent the potato blight, but the English
created the Famine."[15]

In his haughty superiority and unassailable certainty, Trevelyan seems like a stock villain and thus a worthy target of Irish wrath in his time and forever after. If there is any other way of seeing him, the most likely person to find it would be his direct descendant, Laura Trevelyan. In her *A Very British Family: The Trevelyans and Their World,* she devotes a chapter to her controversial ancestor. In his defense she counterbalances Trevelyan's often-quoted derogatory words about the Irish with other, less well-known selections from his writings that cast him in a more favorable light. For example in an 1846 letter, he noted that "it wd [*sic*] be disgraceful to us to have it recorded in History that we allowed our Countryman to die of famine without making every effort to save them."[16] The way in which he defined every effort was, however, via logical deduction from a set of first principles in which he believed without question.

Laura Trevelyan provides what may be the crucial insight into her ancestor's character: "He believed in doing all he could within the intellectual limits he set himself."[17] Those intellectual limits included a set of logical and interlocking principles from which he did not allow himself to deviate. He believed that "the virtues of self-reliance and industry would be undermined by too much aid to Ireland";[18] that physical survival of the Irish was secondary to the avoidance of dependency on big government, which he termed "a system of mendicancy such as the world never saw";[19] and that "an all-wise Providence" had set "a bright light shining in the distance thro' the dark cloud which at present hangs over Ireland,"[20] a light that would be dimmed if too much aid were given to Ireland. Thus he was the epitome of the then-fashionable laissez-faire philosophy: confronted with human suffering, he let it be.

Many historians believe that the generation of Famine survivors did not preserve its memory and did not encourage their children to do so. However, in the past half century, there has been an increasing desire on the part of those of Irish heritage on both sides of the Atlantic—historians, writers of fiction and drama, and readers thereof—to understand the impact of this pivotal event, not only in its own time but also in terms of its effect on generations now living. Literary examples of this phenomenon are William Trevor's short story "The News from Ireland" and Joseph O'Connor's novel *Star of the Sea.*

Coming to Terms: William Trevor's "The News from Ireland"

Trevor's story focuses on an estate, Ipswich, and its residents: the owners, the Anglo-Irish Pulvertaft family, and their household employees. Like many other Planter families, the Pulvertafts obtained their land by royal grant during the reign of Queen Elizabeth I (1533–1603). The present Pulvertaft inherited the house, felt it his "bounden duty to accept the responsibility," and moved permanently to Ireland in 1839.[21] Thus he joins the ranks of those members of the Pulvertaft family who believe that they can call themselves Irish based on the Elizabethan land grant, who feel that they "belong here now. They make allowances for the natives, they come to terms, they learn to live with things" (881). But should one learn to live with famine?

The characters in "The News from Ireland" differ in the way they would answer this question. Analyzing them one by one, from persons of highest to lowest social rank, uncovers a variety of different responses. First consider the residents of Ipswich, the Big House family and its retainers. The characterization of Mr. Pulvertaft, the heir to the estate, is an example of Trevor's insight into the complexities of human behavior. He does not oversimplify the ethical situation by making Pulvertaft and his family a collection of stock villains. The distant relative who left the house to him was "by all accounts a good man," and so is Pulvertaft (884). Charles Trevelyan would have been pleased with such a landlord, as Pulvertaft is accepting local responsibility for what Trevelyan saw as a local problem. Pulvertaft's relief effort is to finance the building of what were termed famine roads on his estate. These roads were a common make-work project in Famine-era Ireland, designed not for their practical utility but to keep the hungry from growing dependent on government handouts. Vestiges of such roads can still be seen, and they are testimony to at least some land-owners' attempts to do the right thing, albeit ineffectively, as they understood it. Pulvertaft's attitudes and actions represent one theory on how to alleviate the suffering of the starving people: private charity from the rich to the poor in the form of make-work projects, with all the paternalism and condescension that it involves and with no significant change in the social order.

Mrs. Pulvertaft also sympathizes with the famine victims, but like many others of her social class, she believes the British government's official explanation of the problem:

> It is nobody's fault, Mrs. Pulvertaft reflects, that for the second season
> the potatoes have rotted in the ground. No one can be blamed. It is a
> horror that so many families have died, that so many bloated, poisoned
> bodies are piled into the shared graves. But what more can be done than
> is already being done? Soup is given away in the yard of the gate-lodge;
> the estate road gives work; the Distress Board is greatly pleased. (893)

To her is attributed the key question regarding the Famine: "what more can be done than is already being done?" The way she frames the question seems to presuppose the answer: nothing more can be done. But to the reader, the question suggests that more could have been done.

Is this awful suffering truly "nobody's fault"? A good woman, though limited like her husband, Mrs. Pulvertaft cannot see that, since the Famine was a natural event, the issue of fault is as irrelevant as if it were an earthquake. But since nature can wreak destruction, the relevant issues are responsibility and response. While Mrs. Pulvertaft cannot imagine anything more being done than meager handouts, make-work projects for men too weak to work at all, and bureaucratic self-satisfaction, it is not her job to find better, more creative ways to resolve the problem. Those whose job it was—officials in London— seem in historical retrospect to have been as limited in their thinking as she is, and not nearly as empathetic.

The Pulvertaft children are self-absorbed, focused on the typical concerns of people their age rather than the disaster on their doorstep. The girls concentrate on what are for them life's key questions: Who will marry? Who will not? Adelaide, in love with her sister Charlotte's intended (to whom Charlotte herself is indifferent but plans to marry anyway), seems doomed to frustrated spinsterhood. For a woman of the Victorian period, Emily has an ambitious plan: to travel extensively, then, her version of wild oats sowed, to return to Ipswich and either live there with George Arthur or marry. George Arthur, the son and heir, is key to the viability of the estate. He must be dissuaded from his desire to join the military and persuaded to take his father's place. If he does then the system will continue. If he does not, especially if he joins the military and is killed in combat, the line will die out. The assumption of the Pulvertaft adults is, of course, that the failure of George Arthur to inherit and then to beget an heir in his turn would be a tragedy; but this is not a belief shared by Fogarty, the butler.

The fate of the servants of the family hinges on that of the house. The English governess, Miss Heddoe, is the most recently arrived member of the household staff. Readers of the English fiction of the nineteenth century (Charlotte Brontë's *Jane Eyre*, for example) will remember how undesirable was the position of governess, how willing a young woman would be to abandon a life in which she fits comfortably neither with family nor with servants. Miss Heddoe differs from the literary stereotype in that she is a "young woman of principle and sensibility" (881). Her sensibility causes her to respond emotionally to the famine victims; her principles are violated by the events around her. She is an outsider who must adjust to the situation in Ireland, leave, or go mad. Her diary is the record of this conflict. At first she is shocked and dismayed at the visible manifestations of the Famine and prays to the Lord to have mercy. She weeps in her bed and appears unable to eat, as if in sympathy with the starving. She tries to make sense of the ancient conundrum of human suffering in a world created by a good and loving God: "The famine-fever descends like a rain of further retribution, and I wonder—for I cannot help it—what in His name these people have done to displease God so? It is true they have not been an easy people to govern; they have not abided by the laws which the rest of us must observe; their superstitious worship is a sin" (900). As much as she empathizes with the Irish, her thought is shaped by her own cultural biases in favor of Protestantism and imperialism. But gradually she acclimates, and despite Fogarty's warning she agrees to marry Mr. Erskine, the estate manager. "Stranger and visitor, she has learnt to live with things" (906). Living with such things as are happening in Ireland requires her to suppress the sensibility and ignore the principles with which she arrived.

Erskine has much in common with Miss Heddoe in that he too is neither part of the Anglo-Irish aristocracy nor part of the native Irish population. A middle-aged Englishman who because of his injury—he has lost a leg—"has ended up in a country that is not his own, employing men whose speech he at first found difficult to understand, collecting rents from tenants he does not trust" (891). Such middlemen as he were among the most hated in Ireland, as it was often their job to enforce the landlord's wishes. Nevertheless marriage to Erskine would enable Miss Heddoe to give up her onerous governess position and rise somewhat in social status. On the other hand, she would also earn a share of whatever hatred was directed toward her husband as representative of an oppressive system.

The Fogartys, poor Irish Protestants, brother and sister, butler and cook, "belonged neither outside the estate gates with the people who had starved nor with a family as renowned as the Pulvertafts. They were servants in their very bones" (905). They supervise the downstairs staff, which position enhances the Fogartys' own social position within the servant class. Fogarty alludes to the fact that their domestic subordinates, Brigid and Cready, are Catholic (889–90). This little hierarchy illustrates the effect of the plantation system on even the best-off of the Irish, regardless of religion; they only live as well as they do because they are serving the interlopers.

Though the Pulvertafts' ascendancy in the little world of Ipswich guarantees Fogarty's own, he regards them with ambivalence: "their fresh, decent blood is the blood of the invader though they are not themselves invaders. . . . they perpetrate theft without being thieves" (881). Of Anglo-Irish roots himself though not a member of a wealthy landowning family, Trevor often depicts his characters trying to cope with the moral complexities involved in benefiting from Ireland's problematic landholding system. Fogarty's own solution would be for the old order to wither away peacefully: "He does not dislike the Pulvertafts of Ipswich, he has nothing against them beyond the fact that they did not stay where they were. He and his sister might alone have attended the mouldering of the place, urging it back to the clay" (881–82). The dissolution of Ipswich would reverse the ancient wrongs. Fogarty, then, is not eager for George Arthur to take over the estate.

The encounter between Fogarty and Miss Heddoe is crucial to the meaning of the story. In the first place, Fogarty is drunk, and he must be drunk to tell the truth: that he has been reading Miss Heddoe's diary and does not think she should marry Erskine. Even more important, he must be drunk enough to release his inhibitions about discussing the Famine. His interpretation of guilt and blame with regard to the Famine contrasts with Mrs. Pulvertaft's: "A blind eye was turned, miss, you know that. The hunger was a plague: what use a few spoonfuls of soup, and a road that leads nowhere and only insults the pride of the men who built it? The hunger might have been halted, miss, you know that. The people were allowed to die: you said that to yourself" (903). It is important to notice that, when Fogarty discusses responsibility for the Famine, he does so in the passive voice: "A blind eye *was turned*," "The hunger *might have been halted*," "The people *were allowed* to die." The passive voice of the verbs allows suppression of the doer of a given action. If Fogarty's sentences were revised, with the passive voice replaced by the active, a doer would have to be identified. Who was it that turned a blind eye? Who might have halted the Famine? Who allowed the people to die? The answer to these questions is too difficult for Fogarty, even drunk, to articulate; due to his involvement with the landlord class in Ireland, he has a stake in the very system he deplores. Fogarty's dream is his way of expressing his hope that Ireland might return to an imagined golden age before the coming of the English; that the landlord class be abolished (by violence if necessary) in order that the true owners of the land might take it back and live as they always should have lived (905).

"The News from Ireland" traces the evolution of an unjust system. The English landlords diverted into private ownership what should have been common property. Then when landlords had destroyed the rural economy, they returned, via ineffectual charitable gestures, tiny portions of what belonged to the people in the first place. This situation was bad enough in the best of times, but during the Great Famine, it was pure evil. Despite this Miss Heddoe decides to marry Erskine. As her fantasy of the pews in church indicates, she is motivated by a desire for security and social position, as well she might be, given the precariousness of her own employment. She is unable to respond to Fogarty's plea, possibly because the fact that Fogarty has revealed these opinions while drunk has diminished their believability for her.

While those inside Ipswich are well-fed and comfortable, outside the Big House, the Famine rages. The famine road, "a road that goes round in a circle, not leading anywhere" (889), is an image of the futility of the relief efforts. But the Pulvertafts see the road differently: "In years to come the road would stand as a memorial to this awful time, and Mr. Pulvertaft's magnanimity would be recalled with gratitude" (885). The famine road issue asks readers to examine their own beliefs surrounding the reciprocal virtues of generosity and gratitude. The landowners were beneficiaries of an unjust system that enriched them, producing sufficient surplus income to allow them to be generous (in fact to appear to be far more generous than they actually were). But the same system reduced the native population to beggars, dependent on the landown-ers for whatever meager assistance might be offered. In an irony obvious to the reader if not to the Pulvertafts, the landowners operate on the assumption that the lower classes should be grateful for receiving as charity a tiny fraction of what had been previously stolen from them.

The recipients of the Pulvertafts' soup illustrate this dynamic. Unlike many other such meager relief efforts during the Famine, there is no religious agenda to the Pulvertafts' effort, and this is to their credit. Unlike some of their core-ligionists, who gave the starving peasants soup only when they would agree to join the Church of England, the Pulvertafts are not trying to get the Catholic Irish to become "soupers," as such converts were contemptuously called. The Pulvertaft women are innocent practitioners of a genteel but inadequate Lady Bountiful form of charity; the soup is to the women what the roads are to the men. The charitable activities of all the Pulvertafts raise the issue of the limits of private charity, which, virtuous though it may appear to be, is often insufficient and merely serves further to cement the destructive inequalities that caused the problem in the first place. Like the roads this pattern of behavior "goes round in a circle, not leading anywhere."

A child with stigmata, miraculous wounds that resemble those of the cruci-fied Christ and are in Catholicism considered a sign of great sanctity, raises the story's meaning from historical-economic-sociological to theological. Given their religious divide, it is natural that the characters also be divided over the question of the nature of these wounds. They frame the question thus: are the wounds indeed miraculous, or were they inflicted by the child's parents in order to single him out for special treatment, that he might survive? Fogarty alone seems to be moving toward understanding when he discusses the theory of leg-end. With regard to the ancient legend of the True Cross, Fogarty remarks that legend "illustrates the truth. It does not tell it" (890). Applying that insight to what might be called the legend of the stigmatic child, it is clear that the real issue is not whether his wounds were truly sent from God or whether they were inflicted upon him by his parents in a desperate effort to save their last child. Rather the truth illustrated by the legend is this: the English are a Christian people yet do not see the face of the suffering Jesus in the faces of the poor. Asking the wrong questions about the child's stigmata causes them to miss the point. Fogarty says that "there is a feeling among them that the child should not have died. It is unpleasant superstition, of course, but there is a feeling that Our Lord has been crucified again" (895). According to Fogarty's own defini-tion of legend, even a superstition illustrates truth, should anyone be sensitive enough to discern it. Miss Heddoe is "astonished" that "all these people had independently dismissed, so calmly and so finally, what the people who were closer to the event took to be a miracle" (896). But the dismissers would have

to acknowledge their own complicity in the death of this child, and by extension all the other famine dead, if they were to accept the truth that the stigmata
story illustrates.

A dream of Mrs. Pulvertaft develops another aspect of the story's theological meaning. In her dream the pastor instructs his parishioners to wash Jesus's
feet. "But Mrs. Pulvertaft is unhappy because she does not know which of the
men is Jesus. They work with shovels on the estate road, and when she asks
them they tell her, in a most unlikely manner, to go away" (898). The Christian
directive to do to all men as one would to Jesus is being violated on the grand
scale during the Famine in Ireland. Mrs. Pulvertaft is troubled in the dream
because she does not know which of the men is Jesus. In the symbolic language
of dreams, this means that she and those like her do not see that all of the men
are Jesus. The Pulvertaft family should not be living comfortably amid Irish
suffering; to do so is to refuse to wash the feet of Jesus. "The descendants of
the people who had been hungry" (905), which includes everyone of Irish descent alive today, might well judge the Pulvertafts and their ilk harshly for their
failure to see the face of Jesus in the faces of their starving countrymen.

"Ocean wild and wide": Joseph O'Connor's *Star of the Sea*

"I think a writer usually writes the novel that he or she would most like to read;
and in the case of *Star of the Sea,* I couldn't think of another novel which ap-
proached the Famine era with the amplitude I felt it demanded."[22] This obser-
vation by Joseph O'Connor (b. 1963) is a true description of his novel, which
is so comprehensive as to serve as a Famine studies curriculum in itself. It is a
historical analysis of the landholding system that led to the Irish dependence
on the potato; a painfully detailed description of the Famine's ravages; a sociological explanation of the relationship between the classes in Ireland; a story
of thwarted love and failed marriage; and a murder mystery. Technically the
novel is complex, but the present discussion will focus on only one aspect of the
novel: it is a sea story, an accurate rendering of the conditions aboard the so-
called famine ships or coffin ships that transported emigrants across the ocean
to the major seaports of North America and beyond. Those who managed
to scrape together the passage money and made the difficult decision to leave
home and family members, usually forever, still had to endure the miseries of
the transatlantic journey under conditions worse than those on slave and con-
vict ships.[23] These conditions are faithfully re-created in the novel. In addition
the ship functions as a microcosm of Ireland itself. Despite what they think
of as insuperable barriers between them, the characters are all interconnected,
their fates intertwined for good or ill.

The route of this particular ship, from Liverpool to New York, is typical.
Those Irish who hoped to immigrate to the United States often left Ireland for

England first, where they were able to board ships for the Atlantic crossing. But as Grantley Dixon, an American journalist, relates, many of these emigrants, uneducated country people, did not grasp the basic geography of their trip. On their journey from Ireland to England, they had gone east; from Liverpool they traveled west again, past familiar seacoasts, thus experiencing all over again the grief of the break with the home country. The ship's route hugs the coast of Ireland, from Dublin, "from where they had fled in the weeks before, resigned— or endeavoring to become resigned, at least—to never setting eyes on their homeland again,"[24] south, then east along the Irish coastline before setting out across the Atlantic. This experience, a "bitter taunt, a poultice being ripped from a putrefying wound," proves too much for one passenger, a "consumptive blacksmith" who attempts to swim to shore, "every last shred of his will employed to bring him back to the place where his death was certain" (xvii). The vast sweep of the novel includes many such pitiful scenes.

The *Star of the Sea* leaves Liverpool in November 1847. This means that, except for the smallest children onboard, the passengers have already survived two years of the Famine, including the winter of 1846–47, which was unusually harsh in Ireland.[25] The ship's captain, Lockwood, estimates that the trip will take twenty-six days, which places it in the middle range of ship speeds for the day,[26] with arrival in New York planned for early December 1847. A November departure risks raw weather during the crossing and upon arrival in New York. The steerage passengers are poorly clothed, a predictable consequence of their poverty but also a corollary of their previous dependence on the potato. Christine Kinealy notes the irony that "the easy cultivation of this 'lazy crop' was blamed for the supposed indolence of the Irish people."[27] Once planted, a potato crop needs little attention, and none in winter; therefore "a great majority of Irish labourers and potato farmers did not normally work much in the winter months, and no one owned heavy clothes."[28] Thus emigrants were more vulnerable to exposure on board ship. Crossing in late fall, they will arrive in New York during the coldest season of the year. An emigrant whose trip took place in the late spring or summer would have warm weather in New York for a few months while he obtained a job, proper clothing, and a place to live before winter. But a winter emigrant, penniless, homeless, dressed in rags, and probably either sick or convalescent, would have no time to make these advance preparations.

Five days into the voyage, Captain Lockwood notes that he has registered an official complaint with regard to "the perennial matter of overcrowding . . . too many steerage tickets have been sold for this voyage, by a factor of thirty percent at the minimum" (34). This he feels has endangered all aboard. It also exacerbates the problem of onboard illness. Famine deaths do not occur from starvation only; as Lockwood observes in the first entry in his ship's log, "infirmity consequent on prolonged starvation" (2) kills three passengers the first day out of Liverpool. Malnutrition weakens the immune system, which means that opportunistic viral and bacterial infections have a ready target. Some would-be emigrants are left behind to die on the dock. The limited diagnostic expertise employed at dockside ensures, however, that some sick persons would be allowed to board; incubation periods for the development of infectious diseases would also result in asymptomatic carriers of deadly illness also being allowed to board. In the cramped quarters of steerage, "the sick and the healthy sleeping side by side" (xv), disease spreads rapidly. Sanitation arrangements are primitive, ventilation poor, and overcrowding rampant. Granted that people of the steerage passengers' social class would not be accustomed to luxury on land; but they also would not necessarily be confined in close quarters with overflowing waste receptacles, contaminated water supplies, and infectious bunkmates. Even healthy people are weakened by the malnutrition and dehydration consequent upon seasickness. The ship's owners provide no medical staff; a passenger physician and his assistant are dedicated but overwhelmed, with nothing but minimal access even to the ineffective remedies available at the time.

All this makes for a perfect storm of misery—at least in steerage. The crew and the first-class passengers are in no danger of starvation or even malnutrition on the ship as long as the journey takes the planned amount of time; their needs have been provided for, more sumptuously in the case of the first-class passengers but adequately in the case of those on whose strength and ability to work depends the success of the voyage. Though separated from the sick in steerage, other passengers would still be liable to contagion. But they are not overcrowded—David Merridith, for example, appears to have his own stateroom, apart from those of his wife and children; his wife and Dixon have sufficient privacy to have an affair on board. Cabin accommodations on the transatlantic ships of the time were available in small numbers and, of course, at a higher price.[29] But cabin passengers would be only a small minority of those aboard. Ships' passenger lists available online from the United States National Archives tend to identify passengers by occupation, and those occupations are seldom upper-class. The equivalent list from the novel mentions "evicted farmers . . . beggared spalpeens . . . a cooper; some farriers, a horse-knacker from Kerry; a couple of Galway fishermen who had managed to sell their nets" (25).

Also according to Edward Laxton's *The Famine Ships,* the ships were old, some never intended to carry human cargo, and at the end of their useful lives, pressed into service for the newly hatched famine emigration market, minimally retrofitted to provide the lowest level of accommodation possible—and with minimal safety considerations. The *Star of the Sea,* according to Dixon, was eighty years old, "a vessel approaching the end of her service" (xviii) set for retirement after the current voyage, and had been used to transport cargo ranging from opium to sugar to slaves. Lockwood notes in his log that although the ship is seaworthy, it also requires substantial repairs due to damage and "bad leaking" (2)—which suggests that his standards of seaworthiness are low. In addition to passengers, the *Star of the Sea* also carries mercury, mail, coal, and even "one grand piano for John J. Astor Esq. at New York" (2). This is clearly a maximal load for a ship built in about 1767 and in need of repairs. The perils of such a journey are highlighted by the captain's reference to the wreck of a similar ship, with the loss of all but three on board.

The presence of onboard food storage and cooking facilities, live animals to be slaughtered, and suitable wines suggests that the *Star of the Sea* had been used for the journeys of the well-heeled before the Famine, since it is hardly likely that these amenities would have been added for the *Star*'s final trip. The function of the ship as a metaphor for Irish society depends on the presence of this first-class section. Like Ireland itself the ship is a small space in which a tiny minority of the wealthy has privileges not available to all the rest. This social class, according to the captain's own passenger list, includes the four Merridiths, members of the hereditary landowning class, albeit now virtually bankrupt; their servant Mary Duane; Grantley Dixon; a physician, Dr. Mangan, and his sister/assistant, Mrs. Derrington; a foreign dignitary; and a Methodist minister (3). Presumably their fares would be much higher than those of the steerage passenger, or else the ship's owners could have easily converted their quarters into steerage facilities, especially since such conversion usually involved merely installing narrow shelves to be used as beds.[30] Whether the rich were subsidizing the steerage passengers' fares or vice versa is not clear; what is clear is that in the little world of the ship, income inequality prevails. There are far more poor people than there are rich people, and those who are poor are desperately so. If the first-class passengers of this ship equal the upper classes of this little society and the captain and crew the working poor, the steerage passengers represent the lowest classes.

As for the upper classes, at sea as on land, their comfort and convenience depend entirely on their assumption that they have somehow deserved their superior privileges. The abject poor may always be with them, below in steerage, but the first-class passengers are protected from seeing them or sharing in any of their suffering. Ironically it is the working poor (the crew members) who provide this barrier between the wealthiest and the poorest members of the shipboard microcosm. This arrangement seems to be, but is not, similar to modern customs such as first-class sections on airplanes. The symbolic barrier of the curtain may on a modern plane protect the first-class passengers from the sight of their inferiors; the aviation aristocrats may receive more services and better food; and of course the upscale seats will cost more, providing a profit margin for the airline and perhaps offsetting some of the cost of coach seats. But the first-class air passenger will not be quaffing the "good port wine and porter-beer" mentioned in the captain's log while coach passengers die of thirst, nor will they be eating freshly butchered "pigs, chickens, lambs and geese" (2) as others starve. Coach-class air travelers may be less comfortable and worse fed but not in a way that would have long-term consequences. And under no circumstances will passengers either endure privation or enjoy privilege aboard an airliner as they would aboard the *Star* for the projected "TWENTY-SIX days at Sea" (1) in the winter of 1847.

But in one essential way, the travelers on a modern aircraft resemble those on this famine ship: as far as health and safety are concerned, they are all in the same situation. If a plane is airworthy, a ship seaworthy, it is so for all aboard, and the converse is true as well. Thus the first-class passengers are in as much danger from the shipowners' carelessness as are the steerage passengers. Here is the point at which the ship becomes a microcosm of Ireland itself. The country is itself a leaky ship in need of repair. While the well-off believe that they somehow pay their way and are entitled to their privileges, in fact they are as threatened by the Famine as are the peasantry. The Merridiths are destroyed financially by the Famine; and the fact that Lady Verity Merridith dies in 1822 from "famine fever" (132) is evidence that disease does not respect social boundaries. It would be in the best interest of the whole society to keep all its members fed and healthy; but those who have the power to do this, the government officials in London, do not.

For the Merridiths and their ilk, comfort depends on not seeing, pretending not to know about, and ignoring their own complicity in an oppressive system. Laura Merridith, Lady Kingscourt, who is regarded with scant respect by her own husband, is an example of upper-class indifference. When steerage passengers die, the captain reports in his log that the women "indulge in 'keening,'" a cry of lamentation for the dead, "a peculiar variety of wailing ululation where they rend their garments and pull at their hair" (32). Laura Merridith, incapable at this point of empathizing with the grieving women, is one of the passengers in first class who "complain about the disturbance . . . concerned that her children might be distressed by the queer proceedings" (33). The next generation of Merridiths, according to their mother, should be protected from any experience that may make them even aware of, much less sympathetic to, the plight of the lower classes. Laura is like those whom Dixon castigates in his newspaper article, those who "chastise the poor for their poverty while regarding [their] own riches as a matter of Divine entitlement" (18). Dixon does not, however, seem to regard this failure of empathy on her part as a barrier to their relationship.

In addition to the sexual rivalry between David Merridith and the American journalist Dixon, their hostility to each other, expressed both in writing and in speech, can be accounted for by the fact that the landlord system can only exist if the full evidence of its injustice is ignored or suppressed, and it is the role of the journalist to pay attention and to reveal. Not that Dixon and the *New York Tribune* are angels of mercy; he is interested only in getting the story, and his employer in selling newspapers. Nevertheless articles such as Dixon's response to Merridith's letter to the editor expose how Irish landowners, native Irish as well as those of British ancestry, conspire to trap the poor in their substandard, overcrowded compartment of the ship of state. As has been noted in the case of Charles Trevelyan, British politicians were in thrall to laissez-faire or free market economic theory, "which preaches that the lust for profit may regulate everything, including who should live and who should die" (18). The modern reader familiar with current historical writing on the Famine will recognize Dixon's response to Merridith as a reasonable summary of the situation in Ireland as the *Star of the Sea* sails westward.

The journey is much as the reader might expect in such marginal vessels. As on most other ships, death is an everyday occurrence in steerage (the only death in first class is a murder). Storms batter the elderly vessel. The beacon of hope at the end of the journey (one meaning of the "star" that guides this sea journey) is the port of New York, gateway to America and to the better life for which all immigrants long. But after the horrors that have already afflicted the steerage passengers, the arrival at New York Harbor is as much of a nightmare as what has gone before. By December 4, 1847, the day on which the ship approaches New York, it was well known there and in other seaports that these famine ships contained diseased passengers, and the mechanisms of contagion were well enough understood that quarantine measures were put into place and disembarkation prohibited. The situation is dire; not only are there the sick people aboard that the harbor officials feared, but it being December, the cold is an additional threat, and supplies are running low. Lockwood estimates that 174 ships are in the same situation as is the *Star of the Sea*. Passengers who have survived the torturous voyage die in the harbor, and bodies cannot be buried either on land or at sea. As befits the political system of New York itself, a certain democracy of suffering has been put in place by edict of the captain: "all provisions now on board are to be shared equally between the steerage passengers, the men and those in First-Class" (352). Pathetic scenes involving "groups of resident New York Irish" hopefully anticipating the arrival of family members who had died at sea or even at dockside in Liverpool are juxtaposed with the threatening arrival of "a party of humble Irishmen" who, unbeknownst to the captain, are checking on Pius Mulvey's completion of his act of retribution (353), which is to kill David Merridith as a representative example of "his class, his genealogy, the crimes of his fathers, for the pedigree bloodline into which he had been born"—the Anglo-Irish (29).

The situation in New York Harbor was foreshadowed several days earlier when, off the coast of Newfoundland, Lockwood boarded a ship returning to Ireland, there to hear from its captain about "horrible events," which Dixon annotates thus: "Captain Lockwood is alluding to the tragedy at Grosse Ile in the summer of 1847, when the Quarantine Station on the St Lawrence river was overwhelmed by an enormous number of sick and hungry immigrants, many from Ireland. Thousands died; Quebec and Montreal suffered devastating fever epidemics" (262). Dixon's term *overwhelmed* accurately describes the historical situation at Grosse Île. The quarantine station had been open since 1832, and during that year it was indeed overwhelmed by the "larger than usual number" of Irish emigrants arriving with cholera.[31] During the years between 1832 and the Great Famine, the quarantine station functioned well. The news from Ireland arrived in Canada in advance of the first 1847 famine ships: "The Canadians . . . did not know the full dimensions of the horror, but they knew a crisis was at hand."[32] Preparations were made under the direction of Dr. George Mellis Douglas, despite whose best efforts the accommodations on land were inadequate. Douglas was therefore "obliged to flout the quarantine law and confine all passengers, healthy and sick alike, on board the ships at anchor in the river."[33] The situation was dire, with disease spreading and medical staff and clergy dying along with patients. The Canadians, though prepared and committed, could neither protect their own population nor care for the sick, and, hoping not to duplicate their fate, New York officials held the famine ships in the harbor.

The modern traveler can visit Grosse Île, which the Canadian government has preserved and maintains in tribute not only to the many immigrants who died on the island but also to the Canadians who tried to save them, many of whom lost their own lives in the process. A monument in the Irish cemetery on the island lists as many of the names of the Irish immigrants buried there as could be discovered. A Celtic cross erected by the Ancient Order of Hibernians in 1909, a dramatic sight from the boat that takes visitors to the island, further commemorates the Irish dead. Visitors to this island are reminded not only of the pathos of the situation from the viewpoint of the immigrants, but also of the heavy responsibility borne by the Canadian government to protect the health of its own citizenry while also rendering humanitarian aid, all in an era before modern medicine and with minimal medical staff and facilities. A similar set of circumstances caused the authorities in New York to set aside Ward's Island "as a secure place to hold immigrants while their applications were processed and their illnesses tended" (376). Neither situation was ideal; medically necessary quarantine was hard to distinguish from nativist rejection. But the mirrored scenes both at Grosse Île and in New York Harbor are a reminder of the huge impact the Great Famine had on both Canada and the United States. Societies unprepared for this flood of destitute, sick, and starving people were asked to compensate for the sins of others, the officials in London and their political supporters, whose callousness set so many adrift.

Yet the novel also includes portraits of those whose journey results, as literary sea voyages often do, in a psychological transformation. The captain is the least surprising of these. From the first day of the voyage, he commemorates the dead in the ship's ledger by name, age, and occupation, not just entering a number, and appends a prayer. By the end of this journey, the empathy that Lockwood shows all along in his way of memorializing the dead leads him to abandon his maritime career and devote himself entirely to the humanitarian mission of the Quakers, who were "the first large-scale organizers of relief for Ireland."[34] Lockwood spends the rest of his life in Ireland. He and his wife "had no previous connection whatever with Connemara; but they saw connections where others who should have seen them simply looked the other way" (385). Such people are the antithesis of the authorities in London who debated economic theories rather than fed the hungry.

More startling is the transformation of Laura Merridith. When first on board ship, she espouses the typical argument of those who, like Charles Trevelyan, regarded the poor as lazy and irresponsible: "Unless strict conditions are imposed they take advantage of the help offered them. . . . Otherwise we merely encourage that same idleness and dependency which have only led to their present misfortune" (14–15). This position seems so indefensible even to her husband, a man whose social status depends on the oppression of others, that he corrects her publicly and harshly. She also, as noted earlier, fails to see the keening women as other than a noisy nuisance. But once in America, this spoiled, silly young matron (and unapologetic adulteress) is transformed, according to her second husband, Dixon, into a passionate advocate for social justice who "fought prejudice and bigotry wherever she saw it" (392). In America she rejects the lifestyle of the idle rich and, though old, crippled, and blind, dies fighting for the rights of women to unionize.

But the most heroic act is that of Mary Duane, who, "when the moment of retribution rolled up out of history and presented itself like an executioner's sword . . . turned away and did not seize it" (366). Mary's act embodies that moral ideal alluded to in the novel's title. Earlier in the novel, when "rumours that the authorities at New York and Boston might turn back all ships deriving from Ireland" (263), the steerage passengers, close to despair, beseech God in the form of a specific type of Catholic prayer, a litany. This litany consists of a collection of devotional titles attributed to Jesus's mother, Mary, interspersed with the Latin invocation *Ora pro nobis*, pray for us. Its culmination is an appeal to Mary as "star of the sea" (265). At a time when navigation by the stars led sailors safely home, it was a religious commonplace to imagine Mary as a guide during life's journey across the turbulent sea, which was itself a metaphor for evil threatening the fragile vessel of the soul. Like many other Catholic women, Mary Duane has been named for the mother of Jesus. Guided by her patron saint, she achieves a moment of moral perfection. The language of Catholicism is true to the thought processes of these characters; but it is not only through organized religion that such acts of reconciliation are possible. Mary's act suggests that when similar moments of retribution arise on the social and political front, one need not necessarily forgive in the theological sense or even the psychological sense. It is enough not to seize the executioner's sword, not to make oneself an instrument of retribution, even if such retribution may seem to be, or in fact is, justifiable.

It is not surprising that both Trevor and O'Connor modulate into the vocabulary of religion: the stigmata of Christ, a devotional title of the mother of Christ, the biblical sword of retribution. One of the greatest ironies of the Great Famine is that the English and the Irish were not only citizens of the same country but adherents of the same Christian faith, albeit different denominations thereof. But in total disregard of the message of the Gospels, political, social, and economic conflicts take precedence over simple humanitarian ethics, much less religious beliefs. Feeding the hungry, giving drink to the thirsty, and comforting the afflicted were replaced by theories that encouraged a contemptuous attitude toward those victimized by the structural inequities inherent in a rigid hierarchical system. When an emergency arrived in the form of the failure of the 1845 potato crop, the powerful in London did not follow the tenets of their common faith.

"A novel should be beautiful, and, hopefully, absorbing, but for me the aim is not art for art's sake. All the strategies of the storyteller and the artist should be at the service of the aim of change."[35] O'Connor's words raise the question of in what way reading such fiction as *Star of the Sea* and Trevor's "The News from Ireland" can effect change in the thinking of the twenty-first-century reader. The villains of the Famine story were the officials of the British government whose responsibility it was to respond to what Charles Trevelyan called "this great calamity." A large body of official writings bears witness to the government's contempt for the Irish. In writings by and to such men as Trevelyan and Prime Minister Lord John Russell (1792–1878) can be found nuggets of breathtaking bigotry. Unfettered by modern standards of political correctness, these nineteenth-century politicos made clear their beliefs that they, and people like them, were the truly important members of their society, superior in every way to their problematic fellow countrymen; that they themselves were essential but others were surplus population, ripe for reduction; that a natural disaster was therefore literally a godsend; that even in the face of terrible suffering, government had no responsibility to intervene, indeed had a responsibility not to intervene in what was believed to be the operation of natural forces.

"But what hope is there for a nation which lives on potatoes?" wrote Trevelyan in *The Irish Crisis*.[36] One possible answer might have been to give them hope by providing them with a substitute food, promptly, in usable form and sufficient quantity. But what hope is there for government officials so enslaved to political theories that they allow their countrymen to starve? The actions and inactions of the British government during the Famine exacerbated the antagonisms that had already festered for hundreds of years over such issues as land ownership and language. Demographically the Irish population has never recovered from the Famine. Politically the Famine made separation from the British Empire inevitable. The political consequences would be a half century in coming, but come they did, in the form of the 1916 Easter Rising.

"Terrible beauty"

The Easter Rising

On the Monday after Easter in 1916, a small group of armed rebels seized the General Post Office on Sackville Street (now O'Connell Street) in Dublin. Like other Irish rebels before them, they were protesting the British government's control over Ireland. Like others before them too, they were defeated and their leaders executed. The doomed revolutionaries rose to Ireland's pantheon of patriots. One of the major literary works on the Rising, William Butler Yeats's poem "Easter, 1916,"[1] commemorates the rebel leaders' ascension from the ordinary to the heroic. But in Ireland as elsewhere, larger-than-life political figures provoke questioning as well as adulation. In Tom Murphy's play *The Patriot Game*, first staged in 1991, a group of actors commemorate the Rising but present the event as more a piece of linguistic, and especially dramatic, artistry than a serious attempt at political change. In Murphy's version one of the historical reasons for the Rising's failure as a military action was that, contrary to the idealistic words of the Proclamation of the Irish Republic, far too few Irishmen and Irishwomen recognized the claims of the Republic to their allegiance. Sebastian Barry's 1995 play, *The Steward of Christendom,* looks at the Rising from the point of view of one such nonrebel, Thomas Dunne, a character based on Barry's own great-grandfather. Read in juxtaposition, the two plays demonstrate the ambivalence of these two playwrights as they depict the lives of those who died, or did not die, for Ireland.

"Easter, 1916," written several months after the events, is often anthologized in college textbooks and thus more likely to be known to educated American readers than any other piece of writing about the Rising. Those who know little else about this event nevertheless might well know that, according to Yeats, the leaders of the Rising were ordinary people whose lives were transformed by the "terrible beauty" of violence. In the poem he expresses some reservations about the necessity of violence; he thinks that it was possible that England might yet "keep faith" (l. 68), presumably with regard to allowing Ireland some measure of what was known as "Home Rule." Yet, even given his reservations, Yeats is in awe of the leaders' absolute commitment, the "excess of love" that "bewildered them until they died" (ll. 72–73). While he is not above taking potshots at Rising participants that he disliked (he considers Countess Constance Markievicz too contentious, her voice too "shrill" [ll. 19–20]; John MacBride is a "drunken, vainglorious lout" who did "bitter wrong" to Maud Gonne, Yeats's longtime unrequited love [ll. 32–33]), he names four men, all of whom were "changed, changed utterly" by the "terrible beauty" of the rebellion (ll. 74–80).

MacDonagh, MacBride, Connolly, and Pearse: Yeats's list of Rising participants is now part of the literary canon. Historians may debate whether the rebellion was poorly planned, hopeless, and especially in the case of Rising leader Patrick Pearse (1879–1916), designed more as a "blood sacrifice" of his own life than to free Ireland;[2] or whether it was less the rebellion itself than the British overreaction to it that moved the Irish people along the path to national independence. Whatever refinements later historians may offer, the main point is that these rebels came to be "central to ideas of Irishness."[3] This despite the fact that, at the time, the Rising surely must have seemed a catastrophic failure. The population did not rise up en masse along with its would-be liberators; those who did participate were disorganized and poorly equipped. The complexities surrounding the event grow rather than diminish with the passage of time. The two political dramas discussed here, first staged in the 1990s, offer their own interpretations of the events of Easter Monday 1916.

"Words! . . . Words?" Tom Murphy's *Patriot Game*

The Patriot Game by Tom Murphy (b. 1935) "concentrates on the build-up to Easter Week, the slow teetering into calamity which becomes a headlong rush. And in that portrayal of Ireland before the Rising, there is no sense of a single, unified people waiting to emerge into nationhood."[4] Murphy sees this process as full of even more contradictions than the usual Irish versus English, Catholic versus Protestant polarities of the past. In this discussion one must keep in mind the distinction between the historical figures (Patrick Pearse and James Connolly [1868–1916]) and their namesakes in the play, Pearse or Connolly. In the play Murphy calls attention to one of the great ironies of the "game" of patriotism in 1916: the leaders of the Rising are playing by different sets of rules. In particular the two key theoreticians of the movement, Pearse and Connolly, disagree on the ideological underpinnings of the revolution. This incompatibility is apparent in the language with which they discuss their theories. While both were political orators, Pearse's thought was an amalgam of Christian theology and Celtic mythology, while Connolly was more interested in international socialism than in Irish nationalism. So in the play, "Language is the rebels' privileged medium and battlefield"; Pearse and Connolly are the main combatants; but the other members of this "poets' and speechmakers' revolution"[5] add their contribution to the war of words. Of the would-be revolutionaries, the Narrator notes that "all they needed was men, money, arms, a date to start the fight and whip up national spirit with speeches."[6] Of these requirements they are best supplied with speeches, Pearse and Connolly in particular. Men kill and die because of words. Literary allusions, semantic distinctions, specialized vocabulary, poems, prayers, songs, slogans, lists, jargon, newspaper articles, words read, written, proclaimed, and signed, when necessary forged; speech acts such as interruptions and hesitations; all have a place in this rebellion made of words, to culminate in that ritual/liturgical speech act, the litany. Murphy's verbal "collage"[7] of different types of linguistic constructs serves the modern reader as an introductory or refresher course in the core beliefs of the rebels of 1916.

England and Ireland had waged linguistic warfare since long before Patrick Pearse was born, as was discussed earlier. Pearse's contribution to this battle was to make a firm connection between Irish language and literature and Irish nationalism and to make both central to his educational as well as political agenda. As a young man, Pearse studied Irish in order to read ancient Celtic literature; his stage counterpart sings in Irish and uses short passages of Irish in his oratory. As headmaster of St. Enda's School, the actual Pearse developed a program of Irish language and literature study specifically to train the boys as future revolutionaries. His biographer, Ruth Dudley Edwards, cites a passage from the Irish-language version of the school's prospectus describing its mission as "to inculcate in [the students] the desire to spend their lives working hard and zealously for the fatherland and, if it should ever be necessary, to die for it."[8] Pearse wanted the St. Enda's boys to imagine themselves as the "boy-troops" of the Cúchulainn sagas, from the Irish mythological tales dating back at least to the seventh century and collected in the *Táin Bó Cuailnge*. This suggests that Pearse thought of himself as Cúchulainn, leader of the boy-troops.

So strong was the influence of this literary character on Pearse's thought that he made it into a tool of his pedagogy as well as a template for his own life. He wrote a play for the St. Enda's students based on the Irish superhero's adventures, gave lectures to them on the hero tale, and exhibited a painting in the school of an armed Cúchulainn.[9] The inscription on that painting was the same words from the *Táin* that Pearse uses to make an explicit connection between himself and Cúchulainn:

NARRATOR: He'd be dreamin' a lot, d'yeh know, an' looking at pictures he had of Cuchulainn an' the likes, heroes of ancient times, being warned by old Druids not to—whatever else in the world they did wrong, d'yeh know?—not to take up arms or they'd die young—d'yeh know?

PEARSE: I care not if my life have only the span of a day and night if my deeds be spoken of by the men of Ireland. (98)

Pearse's words, spoken by Cúchulainn in the *Táin,* explained the historical Pearse's life choices. In life and in the play, the *Táin* quotation is an example of the way in which "words precede reality and lives are lived as roles, according to pre-written script."[10] A life devoted to emulating this particular hero will be heroic, but brief.

Another literary component of Pearse's political theories—the Fenian myth—was expressed in his eulogy for Jeremiah O'Donovan Rossa. O'Donovan Rossa (1831–1915), Irish Nationalist, recruited Irish Americans to the cause, whose support—as the British in the play realize (107)—is crucial to the Nationalist enterprise. O'Donovan Rossa's political followers were dubbed the Fenians to echo the name of a warrior troop, the Fionn, in another of the mythological cycles. The Fionn function in Irish myth much as King Arthur and his knights do in English storytelling, as exemplars of military might in service of the nation. Like King Arthur, who will return from Avalon at the time of England's greatest need, so the Fenians can save Ireland. In his eulogy Pearse elevates O'Donovan Rossa into a paragon of all the Nationalist virtues, an inspiration for the future in the battle against those who "think that they have purchased half of us and intimidated the other half . . . but the fools, the fools, the fools! They have left us our Fenian dead, and while Ireland holds these graves, Ireland unfree shall never be at peace" (101). After O'Donovan Rossa is buried and the Rising is well under way, however, Pearse's funerary oratory is echoed ironically when, at St. Stephen's Green, Countess Constance Markievicz and fellow rebel Michael Mallin are "hemmed in . . . sitting ducks" (138). The Narrator echoes Pearse's own rhetoric in the eulogy regarding the Fenian myth to express the futility of the rebels' vain hope that "help would come. From where? Be-cause, be-cause all Ireland did not rise up once the fighting started: The fools, the fools, the fools, they did not wish to become Fenian dead!" (138). All very well, in other words, to praise famous men: but to die as they did? Except for a core group—most of whom were executed with Pearse— few Irishmen wished to die like a Fenian.

Pearse, however, did. In addition to his identification with the Fenians and with Cúchullain, he also identified with another figure who died young but lives on in the written word: Jesus Christ. Christ's death and resurrection are echoed in imagery associated with the Rising. While in the play the timing of the Rising is depicted as haphazard, the revolutionaries agree on the Easter season be- cause of its religious symbolism (112); having come to this agreement too late in the day on Easter itself, however, they settle on the following Monday (129). Murphy's Pearse says that "bloodshed is a cleansing and sanctifying thing"

(129), and the historical Pearse's poetry reflects his perception of himself as emulating what Christians believe to be the redemptive sacrifice of Christ's death. In a poem written from the point of view of Pearse's own mother and quoted in the play, he equates his mother's suffering with that of Christ's mother, Mary (doubled in the case of Mrs. Pearse, who lost two sons, Patrick and William [1881–1916], in the Rising). Murphy's stage directions, however, allow for a more cynical interpretation of the "mother" poem. He suggests that "the actor playing MOTHER is free in interpretation to question the sentiments" (115). Pearse was not himself a parent and could therefore not have fully understood the impact of his and Willie's deaths on their mother. Once the character named Mother interprets or questions the sentiments, "the male heroic voice of romantic sacrifice dissolves in the mouth of a woman, the rhetoric becoming bitter, incredulous, and grief-stricken,"[11] in effect unsaying itself—yet another linguistic act in a play about the impact of words.

Pearse was not the only poet among the Easter Rising central command; the poetry of Thomas MacDonagh (1878–1916) and Joseph Mary Plunkett (1887–1916), some of which is repeated in the play, is still anthologized alongside Pearse's.[12] Connolly, however, is portrayed in *The Patriot Game* as scornful of his colleagues' literary leanings ("Let's become poets and *eat* poetry" [113; italics in original]). Connolly's own speeches eschew poetic diction and employ the specialized vocabulary of Marxism—"comrades," "ruling class," "despotic government" (108)—rather than either Celticism or Catholicism. Connolly sees the issue confronting Ireland as not specifically Irish but pan-European and class-based. His goal is not so much to separate Ireland from England as to "be the one to set the torch to a European conflagration that will not burn out until the vulture classes that rule and rob the world are finally dethroned. In America, in Russia, in Scotland, in Europe" (103).

Other characters in the play call Connolly's socialist agenda into question as unsuitable for the Ireland of 1916. For one thing the average man on the Dublin street is anything but international in his political thinking. As one listener interjects in response to Connolly's speech about Russia, Scotland, and Europe, "Them're middlin foreign places, sir!" (103). He knows little and cares less about foreign places, apparently making no distinction between America and Russia, and seems unaware not only that Scotland is a close neighbor, but also even that Ireland is part of Europe. The crowd insists that Connolly consider the needs of Ireland first, and he does concede by the end of the scene that the movement will need to "forget Europe and clean up this mess of nationalism first" (104)—not that everyone agrees on the definition of nationalism. A side conversation between attendees at the funeral of O'Donovan Rossa intersperses economic analyses with phrases from the Catholic Hail Mary prayer. The events of 1916 are taking place at a time of agricultural prosperity, and the speakers do not want politics to interfere with this: "what with the high prices for the stock and the grain an' the exportin' wholesale since the war started: we'll be made-up if it lasts, an' secure if the Volunteers don't go upsettin' us" (102). Connolly's socialist message will have little resonance in a time of war-fueled prosperity but will only be "upsettin'." Connolly, then, is persuaded to switch his approach from Marxism to nationalism, a change that he believes to be temporary.

On Easter Monday 1916, Pearse read the Proclamation of the Irish Republic outside the General Post Office, and in the play this key document in Irish history is included in its entirety (136–37). The Proclamation is the point at which speech, writing, and theater intersect; it is the culmination of all that had gone before and the cause of all that was to come after, including Pearse's own death. The power of words to shape a life even involves the values embodied in one's name: Patrick Henry Pearse, named for the American revolutionary whose famous ultimatum, "Give me liberty or give me death," had inspired rebellion in the Colonies. The Proclamation of the Irish Republic combines more language echoing that of the American Declaration of Independence ("national freedom," "religious and civil liberty," "happiness and prosperity of the whole nation") with the language of Roman Catholicism ("We place the cause of the Irish Republic under the protection of the Most High God, Whose blessing we invoke"). Both language systems are emotionally resonant for the Irish and are thus rhetorically effective. The scene ends with Connolly and Pearse sharing a moment of triumph.

But at the same time the might of empire, personified by Gen. Sir John Maxwell, is mobilizing against them. Maxwell's own speech, with its long sentences laden with military jargon, mark him off as the quintessential bureaucrat: "I will take all such measures as may in my opinion be necessary for the suppression of insurrection here and I am accorded a free hand in regard to the movement of all troops now in Ireland or which may be placed under may command hereafter and also in regard to such measures as may seem to me advisable under the Proclamation dated 26th April under the Defence of the Realm Act" (144). Maxwell's Proclamation competes with that of the rebels, and it is clear that Maxwell will win. What is really meant by all his bureaucratese is contained in a casual aside: "Dig a grave for a hundred men" (144).

Coexisting alongside the elevated diction of the Proclamation or Maxwell's jargon are slogans and song lyrics, oversimplified but motivational for the average Dubliner. The play is full of songs, opening with a "distorted version of 'God Save the King,' the British National Anthem" to express the disillusionment of the Irish people with regard to their poor-relation status in the British Empire; the relationship, like the recording of the anthem, has long since "unwound itself" (93). A singer offers a rendition of Yeats's poem "The Rose

Tree," the theme of which is the uselessness of "lightly spoken" words compared to bloodshed—only the "red blood" of martyrs can nourish the "rose tree" of a free Ireland (119). Like many other political protest songs in Ireland, "The Rose Tree" includes those elements of deniability that protect a subordinate people in that the meaning of the central image, the rose tree, is vague. Does it symbolize freedom from empire or some other lofty, but unthreatening, ideal? Other singers interject scraps and phrases of similar rebel songs, as for example when the Narrator quotes the rebel song "Kelly, the Boy from Killane," in praise of one of Ireland's "brave sons who died/For the cause of long-downtrodden man" (139)—here again, the cause for which Kelly dies nobly is left unspecified. The rebel songs in general, with their bouncy rhythms and rousing choruses, make military action seem almost a form of manly camaraderie. When the singing stops, however, the death and destruction of war is represented by a drum-beating man. This character's drumming, along with his memento mori function, highlights how the synergy of words and music increases the emotional appeal of the ideas contained in the lyric.

A political play, not surprisingly, uses the verbal tags of its movement. Catchy phrasing is the stock in trade of the political sloganeer; at best these word bytes encapsulate the highest ideals of a movement, at worst they substitute oversimplifications for deep, or even rational, thought. Because England was involved in World War I in 1916, this may have been a good time for Ireland to challenge the status quo: "England's difficulty is Ireland's opportunity" (94). Short and punchy, with rhythmic, repetitive phrasing juxtaposing *difficulty* with *opportunity*, the slogan seems convincing, distracting attention from the practical logistics that Ireland faces in seizing said opportunity, assuming that it in fact exists. When Connolly cautions his hearers against working for the British government, his slogan "Don't take the shilling!" (111) ignores the realities of supporting a family in nonagricultural areas such as Dublin. Announcing rebellion, Connolly appropriates (without attribution) the phrase of labor leader James Larkin (1876–1947) from the Dublin Lockout three years earlier: "The great appear great because we are on our knees! Let us rise!" (115). But will enough people consider themselves sufficiently part of "us" to risk rising? And what form will that rising take? Finally, adopting the Nationalist slogan "UP THE REPUBLIC!" (149), as the hitherto skeptical Narrator does by the end of the play, does not necessarily guarantee that the Republic will achieve the hoped-for elevation.

The rebels act on the basis of words, but words are slippery. Characters cannot agree on the definition of important terms, and misinformation abounds. Even sympathetic characters such as Connolly, in an argument with Eoin MacNeill, leader of an opposing Nationalist group, combine sloganeering with ambiguities of language. "Constitutional action in normal times, revolutionary action in exceptional times. These are exceptional times," he says, assuming that he, not MacNeill, will define *normal* and *exceptional* (96). A group of comic characters who are reminiscent of the stereotypical "culchies" or perhaps the stage Irishmen of comedy—Molly, Biddy, Jim, and Mick—are, in the midst of the Rising, "huddled together, waiting, trying to get into a pub" rather than joining in (140). Meanwhile they report absurd untruths: the Pope has been killed; London has been taken by Irish Volunteer Reserves; Jim Larkin is marching from the West "with a million even American soldiers" (140). This last, a variant of the Fenian myth, shows that some of the would-be revolutionaries are coming to believe their own legends. Forgeries and counterforgeries turn the plot, and the media of the time, a local newspaper, plays its role. MacNeill, heading a rival Nationalist group, issues orders countermanding Pearse's: "he composed a longer an' a better notice an' put it in the *Sunday Independent* that everybody'd be readin'" (124).

The British are no better at confronting linguistic ambiguity than the Irish are. The Prime Minister of England apparently thinks that changing the names of things or adopting conciliatory language is going to help; so Asquith offers an "Irish Brigade" or "Irish Army Corps" to encourage Irish recruitment to the war effort, so that they can maintain their national "identity" while simultaneously helping England with the war effort and draining off manpower from Ireland's Nationalist cause (109).

The Narrator ponders from time to time on the meaning of loaded words: *hatred, Home Rule, freedom*. This character represents the second thoughts of all but the most committed ideologues: "Weren't we all right the way we were? And we don't really *hate* the English, do we? Wasn't Home Rule on the way? Whatever that is. Wouldn't we be free sometime? Whatever that is" (139). Anything, according to the Narrator at this point in his or her ideological evolution, would be better than what has just happened: the random killing of a nurse who had arrived to help the injured. The Narrator at this point rejects all political beliefs in favor of basic survival: "I hate nationalism. . . . I love life" (129). No sooner does the Rising begin than the Dublin populace resorts to looting, issuing their own proclamation justifying it: "It's a free country!" (142). Characters interrupt and contradict each other, demonstrating the lack of clear channels of command; pauses and hesitations connote insecurity; and "one central scene consists in a cacophonic speech contest between Asquith, Redmond, MacNeill, Pearse, and Connolly, all speaking at the same time and trying to recruit for the British army, the Volunteers, the IRB or the ICA."[13]

At various points in the play, it is tempting to see the cast of participants in the 1916 Rising from Connolly's exasperated viewpoint, as "comic-opera revolutionaries" (116). But in the last scene of the play, as the prisoners make their final speeches and are executed, the play achieves a "balance between human sympathy for the rebels and refusal of hero-worship."[14] Their nobility moves even the cynical, worldly wise Narrator, who, it must be remembered, is a character from the 1990s who began the play with contempt for the idealism of 1916. The incantatory, quasi-liturgical recitation of the names, which contributes the "air of a religious rite, a search for redemption through sacrifice,"[15] echoes both the Proclamation and Yeats's "Easter, 1916." The play ends with the Narrator reciting a poem by John Stephens (1882–1950) that mourns but also celebrates the "last journeying" of the rebels (149). Contrary to the historical record, Pearse is not executed as his real-life counterpart was. Instead he waits by the exit for the Narrator, as if ready to guide that person from the future on the path set down by the revolutionaries. For all the questioning of Pearse's motives, his expertise, his management of the Rising, the play ends with him still alive, his place in history secure as, after all the linguistic confusion, he calls not just the Narrator but all Irishmen and Irishwomen to a simple goal simply expressed: "Come on home" (149).

"Nets of history": Sebastian Barry's *The Steward of Christendom*

Whether the rebels were heroes or not is, in *The Patriot Game,* debatable; but those who supported the Loyalist cause during the Rising certainly seem to have been on the wrong side of history. Such a one is Thomas Dunne, in *The Steward of Christendom* by Sebastian Barry (b. 1955). Based on Barry's own great-grandfather, Dunne, though a Catholic, remained loyal to the British Empire during the Easter Rising and through the period of political violence that followed the Rising and peaked after the signing of the Anglo-Irish Treaty of 1921. Barry's play explores the consequences of not seizing the day, not rising to the occasion, not being part of a transformational moment in history.

Much of Barry's work explores the lives of such men as these, whose lives call into question what is "perhaps nationalism's most sacrosanct myth . . . its idea that Irish history can be read as an uninterrupted chronicle of pan-nationalist resistance against British rule."[16] When Pearse read the Proclamation of the Republic, he described a consistent pattern of Nationalist uprisings: "In every generation the Irish people have asserted their right to national freedom and sovereignty: six times during the past three hundred years they have asserted it in arms." Pearse could have added some modifications to this ringing declaration: in *some generations, some* of the Irish people asserted their rights in arms *about every fifty years or so.* In between many of them, perhaps even most of them, lived as British subjects. But qualifiers make for bad oratory, and so some people, maybe most people, get left out of the historical record. Like William Trevor, whose novel *The Story of Lucy Gault* centers on the Anglo-Irish, a group that does not fit neatly into the "sacrosanct myth," Barry dramatizes the lives of another such group: Catholic Loyalists. Such people "find themselves without a place or a narrative of identity" in the Republic.[17] Men and women without a country, they have been "edged out of the Irish mainstream because certain histories of Ireland have been accepted and others have been rejected."[18] A man such as Dunne represents "a complexity that Irish nationalist histories quickly eliminated, preferring instead a past in which Catholics were Nationalists, Protestants were Unionists, and few confusions over loyalties had or would ever exist."[19] The "binary narratives" of Ireland are disturbed by such anomalies.[20]

For the reader of Barry's work who is not Irish, and perhaps even for some who are, one of the main challenges is to unscramble the time sequence of events in Irish history, so as to correlate the public events mentioned in the play with the private lives of Dunne and his family. Like many modern literary works, *The Steward of Christendom* operates according to the nature of human memory. Dunne's memories explore the past, his own and his family's. But events are not remembered in neat chronological order, and the nonlinearity of memory is only one factor distorting time. The play premiered in 1995; the present-time action of the play takes place in 1932. While Thomas can know nothing that happened after 1932, the Irish audience can fill in the gaps in the historical record up to 1995. They know on what points he was less than prescient and judge him accordingly. The audience remembers events that are still in the future for Thomas, and this adds another dimension to the chronology/memory component of Barry's play.

Thomas is based on Barry's great-grandfather, the last man to hold the position of chief superintendent of the Dublin Metropolitan Police (DMP) under the British government. Ten years after the signing of the Anglo-Irish Treaty, in the present-time action of the play, Thomas is in a mental institution, his present life as bare as the stage set. His glory days with the DMP—when Queen Victoria, then her son Edward, reigned, when Thomas's beloved wife, Cissy, was alive—are all in the past. Thomas is not ready for the new regime ushered in by the coming of the Republic; his way of thinking is rooted in a trio of interrelated hierarchical values passed down to him from his forefathers: service, loyalty, and stewardship.

The concept of stewardship is intrinsically hierarchical in that it implies serving a master, being a caretaker of the master's possessions; so it is depicted time and again in the Bible, as Thomas seems to recognize.[21] His father was a steward, and his great-great-grandfather was a steward, both of Humewood, the Big House of an Anglo-Irish family. When Thomas says this, he is boasting that his father was a servant. He believes that to be in service is an honor. The extent of a master's possessions, the size of his house in particular, is a status indicator for the servant as well as those served; and so being the steward of so large an establishment, as opposed to being in service in a small one, means basking in the reflected glory of the Ascendancy, even several generations later. But the high status of masters would not be possible without the low status of servants; the servants must be complicit in a structure of subordination for the hierarchy to endure. When in 1913 labor leader James Larkin questioned the assumptions on which the master/servant relationship was based, his words threatened to upend a whole social system, to render it, in Thomas's words, "all topsy-turvy."[22]

Although Thomas does not follow his father as steward of Humewood, he does follow the same principles of service, loyalty, and stewardship. As a member of the DMP, he sees himself as protecting the queen's property much as his father cared for the grand estate, in a similar aura of reflected glory. Thomas, born in 1857, grew up thinking of himself as an Englishman. Queen Victoria had been on the throne since 1837 and would be until he was forty-four years old. Thus when he is employed by the government, he understands it to be his own government, and he is not alone in that sentiment: "Until 1916 . . . crown employment was a fact of life rather than a cause for patriotic self-doubt. Numerous poor Catholic men also took the Saxon Shilling."[23] Thomas's pride in his work comes from his loyalty to the queen, "the principle of order" presiding over "a perfect chain of being."[24] His job is to keep Victoria's realm safe and orderly: "the great world that she owned was a shipshape as a ship. . . . men like me were there to make everything peaceable, to keep order in her kingdoms" (15).Thomas's loyalty to Victoria is rooted in his own love for order: "The world was a wedding of loyalty, of steward to Queen, she was the very flower and perfecter of Christendom" (15). He is the queen's steward, not just of Dublin but of the empire.

So strong was his loyalty to Victoria that he found it "difficult to go from her to the men that came after her, Edward and George" (15). Edward VII, Victoria's son, took the throne upon his mother's death in 1910; then, only nine years later, he died, to be succeeded by his son, George V. If Thomas could not shift his loyalties at the stately pace with which monarchs succeeded one another on the British throne, how likely is it that he could question the idea of monarchy itself, much less adjust to a Republican revolution? As historian John Wilson Foster points out, the loyalty of people such as Thomas is "at first glance foolish and justifies their apparent status as time's laughingstocks," but as the play progresses, the audience is asked to "re-evaluate the once deplored loyalty" of the Dunne family, which is not an aberration but rather "represent[s] those tens of thousands of Irish who shared their values."[25] Later events will place Dunne and his fellow Catholic Loyalists on the wrong side of history; but for him history ends in 1932. Barry's play asks for understanding, if not necessarily approval, for people who had to work with the values, not to mention the information, available to them at the time.

Through wearing the uniform of the DMP, as did Thomas, or of the British army, fighting in World War I like his son Willie, Irishmen like them demonstrated affiliation and loyalty. Clothing, and changes of clothing, are always of major importance in theater; and in this play the significant costume is Thomas's police uniform. As is the point of uniforms, this one makes its wearer a part of something larger than himself, something with dignity, even grandeur. The uniform is the centerpiece of one of his favorite memories, of his daughters tending to him and showing pride in him via their maintenance of his uniform: "And Dolly my daughter . . . polished my policeman's boots, and Annie and Maud brought me my clothes brushed and starched in the mornings, as the castle of soldiers and constables woke" (12). As he serves the Crown, they serve him, reinforcing their place and his in an orderly world.

But the gold trim missing from his uniform highlights by its absence the paradox of Thomas's life as what was contemptuously termed a "Castle Catholic." Because historically the ruling class in Ireland under the Ascendancy was largely Protestant and the ruled class largely Catholic, a crossover alliance between Catholics and the British Empire was thought by those of a Republican bent to be a betrayal of Nationalist principles as well as Catholicism itself. By working for the DMP, Thomas protects Dublin Castle, the seat of British power in Dublin, thus exposing himself to discrimination. Nevertheless he is proud of his success within a Protestant-dominated force; he brags of rising as high as a Catholic could, apparently insensible to the irony that even a competent and loyal steward would hit a low glass ceiling because of his faith: "If I had made commissioner I might have had gold, but that wasn't a task for a Catholic, you understand, in the way of things, in those days" (10). Dunne is not one to question "the way of things," discrimination against Catholics by the British government; he assumes that his hearers will understand it too and makes his way in the system as it is, accepting its limitations as if they were divinely ordained. Even when he thinks that he should have "a beautiful pension for [his] forty-five years of service" and finds out from Annie that he does not (32), he does not question the system that got him and his family to this point. Instead he pledges allegiance to the past: "My father was the steward of Humewood, and I was the steward of Christendom" (33).

By 1932 all that Dunne's uniform once represented had been rejected by the Irish people; the DMP was disbanded in 1925. This erased his entire work history. In the present-time action of the play, not only does he not have the gold, he does not have the uniform either; early on he is stripped naked by the orderly Smith, and the seamstress Mrs. O'Dea measures him for the black suit linking him not to his beloved monarch but to the madhouse. While the seamstress, in the condescending way people have with invalids, describes it as a "fine suit, as good as my own attire," Thomas knows that it is not as good as his uniform and begs for "a bit of gold or suchlike for the thread" as a consolation prize (7). Reinforcing the clothing symbolism, all Thomas has of Willie is the muddy uniform in which he died as a soldier of the British army on the Western Front.

In his DMP uniform, in his heyday, Thomas was charged with maintaining public order. But maintenance of order to some is suppression of freedom to others. His role in the 1913 Dublin Lockout earned him the resentment of those on the labor side of this labor vs. management dispute, and that long-ago conflict has consequences even in Thomas's life in the asylum. The hospital orderly Smith holds him responsible for the violence with which the lockout was suppressed. Smith's "verbal and physical abuse of Dunne casts him as a brutal personification of nationalist fanaticism and bigotry":[26] "Chief superintendent, this big gobshite was, Mrs. O'Dea, that killed four good men and true in O'Connell Street in the days of the lock-out. Larkin. Hah? His men it was struck down the strikers. (*A gentle hit with the drying cloth.*) Baton-charging. A big loyal Catholic gobshite killing poor hungry Irishmen. If you weren't an old madman we'd flay you" (9).

Thomas, of course, sees the Lockout as a highlight of his career: "When I went out that day to stop Larkin in Sackville Street, all the world of my youth, the world of Ireland that I knew, was still in place, loyal, united and true. I had three lovely daughters, and a little son as glad as a rose. And I had risen as high as a Catholic could in the Dublin Metropolitan Police. And we were drawn up, ready to dispel them" (53). The Larkin of whom the two men speak is the same labor organizer who worked closely with 1916 revolutionary James Connolly. The incident in Sackville Street (the fact that Smith calls it by its post-Republic name, O'Connell Street, and Thomas by its pre-Republic name is significant in itself) pitted Larkin's union against one William Martin Murphy, a business leader. When Murphy fired the members of Larkin's union, the union declared a general strike; businesses responded by locking out twenty thousand workers. On August 31, 1913, "Bloody Sunday," violence broke out; Thomas's historical counterpart "is remembered in Barry's family for ordering the vicious baton charge that dispersed a largely peaceable crowd of strikers."[27] The four men of whom the orderly speaks were killed, and the union quashed. Does Smith mean that Thomas personally killed the four men or that the DMP did? Prolabor citizens would see little distinction: the DMP's de facto role was protecting management, and the its public image suffered. Three years later the DMP would be called upon again to preserve order in the midst of an even more violent event.

The Easter Rising is the point of connection between the two plays discussed here. As has been discussed with regard to *The Patriot Game*, the Rising faced an uphill struggle against the perception of men such as Thomas Dunne that they were Englishmen, part of a great and glorious empire. In the early 1900s, "Ireland, like the rest of the United Kingdom, experienced a period

when pride in empire reached unparalleled heights."[28] For years various movements and organizations were developed with the goal of retraining Irish men
and women to think of themselves as other than British. The Gaelic League,
for example, founded in 1893 by language scholar Douglas Hyde (1860–1949),
encouraged the Irish to "de-Anglicise" through language, music, sports, and
nomenclature. The Abbey Theatre, founded in 1899, put on plays such as John
Millington Synge's *Riders to the Sea* (1904), Lady Augusta Gregory's *Rising
of the Moon* (1907), and William Butler Yeats's *Cathleen Ni Houlihan* (1902),
all of them on Nationalist topics. In fact Barry's own mother acted the part
of the old woman, symbol of Ireland, in *Cathleen,* and Barry remembers the
impact the play had on him as a child in the audience at the Abbey.[29] Reading
the literature of the Irish Literary Revival teaches the modern reader how intent
literary Nationalists were on revising the Irish people's idea of themselves not
as citizens of the British Empire but as heirs to a proud Celtic heritage. That
identification with England would not have needed revision had it not been
firmly embedded in the minds of many.

But the audience for the literary Nationalists' translations of folklore, for
their poetry and drama, would be people interested in poetry, fiction, and
drama and open to new ideas, not such a man as Thomas Dunne. Thomas, presumably like many others, is not interested in what he perceives as a highbrow
"Irish Ireland" movement. When the Easter Rising finally does come, he is one
of the many who, when they heard of the capture of the General Post Office by
a small band of rebels, did not rush to swell their numbers; indeed they supported the other side. *The Patriot Game* provides insights into why the popular
uprising for which Pearse and Connolly had hoped did not materialize; *The
Steward of Christendom* provides others. In addition to Dunne, his son Willie
is a reminder that "many more Irishmen chose to serve in the British Army during the Great War than those who took part in the Easter Rebellion."[30] If Pearse
and Connolly imagined themselves as embodying the spirit of Ireland, perhaps,
at least in 1916, such men as Thomas and Willie Dunne did as well.

To Thomas the Rising is not a turning point in Irish history, much less in
the history of Christendom, but merely "that rebellion at Easter time, that they
make so much of now" (10). His dismissive remark suggests that, in his mind
at least, it was not the rebellion itself, but the "making much" of it by later
Nationalists, that was significant. If the Rising was not a pivotal event in Irish
history, then the role of his own organization in suppressing it was just an ordinary day's work. According to him the DMP consisted of "mostly country
men, and Catholics to boot, and we loved our King and we loved our country"
(10). Questioning the legitimacy of the status quo was not on their job description, but keeping order in the Dublin streets surely was: "We did our best and
followed our orders," being "just ordinary country men keen to do well" (11).

A married man with three children, then a widower with four, Thomas was nothing like the political idealists who, in Yeats's "Easter, 1916," "dreamed and are dead" (l.71). In the present-time action of the play, dreamers are replaced by survivors, and the Irish people—even those who, like Thomas, did not support the Rising—are being asked to transfer their loyalty to Michael Collins and Éamon de Valera.

Collins (1890–1922) fought in the Rising but survived to become "*de facto* leader of the entire revolutionary movement."[31] In his role as chairman of the provisional government, he was a signatory to the Anglo-Irish Treaty of 1921–22; he was assassinated shortly thereafter by opponents of the treaty. Because "Collins was perhaps the outstanding talent of the Irish revolution, combining formidable powers as administrator, soldier, negotiator, counter-intelligence chief, and ruthless terrorist," the movement's loss of him at the age of thirty-two was a major blow.[32] His fellow revolutionary Éamon de Valera was sentenced to death for his role in the Rising, but in the time interval between the first execution and that intended for de Valera, "a revulsion in public opinion" saved him.[33] The fact that de Valera was born in New York and so held American citizenship also contributed to his being spared. His political career took him to many of the highest positions in the new Irish Republic; but his complicated relationship with his fellow revolutionaries, including Collins, made him some enemies. By virtue of his long political career (he lived to age ninety-three), de Valera played a mighty role in the development of the new republic. But in 1932, at fifty, he had some of his best years ahead of him. In 1932, when the present-time action of *The Steward of Christendom* takes place, Collins was ten years dead, and de Valera was in the process of undoing his old rival's final accomplishment, the Anglo-Irish Treaty.

As in 1913 and 1916, during the events surrounding the Anglo-Irish Treaty, Thomas is again on the wrong side of history. As he explains his role as chief superintendent of B Division of the DMP after the 1922 treaty signing, his task was to defend Dublin Castle, "to protect the city while the whole world was at each other's throats" (11). Keeping order in the face of such disorder was neither an easy nor a gratifying job, but Thomas is satisfied that he and his colleagues did it with the minimum of violence. Men such as he, conscious of their "proper duty," are, he thinks, "part of a vanished world" (11). Thomas struggles with the idea of transferring loyalty to the new leaders. After the establishment of the Republic, the men he would have been expected to serve do not measure up to what he sees as the greatness of the past. His loyalties are to Victoria and Edward. His daughter Annie reminds him that now, if he is a servant at all, he is a servant of Michael Collins, not King Edward: "Collins is no king either. . . . With a tally of carnage, intrigue and disloyalty that would shame a tinker" (37). Thomas is too deep into his melancholy to do anything more than reiterate the credo by which he has lived his life: "I served that King, Annie, and that will suffice me" (37). The king to whom he refers is Edward.

But when Thomas discusses Collins with his other daughter, Dolly, a more nuanced and ambivalent reaction to Collins emerges. Thomas is impressed with Collins, with his graceful yet athletic way of carrying himself, with his height and good looks, "like one of those picture stars that came on the big ship from New York." He allows as how Collins might have been successful in the police force and moreover that he even "would have been proud to have him as my son" (44). Comparing himself to Collins, Thomas feels again the sting of his limited opportunities as a "Castle Catholic." Collins offers a glimpse of a new world in which a man would not be held back by his religion, and Thomas is beginning to understand why he commanded such loyalty, suggesting that had he lived, he might have earned Thomas's loyalty in time. Thomas appears to have been present at the 1922 ceremony conveying Dublin Castle to Collins as representative of the new Irish government: "And for an instant, when the Castle was signed over to him, I felt a shadow of that loyalty pass across my heart. But I closed my heart instantly against it." Whether that shadow of loyalty might have developed further is a moot point. Had Collins been able to maintain order as Victoria did, Thomas might have reopened his heart. But urban chaos ensues, with the streets that Thomas sees as his own becoming "places for murder and fire" (44).

Then Collins is assassinated, and Thomas has to start all over again to try to develop loyalty to his sometime rival de Valera; all this is more revolution than evolution to Thomas, and he cannot cope with the rapid pace of change. To him Edward is the "true king," far superior to the man who Mrs. O'Dea calls "King De Valera" (24). Such men as de Valera will never be able to raise the status of such as Thomas. Thomas is not alone in his contempt for the sort of man who has risen to power. Annie also questions the right of Collins to rule: "Why Collins of all people to give the Castle to? Couldn't they find a gentleman?" (16). Neither Thomas nor Annie understands that the whole hierarchical principle has been cast aside: hereditary nobility need not apply. He is right when he thinks that there is no place in Ireland for a Loyalist like himself, "a man that loves his King" (24).

"It is difficult to write about anyone without finding them enmeshed in the nets of history, poor fish of circumstance that we are."[34] Barry's insight applies particularly to *The Steward of Christendom,* "a history play about the future,"[35] with "the future" meaning anything that happened after 1932. With every new production of the play, that future expands, as do the audience's perceptions of Thomas Dunne. At the time he was a member of the DMP, Thomas boasts that he could "name every lane, alleyway, road, terrace and street" in Dublin (31). By 1995, when the play was first staged, the fiftieth anniversary of the Easter Rising had come and gone, and if Dunne walked the streets of Dublin, he would have to learn many new names before he could again take pride in knowing his city. The General Post Office is still there, but not on Sackville Street; the street has been renamed O'Connell Street, after nineteenth-century Nationalist Daniel O'Connell. Inside the GPO a statue of Patrick Pearse's mythological role model, Cúchulainn, commemorates the Rising. If Dunne continued to walk along O'Connell Street, he would find a statue of James Larkin, the very labor organizer against whom he rallied his officers during the 1913 Lockout. Railroad stations are named after Connolly and Pearse. Kilmainham Gaol, where they and twelve others died, is now a major tourist destination, and visitors and Dubliners alike can pay their respects to the long line of Irish rebels at the Garden of Remembrance, which opened in 1966. An army barracks named after Collins is now a museum. Conversely many relics of the British Empire that existed in Dunne's time are now gone. Nelson's Pillar, opened in 1809 to honor the then-revered British admiral, was blown up in 1966, presumably by activists eager to rid Dublin of imperialist relics.

These changes in the streetscape of Dublin are not as drastic, however, as the ideological shift regarding the Easter Rising. What Willie Dunne calls, dismissively, "the ruckus at home" (50) has now risen itself to historical archetype: "Our notions of the legitimacy of nationalist struggle, of the acceptability of violence in the pursuit of democratic goals, of the role of heroism and sacrifice in political conflict, and of the dignity of small nations in the face of superior force, have all been decisively influenced by what occurred during Easter week in Dublin."[36] Conversely the worldwide empire that Dunne served has shrunk to one small island, hanging on desperately to a small portion of its neighbor.

Even Dunne's loyalty, his most admirable trait, seems like another relic of the bad old days. By 1995 citizens of the Irish Republic would be likely to see loyalty in a very different light, since "we know today what we think of those who follow orders at all costs."[37] By 1995 Collins was considered "a founding father of Irish democratic independence";[38] a year later an adulatory film drama about his life was a box office and critical success. Éamon de Valera, for all the controversial decisions and therefore enemies that he made in his long political career, mattered greatly to his country.

At the same time, as can be seen in these two plays, artists such as Murphy and Barry are doing what artists have always done: challenging the received wisdom of their time. Could it be that the rebels of 1916 made every possible strategic error, were wholly unequipped for the military role to which they assigned themselves, suffered from internal divisions and ideological confusion, yet prodded their country along a historic path nonetheless? And that those who refused to join them, whose inaction and misplaced loyalties surely contributed to the revolutionaries' death, nevertheless played their own chosen roles with dignity and integrity? Colm Toíbín says, in a review essay concerning the Rising and its meaning for Ireland in the present, "I know that ambiguity is what is needed in Ireland now."[39] If so then the complex vision provided by these dramatists is also needed.

After the separation from England was achieved, all was still not well. The compromise arrangement, the two-country solution that separated Northern Ireland from the Republic, generated its own set of problems. The small island was still divided. Language was affected, especially in terms of place-names, which in the Republic were often de-Anglicized (reversing the process described in Brian Friel's *Translations*); eventually street names in Dublin would be re-named after the heroes of the Rising. In the Republic these processes left in an anomalous position those descendants of Edmund Spenser's compatriots, the Anglo-Irish. Residents of Ireland, sometimes for hundreds of years, but of British heritage, these Anglo-Irish, as they were called, still owned land, and the houses upon that land, to the chagrin of those who believed themselves to have been treated ill in the past.

Chapter 6

The Big House

Symbol and Target

Novelist and short story writer Elizabeth Bowen (1899–1973) spent childhood summers in County Cork, at Bowen's Court, a house built on land given in 1749 to her ancestor, Col. Henry Bowen, as a reward for his service to Oliver Cromwell's government. Though she loved the house and her life there, when she inherited Bowen's Court in 1930, the cost of its upkeep was an immediate problem; and by 1960 Bowen could no longer afford to keep it. In her memoir named after the house, as well as in several of her novels and essays, she memorialized not only the house but a way of life. Bowen's writing survives, but Bowen's Court did not; its new owner tore it down.

Transmuted into a literary setting, a house such as Bowen's Court is known as the Big House, and its meaning depends on the larger story of the troubled relationship between England and Ireland dating back at least to the era of the Tudor monarchs, who made land grants to the so-called Planters. Not all Anglo-Irish landholders were British nobility; some, like Bowen's ancestor, and probably like the Gault family in William Trevor's *The Story of Lucy Gault*, benefited from the government's policy during the time when Cromwell was lord protector of England (1653–58) of using Ireland "mainly as a vehicle for paying its debts to soldiers and adventurers."[1] The nouveaux riches of their age, such people and their descendants joined with the Planters to form a "minority culture" that dominated the majority; at the same time, the Planters came to form an "Irish identity, however different that may have been from the Catholic Irish."[2] As time passed, the residents of the Big Houses dominated local culture, society, and government. The eighteenth century, the period of their greatest power, came to be known as the Protestant Ascendancy.

Historians agree that the Big Houses of the Ascendancy were not so big, were in fact smaller versions of their counterparts in England, but they received the epithet in contrast to "the one-room hovels that were inhabited by the native Irish."[3] In addition to social and economic disparity between the haves and have-nots, religious tensions exacerbated relationships between the two groups. "The definition of the term Ascendancy," says historian R. F. Foster, "revolved around *Anglicanism:* this defined a social elite, professional as well as landed."[4] The Great Famine exacerbated the already tense relationship between the haves and the have-nots. Before the Famine the Anglo-Irish imagined their relationship to the Celtic population in terms of the feudal system, with English lord and Irish retainers in a symbiotic relationship of reciprocal duties and responsibilities, as if re-creating a bit of medieval England, albeit an idealized version thereof, on Irish soil.[5] According to Irish studies professor Vera Kreilkamp, the Anglo-Irish envisioned their society as based on both a strong sense of tradition and an assumption of their own innate superiority over the native population: "Behind the historical tenant-landlord relationship in both Ireland and England lies a literary formulation of an ideal feudal community of hierarchical reciprocity, a lost Eden in which loyal vassals serve their beneficent lords in exchange for economic security and stability."[6] The reality was less a single organic community than a pair of communities living in the same space but in mutual enmity: "the high walls of the Big House were to separate for seven centuries the Gaelic population from the English invaders and this partition gave birth to two separate worlds, both perfectly alien and yet close to each other."[7] The feudal myth, never convincing to the Irish, collapsed completely when the landlords' behavior during the Famine gave the native population conclusive evidence that any loyalty they might have had to the owners of the Big Houses was misplaced. While some Big House families assisted the starving, it was more common for landlords to take the same laissez-faire position as did the government in London. Anglo-Irish indifference to the suffering of the native Irish made the Big House itself, post-Famine, "an obnoxious symbol of English imperialism."[8]

Tensions surrounding the British presence in Ireland had simmered for centuries. By the late nineteenth century, popular media as well as Nationalist organizations spread "emotive ideas of the Irish past and Irish identity. . . . The emphasis on past battles, and rebellions, and the high value put on 'dying for Ireland,' helped inculcate a verbal cult of physical violence" that became "inseparably part of Irish nationalism from this time on."[9] These emotions came to a boil with the Easter Rising. Despite the establishment of the Irish Republic six years later, civil unrest beset the country from 1918 to 1923. Given the history, the Big Houses were obvious targets of revolutionary wrath. To some citizens of the new Republic, the presence of these relics of the past—houses and inhabitants both—in an independent Ireland was too obvious a reminder of the bad old days. Scenes of "great destructive conflagrations" due to posttreaty violence, appearing often in fiction, were based on historical reality.[10] Arson, however, may not have been the Big Houses' fate as often as abandonment.[11] Many historical Anglo-Irish families behaved just as did the fictional neighbors of the Gault family in *The Story of Lucy Gault*, the Gouvernets, the Priors, the Swifts, and the Boyces: "the owners of the Big Houses, some of which were in vulnerable rural areas, abandoned them for one of their safer residences (many had several) or left for England."[12]

But to other Anglo-Irish, some of whose families had regarded Ireland as home for centuries, the violence directed against them threatened to uproot them from the only country they knew. For these the move was no simple matter. It might have been, as Bowen sees it, that they were motivated by "myth, lack of means, concentration of interests, [and] love of their own sphere of power";[13] or they might have been motivated by love for the houses, for the lifestyle, or even for Ireland itself. In the fiction based on their experiences, the decaying, destroyed, or abandoned house symbolizes a "broken world,"[14] and "the image of the collapsing great house" became a "metaphor for loss and ruin."[15] Lost and ruined in Big House fiction are the house and the family for which the house is a metaphor (as in, for example, the House of Atreus in Greek tragedy or the Ushers in Edgar Allan Poe's "The Fall of the House of Usher"). The Big House family had assumed that it could bequeath intact to future generations not only a structure but a way of life; the house lost, the family's sense of itself is lost also. The collapse of the Big House in Irish fiction is usually the culmination of a set of historical circumstances against which its current inhabitants are powerless.

In Big House fiction, the relationships among the characters can at least preliminarily be discussed in terms of the following equivalencies:

Big House = Anglo-Irish = Protestant = landowner class;
Cottage = native Irish = Catholic = tenant class.

In such fiction "the gentry life of the Protestant ascendancy"[16] is, from their point of view, a golden age shaped by a "set of manners and a certain life style, above all the idea of leisure."[17] The fact that this leisure had always depended on the poorly remunerated work of others was glossed over. To the gentry the native population constituted an "imagined community of loyal tenants"[18] who were happy to maintain the Big House lifestyle.

But, as might be expected, the native population did not see matters as the Anglo-Irish did. To them the story of the English in Ireland was one of expropriation followed by oppression. The Big House, built on land that they regarded as stolen from their ancestors, "evoked memories of dispossession, exploitation, and injustice."[19] Hence it is a convention of Big House fiction to "describe the decline of Protestant authority and employ as metaphor the decay or destruction of the house itself."[20] As the house goes, so goes the family;

"the imperial place . . . declines into a shabby edifice" at the same time as a "decaying family line" declines also.[21] Due to the sins of the fathers, Big House families do not flourish either physically or psychologically: "ascendancy families fail to produce heirs, and legitimate lines of succession are threatened."[22] Whether destroyed or abandoned, the Big House is doomed, as is the way of life lived so unjustly for so long.

Ascendancy Economics 101: Maria Edgeworth's *Castle Rackrent*

To understand contemporary fiction set in one of these houses, it is necessary to examine the first and still the best-known Big House novel, *Castle Rackrent* by Maria Edgeworth (1768–1849). Published in 1800 but set, according to its title page, "before the year 1782," it traces the decline and fall of one Ascendancy family. Herself a member of the social class that she criticizes, Edgeworth learned the financial aspects of Ascendancy landholding in her role as assistant to her father, Richard Lovell Edgeworth, who returned in 1782 to his family's property in Ireland to administer it hands-on as opposed to as an absentee landlord. As a young girl, Edgeworth had to learn money management on a great estate. When she uses that knowledge in her novel, she makes it clear that the custom of primogenitive inheritance does not necessarily provide the great estates with the best possible conservators. The Big House family may live a leisured, cultured life; but one of its members must support it in that lifestyle by managing the estate. Property management is a demanding job, requiring commitment and a specific skill set, particularly financial. Over several generations of Rackrents, however, the male heirs behave as if the accident of birth is enough to guarantee their competence as estate managers. Edgeworth herself, judging from the intricate financial and legal insights that she articulates through her character Thady, must have worked hard as a young woman to learn her job as her father's administrative assistant. But the Rackrent men make no effort to improve even their behavior, much less their skills. Edgeworth's own understanding of the economics of estate management gave her the ammunition with which to attack the Rackrent men for the financial know-nothingism that causes them to neglect their fiduciary responsibilities to later generations. They make the most elementary mistakes in handling money, thus dooming the Rackrent family and, by extension, the Big House culture of which the author and her family are a part.

When Edgeworth came to write her novel, she chose as her viewpoint character not an Anglo-Irish Protestant like herself but rather Thady Quirk, né M'Quirk, peasant retainer of the Rackrents, modeled on an Edgeworth retainer, John Langan. This viewpoint choice, innovative at the time, has gained *Castle Rackrent* much critical attention. The story is told in the vocabulary and from the perspective of a person of questionable veracity, not just because of his lower social class or the supposed linguistic limitations of his dialect, but more because he is vulnerable to reprisals by those whose tale he is narrating. The Rackrents are Thady's employer; therefore he must seem to be loyal to the family. This makes him sound naive, even sycophantic; but at the same time, he conveys Edgeworth's own contempt, and her precise reasons for it, to the reader. He does this by speaking in a coded language, wherein the surface meaning of his words is different from their implied meaning, and his words are phrased in such a way that he can protect himself by denying that he meant anything by them.

An example of this coded language in action is Thady's description of Sir Condy's unsuccessful legal career: "born to little or no fortune of his own, he was bred to the bar, at which having many friends to push him, and no mean natural abilities of his own, he doubtless would in process of time, if he could have borne the drudgery of that study, have been rapidly made king's counsel at the least—But things were disposed of otherwise, and he never went the circuit but twice, and then made no figure for want of a fee, and being unable to speak in public."[23] Thady is saying that Sir Condy needed to make a living, was encouraged to study law by his friends, and had the ability to study the subject but found it tedious. Had he worked at his chosen profession, he would have been successful; but he did not work hard, did not make money, and also had no knack for public speaking. In other words he was completely inept at the law and lazy to boot; and this at a time when, since there was little likelihood of his inheriting the Rackrent estate, he needed to earn a living. It gradually emerges in the course of the narrative that Sir Condy's sluggishness is contrasted to Thady's son Jason's energy and ambition; the Quirks may not inherit the earth, but by means of Jason's hard work, they will buy it.

How such people as the Rackrents came into possession of their land in the first place is part of the long backstory of Ireland's relationship with England. As Thady explains it, the family of the Rackrents (né O'Shaughlin) was "one of the most ancient in the kingdom" (8). Since in terms of lineage older is always better, Thady flatteringly places the Rackrent origins in a dim past, "before [his] time" (9). But a complication arises here: if the family is very old, "related to the Kings of Ireland" (8–9), the family must have been Catholic. The O prefix to their original name would be an indicator of their Celtic, rather than Anglo, origins. Such a name change, from O'Shaughlin to Rackrent, was common among "native Irish families who had become part of the Ascendancy caste (or aspired to do so). . . . [They] cannily disguised their Gaelic origins (and the Catholic allegiance that often went with them) by dropping their patronymic 'O' and 'Mac,' or by assuming English names."[24] They did so for practical reasons.

During the early eighteenth century, the Penal Laws restricted land ownership to Protestants. Since land ownership conferred social status, it followed that Protestantism was necessary to high social status. Conversely Catholicism came to be associated with the landless poor (as was the purpose of the Penal Laws). Historian Roy Foster points out that although Ascendancy families might occasionally have had "ancient Gaelic" rather than Anglo roots, it was "Anglicanism [that] conferred exclusivity . . . and exclusivity defined the Ascendancy, not ethnic origin."[25] Ethnicity is forever, but religion can be altered, and so the O'Shaughlins, not overburdened with principles, changed their name and their religion to sidestep the Penal Laws and thus retain possession of their land.[26] Even if his family received its land directly from the kings of Ireland, then, Sir Patrick O'Shaughlin kept it in a morally questionable manner, which tarnishes the family heritage ever after. Not a man of high accomplishment himself (though Thady, damning with faint praise, notes that Sir Patrick was "said to be the inventor of raspberry whiskey" [10]), his heirs are even less worthy, acquiring their holdings simply by virtue of being born.

Castle Rackrent's owners are responsible for maintaining it for themselves and for the next generation, and this task requires income. The inheritance consists of the land and the buildings upon it; such cash as is needed to run the estate must be obtained from overcharging, or racking, rent, supplemented by the "duty" gifts required and the "duty work" owed by the tenant to the landlord. Sir Patrick sublets the property to a roster of tenants but has apparently been dilatory about collection—he "let 'em all get the half year's rent into arrear" (14). This behavior, however, may not have been quite as lackadaisical as it seems. The custom, called the "hanging gale," was a control mechanism; landlords allowed "new tenants [not to] pay rent for at least six months," but the apparent favor was really intended to put the family in immediate debt to the landlord, which constituted a constant threat of a sudden demand for payment; Edgeworth makes a specific reference to the practice, calling it a "hanging half."[27] If the landlords observing this custom can afford to defer income for a half year, it would seem that they were in a fairly good cash position themselves. This is not in fact the case for the Rackrents.

Sir Patrick's heir, Sir Murtagh, seems to be less interested in emotional blackmail than in cash flow. According to Thady he "knew well how to enforce" his rights as a landlord: "in all our leases there were strict clauses with heavy penalties . . . so many days duty work of man and horse, from every tenant, he was to have, and had, every year" (15). Both he and his wife ("of the family of the Skinflints" [12], the possessor of "Scotch blood" [13]), squeeze every possible advantage from the landlord-tenant relationship. This particular Lady Rackrent furnishes the dinner table of Castle Rackrent with meat and produce supplied free by the tenants, exploiting charity-school children to spin the "heaps of duty yarn" (13), also supplied free. Since the rent money was not spent on food or clothing, it is available for other purposes to Sir Murtagh and his Skinflint wife. Neither of them has any ability to generate income on their own and so to cover their expenses must depend on extracting income in cash, goods, and services from the tenants.

Another major source of ready cash for the Rackrents over the years was that brought to the family via financially advantageous marriages. Sir Kit Rackrent, younger brother and heir to Sir Murtagh, arranges a marriage to a young woman Thady refers to as "a *Jewish*" (25), rumored to be "the grandest heiress in England" with "tens of thousand pounds to her fortune" (23–24). This unhappy marriage, worsened by the lady's refusal to give her cash-strapped husband a diamond cross and his imprisoning her for years in retaliation, produces no heirs. On Sir Kit's death, the estate passes to Sir Conolly (Condy) Rackrent, from a "remote branch of the family" (38) but with many of the family traits nonetheless. His wife, Isabella Moneygawl, marries without the permission of her father and therefore loses her dowry; but "she had a few thousands of her own, which had been left to her by a good grandmother, and these were very convenient to begin with" (48). As Thady's phrase "to begin with" suggests, Sir Condy and Isabella run through this money quickly. The story was given out (Thady does not say by whom) that "her father had undertaken to pay all my master's debts," on the strength of which (false) report, "all his tradesmen gave him a new credit" (48). This leads to predictable results: she and Sir Condy deplete her inheritance, becoming poorer and more debt-laden than ever.

Down through the generations, all the Rackrents seem congenitally inept at managing money. Sir Patrick overspends on drink and hospitality. Upon his death Sir Murtagh refuses to pay his father's debts, declaring an informal sort of bankruptcy, which should, dishonorable though it is, save him some money. But despite his wife's reputed Scotch blood, Sir Murtagh does not benefit from her frugality, as he more than counterbalances her saving with his own characteristic area of profligacy, his passion for litigation: "those suits that he carried cost him a power of money" (16). His heir, Sir Kit, "valued a guinea as little as any man—money to him was no more than dirt" (20)—but feeds his expensive gambling and womanizing habits not only by reneging on his debts to the tenants but also by constantly demanding remittances from them to support him during his long absences. So demanding is he that his agent resigns, and Jason Quirk takes his place. Despite Sir Condy's efforts to extort money via confiscating his wife's jewels, he fails, and by the time of his death, "Castle Rackrent was all mortgaged, and bonds out against him, for he was never cured of his gaming tricks" (32). All of this profligacy results in a greatly diminished patrimony, its value reduced by loans and liens.

Enter Sir Condy, from a remote branch of the family, taking over this heavily encumbered real estate. Sir Condy seems to be a compendium of all the family character flaws. As noted earlier he was "bred to the bar," provided with an expensive education, but neglectful of his legal career. Thus he too finds himself in a state of financial embarrassment, which he attempts to remedy by borrowing: "secretly many of the tenants, and others, advanced him cash upon his note of hand value received, promising bargains of leases and lawful interest should he ever come into the estate" (40). Borrowing against the residual value of an already heavily mortgaged property before even inheriting it is a risky financial move. Although at last he does in fact inherit, "he could not command a penny of this first year's income, which, and keeping no accounts, and the great sight of company he did, with many other causes too numerous to mention, was the origin of his distresses" (41). He has compromised his earning power by virtue of the "bargains" he has promised, depressing his income for an indefinite period into the future. In order to set his affairs in order, he hires Jason, Thady's son, as his agent. Since Sir Condy has been keeping no accounts, he is in no position to evaluate either Jason's professional competence or his honesty. As narrator Thady would never admit that his son was cheating Sir Condy, and perhaps Jason was not. Sir Condy is so inept that the more financially sophisticated Jason may have bested him merely by striking a complicated deal (41). Sir Condy has already self-sabotaged by running up so many debts that almost his whole cash income (the rent-roll) goes to debt service and none to paying down principal. Since the principal never decreases, and since new debts are added thereto, the interest accrues to the point that the principal is doubled. This means he has to take out new loans, and a dismal cycle of debt is set in motion. Sir Condy has an added expense in that he has hired Jason, so now owes him salary, in addition to back salary for work done free (either by Jason himself or by other family members) in the past.

This leads to the next step in Sir Condy's financial ruin and to Jason's moving up the socioeconomic ladder to take his place as master of Castle Rackrent. Not wanting to take charge of his own money, being in denial of the extent of the problem, Sir Condy devises (or agrees to Jason's suggestion of) a scheme that makes the situation worse. Like many Irish landlords, Sir Condy leased out portions of his land to subtenants in return for rent payments, which become part of the landlord's income. One of these parcels being available, Sir Condy leases it to Jason, in a favorable arrangement meant to serve as partial payment for Jason's services, at what Thady calls a "reasonable rent" (41). But rather than pay the rent on this sublet parcel out of his own pocket, Jason subdivides and sub-subleases it to several other tenants for enough money that not only is his rent bill to Sir Condy paid, but he also accrues a profit of two hundred pounds per year. This profit finances Jason's next investment. Not profligate like the Rackrents, he accumulates the money generated by this sublease arrangement so that he can buy the land two years later, "when Sir Condy was pushed for money" and thus presumably ready to accept less than market value

(41). The purchase price is further reduced by an allowance for any improvements Jason made on the land in the intervening two years, further reducing the cash price. The phrase "at twelve years purchase" (41) appears to describe a mortgage arrangement, so Jason has bought the land effectively for nothing, as he has used the surplus rent (other people's money) as his down payment and will make the mortgage payments out of the same surplus rent, thus acquiring the land for no out-of-pocket expense and financing the whole deal out of his rental profits. Unlike Sir Condy, Jason will hold onto this land and even increase the extent of it, rising in power and prestige as Sir Condy falls.

Matters worsen for Sir Condy because of his improvident marriage. He courts a rich man's daughter, Isabella Moneygawl, but her father disapproves of him and so withholds his daughter's dowry. The marriage thus begins with a financial setback. Isabella has a small inheritance but is a big spender, having been raised in an affluent family, "never being used in her father's house to think of expence in any thing" (48). These Rackrents live in the grand style, Isabella occupying herself with expensive renovations and Sir Condy living in his usual state of fiscal denial: "she went on as if she had a mint of money at her elbow; and . . . Sir Condy said nothing to it one way or another" (49). Credit is extended to the couple on the strength of the (false) rumor that Sir Condy's debts would be paid by Captain Moneygawl; bills mount, collection efforts ensue; Sir Condy, like other Rackrents before him, drinks and entertains more than he can afford. So within a year the whole household is living "from hand to mouth" (52) to the point that there are no candles in the household and no turf with which to cook or heat the house. On top of all that, the wine merchant is dunning the Rackrents for unpaid bills.

Rackrent's misery is Jason's opportunity again. Jason had long desired to own the hunting lodge adjacent to his own newly acquired property. He has money, Sir Condy has none, and the latter is about to be arrested for debt. "So Sir Condy was fain to take the purchase money of the lodge from my son Jason to settle matters; and sure enough it was a good bargain for both parties, for my son bought the fee simple of a good house for him and his heirs for ever for little or nothing, and by selling of it for that same my master saved himself from gaol" (54). Thady makes the precise legal point that Jason "bought the fee simple" of the house, that is, bought the house in such a way that he has absolute ownership and the ability to will the house to heirs, thus potentially establishing his own landed family—as opposed to purchasing a leasehold, a long-term rental agreement, which would give him use of the property for a time but leave ownership with Sir Condy. While Thady claims to pity Sir Condy for the collapse of his fortunes and to regard his own son Jason as one of the "vultures of the law" who are feasting on his "poor master's fine estate" (62), it is clear that he is actually proud of his son's financial acumen. As Sir Condy was frittering away his time, Jason "had been studying the law, and had made himself attorney Quirk" (71–72). Sir Condy's wife also leaves him, which leads to even more expense—a "five hundred a year jointure he had settled upon my lady" (75), in effect spousal support, which he arranges without the consent of his legal counsel, Quirk. This payment is an "incumbrance on the land" (76), a lien against the estate that reduces its net value. Nevertheless Jason, buyer as well as buyer's broker and buyer's lawyer, offers to buy the land, and Sir Condy, swamped by the magnitude of his problems, consents. The list of his creditors takes up almost a full page, including, but not limited to, the butcher, the baker, and the candlestick maker.

At this juncture Thady professes great concern for the Quirk family's reputation when the nature of this transaction is discovered: "what will people tink and say, when they see you living here in Castle Rackrent, and the lawful owner turned out of the seat of his ancestors, without a cabin to put his head into, or so much as a potatoe to eat?" (77). This amazing reversal of fortune, with "cabin" people living in the Big House and vice versa, appears on the surface to astound Thady, but his coded language, once translated, could just as easily be a boast. Jason, not burdened with the appearance of servility that his father's peasant status demands, proclaims his entitlement, telling his father that the land was, even before his purchase of it, "lawfully mine was I to push for it" (76). Jason argues that he has in fact undercharged Sir Condy for his professional services all along; that Sir Condy was welcome to find another, better purchaser should he have wished to do so; and that since no other such materialized, Jason's own is the best offer that Sir Condy is likely to get. But the allusion to Irish history is clear: if Jason represents the native Irish and Sir Condy the Anglo-Irish, this land transaction rights ancient wrongs.

Judging by the fate of the Rackrents, Edgeworth seems to see the demise of her own class as inevitable given the multiple injustices that they represent. The fake funeral of Sir Condy, followed by Lady Rackrent's near-fatal accident, compounded by the loss of the land, followed by Sir Condy's actual death (alcohol-related, in the family tradition) all combine to suggest that Edgeworth judges this way of life to be doomed. The Anglo-Irish Ascendancy is like, in Thady's words to Sir Condy, "the ducks in the kitchen yard just after their heads are cut off by the cook, running round and round faster than when alive" (58).

When Edgeworth's father, Richard, returned to Ireland from England in 1782, he did so to prove himself and his family "to be a breed apart from their improvident and uncaring ancestors," so he "took it upon himself to correct the wrongs that had been done to his estate and his tenants."[28] In this project he enlisted the help of Maria, then fifteen years old. This work with her father provided the imaginative impetus for *Castle Rackrent* and accounts for the dual vision with which she saw the Ascendancy situation. On the one hand, people like her father (and, after his death, herself) were trying to play the "civilising leadership role"[29] that they believed justified their relationship to the native Irish population. On the other hand, she literally, and literarily, could see the situation from the point of view of those who, like Thady Quirk, had to pretend to respect, even love, their exploiters while simultaneously perceiving the inferiority of these outsiders to their own upstart progeny, the self-made men of the future.

Never Over: William Trevor's "The Distant Past"

As mentioned earlier, William Trevor is of Protestant, middle-class origins and was raised in the Republic. On the one hand, he is excluded by social class, though not religion, from what remains of Anglo-Irish society; on the other, not being Catholic, he is also not perfectly in tune with life in the Republic either. He sees this outsider status as an advantage for a writer of fiction: "I was fortunate that my accident of birth actually placed me on the edge of things. I was born into a minority that all my life has seemed in danger of withering away. This was smalltime Protestant stock, far removed from the well-to-do Ascendancy of the recent past yet without much of a place in de Valera's new Catholic Ireland."[30] Trevor's allusion to Éamon de Valera calls to mind the passage in the Irish Constitution of 1937 that specifically ties the Irish state to the Catholic Church, thus placing families such as Trevor's in an anomalous position. The sense of being peripheral—Protestant but not wealthy, Irish but not Catholic—helps Trevor to see both sides of the Ascendancy equation.

Before beginning Trevor's *The Story of Lucy Gault,* the reader would do well to read his short story "The Distant Past." The story's title raises the crucial issue: How distant is the past? What is its impact on the present? To situate the story within its historical context, consider the following time line. Historical events in the larger world are in ordinary type, fictional events in the town and in the story's main characters, the Middleton family, in italics.

Eighteenth Century: Heyday of the Ascendancy

1727–60: Building of the Middletons' Carraveagh, a Big House in the south of Ireland

1801: Act of Union with Great Britain, which placed Ireland under British government

1916–23: Easter Rising, followed by the Troubles

1921: Anglo-Irish Treaty, partition of Ireland into an independent Republic in the south and a Loyalist Northern Ireland

1924: Death of the Middletons' father; discovery of his financial mismanagement

1968: Upsurge of political violence in the North, also called the Troubles

Carraveagh, "built in the reign of George II," 1727–60, is "a monument that reflected in its glory and later decay the fortunes of a family" and an empire.[31] Like the real Bowen's Court or the fictional Castle Rackrent, Carraveagh is in need of expensive maintenance, but finances are inadequate. The leaky roof, unpolished furniture, and fading wallpaper all mark the house as, like Castle Rackrent, a symbol of a way of life in decline. On the other hand, the portrait of their father in full Loyalist regalia and the Middleton family crest stressing their British origins mark the house and its owners as relics of a once-proud culture.

The Middletons' fortunes have been in decline since 1924, when the death of their father unmasked him as a poor manager in the Rackrent tradition and revealed that the family's financial position is not what they thought it was. The loss of much of the family fortune is all the more bitter to them in that it has been lost to a Catholic from Dublin. At the same time, what remains of their property, once part of the British Empire, is now in the Republic of Ireland as per the Anglo-Irish Treaty of 1921. The family's history parallels Ireland's own in that the father's mistress, the "Catholic Dublin woman" (349) to whom their heritage was lost, represents to them the entire Celtic Catholic population whose power waxes as that of the Protestant Anglo-Irish wanes. The father's selling off pieces of the land mirrors the reduction in power of descendants of Ascendancy families; now, no longer a powerful elite, they are at best harmless holdovers, at worst threatening reminders. The Middletons blame the Catholic woman as well as the Republic that she symbolizes because it is easier to do so than to look at their own rotting house—the corruption that dooms their way of life.

The Middletons' "continuing loyalty to the past" (349), an unreflective response, manifests itself in matters of religion (Church of Ireland) and politics (Loyalist). Though even their fellow Protestants Loyalists begin to see them as "an anachronism" (350), they live this way uneventfully for many years. In times of peace, the town is a model of how the Catholic/Republican and Protestant/Loyalists can handle their differences: "The visitors who came to the town heard about the Middletons and were impressed. It was a pleasant wonder, more than one of them remarked, that old wounds could heal so completely, that the Middletons continued in their loyalty to the past and that, in spite of it, they were respected in the town" (352). But the Troubles disrupt this harmony.

A significant minor character, Fat Cranley the butcher, highlights the potential for violence inherent in the unstable political situation. The episode in the past in which he and his fellow Republicans occupy the hall of Carraveagh highlights the dichotomies of Irish life: Celtic Catholic versus Anglo-Irish Protestant, butcher (and friends) versus Big House owner, lower class versus upper class. This episode could have escalated into violence but did not (a similar event, but with radically different consequences, begins *The Story of Lucy Gault*). The story of Cranley and friends invading the Big House takes its place in the collective memory, and the event seems to have no repercussions. As if in repentance for his role in the incident, Cranley is generous with the Middletons. In their different ways, both Cranley and the Middletons represent Irish tradition in that all three of them have difficulty letting go of the past: Cranley is too old to run his shop; the Middletons are too old and poor to maintain Carraveagh.

None, however, are able to abandon either butcher shop or Big House, as both structures link them to the past: "Instinctively they had remained at Carraveagh, instinctively feeling that it would have been cowardly to go. Yet it often seemed to them now to be no more than a game they played, this worship of the distant past. And at other times it seemed as real and as important as the remaining acres of land, and the house itself" (353). In peacetime the Middletons could dither along in their decaying house; but Ireland is changing around them. Tourism (which depends on peace) is an ever more significant economic factor. Economic change has increased access to the amenities of life, which in turn leads to changes in the social hierarchy. Social events such as Mrs. Duggan's parties demonstrate that boundaries have become more fluid, and social climbing, fueled by discretionary income, has replaced a more traditional social order based on inherited status. Even in peacetime the Middletons, like other old Anglo-Irish families, have become irrelevant, but harmlessly so.

In 1968, however, a resurgence of violence in the North threatens the peaceful coexistence of Catholic Republicans and Protestant Loyalists in the town. "'A bad business,' Fat Cranley remarked, wrapping the Middletons' meat. 'We don't want that old stuff all over again'" (353). The business to which Cranley refers is political unrest. His point of view is that, in the south at least, they have been there, done that, and want no more of it: the Republic is, for Cranley, a fact of life now. He apparently is content to live with the political division of Ireland into north and south, as he does not think it worthwhile to return to the "old stuff": Ireland's violent history. And when he uses the term *we*, he evidently means to include the Middletons and himself, the Protestants and Catholics in the town and, by extension, the Republic, who by 1968 were learning to coexist.

But the town feels the consequences of violence in Belfast and Derry along with other, less well-known border villages. Violence scares off the tourists, and worse, it disrupts the social arrangement that has incorporated the Middletons into Catholic/Republican society. Because of political violence in the North, they are snubbed and scorned in the little village in the south in which they had hitherto carved out a niche as period pieces. Now, primarily because of their association with all the negative connotations of the Big House tradition, they become a symbol of the enemy (as the German couple was during World War II). Their religious and political positions are no longer regarded as mere eccentricities: "had they driven with a Union Jack now, they might, astoundingly, have been shot" (355).

Why "astoundingly"? Because the threat to civil order inherent in the Troubles in the North makes deviance, even in the genteel, slightly dotty version practiced by the Middletons, threatening. The implied social contract that allowed them to live in peace has been breached, and the cease-fire is over. The Middletons are reminded that their house, in both the structural and familial senses of the term, is now destroyed. They cannot manage it, and there is no one to inherit it; their brother-sister relationship is by its nature sterile; Anglo-Irish culture has reached a dead end. Like many other Trevor characters, they are caught up in a historical process they did not initiate and cannot control. Ireland's being, in Bowen's words, a country in which "nothing . . . is ever over,"[32] has made life there impossible for people such as the Middletons: "Because of the distant past," which has led to the present Troubles and so is not really past, "they would die friendless. It was worse than being murdered in their beds" (356).

Political violence upsets an already precarious balance that people have worked out for themselves. Like Sebastian Barry's character Thomas Dunne in *The Steward of Christendom,* the postindependence fate of those Irish who were loyal to, worked for, or in some way collaborated with the British government during the imperial period found themselves displaced in the new Republic. Such people represented the past, and it was difficult for them to incorporate themselves into the present. As in "The Distant Past," in *The Story of Lucy Gault* the Anglo-Irish and the Irish must, and to some extent do, establish a way of living together. Violence, however, disrupts this precarious truce.

"They don't want us here": William Trevor, *The Story of Lucy Gault*

As in "The Distant Past," in *The Story of Lucy Gault* Trevor describes what novelist and reviewer Thomas Mallon calls "the capitalized Troubles of his native land and the personal lowercase ones of his characters."[33] Lucy's story begins on June 21, 1921, during the period of posttreaty civil unrest that had already sounded the death knell to the Ascendancy way of life. Capt. Everard Gault's "single shot" in the night[34] is only the logical consequence of the long history of division between the Big House residents, represented by Gault himself, and the Celtic Catholic population, represented positively by Henry and Bridget and negatively by Holahan and his two companions. Trevor pinpoints the novel's key issues in a single word in the first paragraph: *trespassers* (3).

In Gault's eyes the three young men are trespassers on the grounds of Lahardane, which he believes has been his family's property for centuries; but those who believe that the Gaults and their fellow Anglo-Irish had no right to the land would see *them* as trespassers and the three young men as representatives of the rightful owners of not only Lahardane but also all Ireland. A political novel in the Big House tradition, *The Story of Lucy Gault* is also a theological meditation on the biblical concept of "trespass" as a term for sin. In the Lord's Prayer, Christians beseech God to "forgive us our trespasses, as we forgive those who trespass against us," that is, forgive sinners as sinners forgive each other. In the novel saying such a prayer seems a risky business in Ireland. Forgiveness is the work of generations; guilt is experienced by the wrong people; and reconciliation is often futile for being too long delayed.

"The origins of the Gaults in Ireland had centuries ago misted over" (4). According to historian R. F. Foster, such arrivistes as the Anglo-Irish "sought— at the subconscious level no doubt—to convince themselves and others that they had been there a long time,"[35] like Edgeworth's Rackrents. The story of how the Gault family achieved the land and social position it now holds is partly legendary: "Previously of Norfolk—so it was believed within the family, although without much certainty—they had settled first of all in the far western regions of County Cork. A soldier of fortune had established their modest dynasty, lying low there for reasons that were not known. Some time in the early eighteenth century the family had moved east, respectable and well-to-do by then, one son or another of each generation continuing the family's army connection. The land at Lahardane was purchased; the building of the house began" (4). The Gaults, then, are descendants not of a Tudor Planter but rather of a self-made man who established the Irish branch of this English family. Over generations the family increased its wealth and power. And most significantly the land on which Lahardane was built was purchased, not granted. Such distinctions as these, however, vanish in the climate of civil unrest that permeates the country.

The Gaults are also not judged on the basis of their own family history, which follows the Anglo-Irish pattern but on which Everard has placed his own individual stamp. The incremental improvements to the size and quality of the property are testimony to the Gaults' commitment to their life in Ireland. But they too have their Rackrent-like profligates, who diminish the patrimony: in 1872 "field after field was lost to the neighboring O'Reillys" due to gambling debts (5). Unlike the Rackrents, Everard Gault works at being a good conservator, doing his best to "keep in good heart what had been his inheritance" (5) with an eye to the next generation and the one after that. Despite his efforts, however, "the style of the past was no longer possible at Lahardane" (6).

Even that diminished lifestyle is far superior to that which is possible to members of the lower classes such as Holahan and his two companions. These young men represent, from the Anglo-Irish point of view, the forces of disorder unleashed by political changes in Ireland and, from the Nationalist point of view, the formerly oppressed classes rising to claim their birthright. In any culture, however, young men like these, with nothing to lose, are a potential threat to public order. They do not represent all Celtic Catholics, however. The Gault family had been living peacefully at Lahardane for years with Henry and Bridget, their household help, who live in the gate-lodge as befits their employee status. Trevor seems at first to be deploying a stereotype in his development of these two characters. In the Big House novel, according to Vera Kreilkamp, "generally, Catholics are acceptable only when they adhere to the roles set up by traditional landlord-tenant relationships."[36] This servant-class stereotype is better represented by the "bedroom maid" Kitty Teresa (6), while Henry and Bridget become the moral touchstones of the novel, wholeheartedly embracing Lucy, raising her as if she were their own child, and respecting her Church of Ireland heritage. When they move into the Big House, it is truly for Lucy's sake; there is no trace of possessiveness, ambition, social climbing, or politics in them.

After the shot in the night, Everard and Heloise Gault decide to leave Lahardane. Gault tries to explain this to Lucy:

"Why must we go?" she cried.
"Because they don't want us here," her papa said. (22)

It seems as if Gault has oversimplified the situation to correspond to the level of understanding of a child, but in fact his six-word explanation is an effective condensation of eight hundred years of Irish history. "Here," is, of course, Ireland, where Gault's family has lived for so long that they know no other home. And "they," Irish Nationalists, Celtic and Catholic, want him and his fellow Anglo-Irish banished in reparation for the sins of the past. They are in the ascendancy now, and they want to destroy the Big Houses, their inhabitants, and the disgraceful past of which both houses and people are painful reminders.

But for Gault, to be Anglo-Irish is not to be English, although he knows that others see him as such. When asked in Ghent what his nationality is, he exhibits momentary confusion: "'You are English?' he was asked in his guest-house and for a moment he hesitated, not knowing in that moment what he was. Then he shook his head. 'No, I'm an Irishman'" (147). According to Foster this ambiguity had long characterized the Anglo-Irish: "The confused but strongly felt identity of colonial nationalism is reflected in the use of the word 'Irish.' Those who in the 1690s called themselves 'the Protestants of Ireland' or even 'the English of this kingdom' could see themselves as 'Irish gentlemen' by the 1720s. In between, there was some doubt as to whether they wanted to be *called* 'Irish'; but they increasingly felt that this was what they were."[37] The confusion with regard to national and personal identity is a minor issue, however, compared to the moral ambiguities upon which the plot turns.

As Kreilkamp notes, "Because Anglo-Irish fiction emerges from a history of conquest and occupation, to study the genre of the Big House novel is to trace the gradual evolution of a literary symbol set against the political history of class and sectarian conflict, rather than conciliation."[38] Conquest, occupation, class conflict, sectarian conflict: Kreilkamp's terms sum up the way in which the sins of the Planter fathers are visited upon their children, sometimes centuries later. Individual moral acts, no matter how long ago, are like ripples resulting from a stone thrown in the water. The English divided and conquered Ireland, exploited its land and people, attempted to destroy its language and culture, and even let the Irish starve. As a result the Irish rose in rebellion against their oppressors, which led to an environment of discord following a treaty meant to resolve their differences. These historical events led three fictional young Catholic men to threaten the Gaults and led Gault to fire. The elder Gaults decide to remove Lucy from the only home she has ever known; so she runs away and is presumed dead, and so her parents live in self-imposed exile from the scene of all this suffering. Heloise never sees her daughter again; Everard suffers years of misery. Back in Ireland, in one of the few good consequences of bad deeds, Henry and Bridget demonstrate parental devotion to Lucy, bridge the social and religious gaps that might have separated them from the child, and in return receive her gratitude and love. Even this, however, does not, at least in Lucy's mind, constitute reconciliation. Repentance is still needed.

One of the more paradoxical consequences of the sins of the fathers is that guilt is experienced by people who were not morally responsible for the original act. This is the case with Lucy. She spends the rest of her life as a "self-lacerating penitent [in] atonement for the sins of history,"[39] as well as for her own perceived moral failing, her childish decision to run away. For her repentance requires her to live in the past, wearing her mother's clothes, reading the old books in her father's library, living in the world created in her mind by the books. She allows for no mitigating factors—as for example her age and immaturity—and so cannot forgive herself for her trespasses. Her self-imposed penance involves not only remaining at Lahardane in case her parents return, but also removing herself from any possibility of conventional happiness there. Lucy thinks of her refusal to marry Ralph as "keeping faith" (81), but it is not clear to what or to whom Lucy is faithful or in what way her marriage to Ralph would constitute infidelity. He is willing to join her at Lahardane, and both of them could tend the flame of Lucy's repentance as well as the Big House itself. She seems never to realize that her choice to repent in the particular way she does dooms the house/House of Gault to extinction.

What might not be easy to remember in these tales of the Anglo-Irish Ascendancy is that both sides of the political spectrum consist of supposed Christians. As such they (theoretically at least) believe in the same basic doctrine of sin. Flawed human beings are capable of evil but also of repentance; having sincerely repented, they are forgiven by a good and loving God. Punishment for sin (as opposed to penalties for civil crimes) is the province of God alone, and flawed as they are, human beings have no right to judge, much less condemn, one another. Restitution is a corollary of repentance, and it is the duty of the repentant sinner to find ways to make reparation. These are simple theological principles, but they are difficult to practice due to the complex nature of moral choice. Every decision in the novel seems to involve ethical dilemmas that cloud the distinction between right and wrong.

For starters the characters in the novel are not presented with examples of absolute good on the one hand and absolute evil on the other, for if they were, almost all of them would choose the good; they are at base good people. Due to the limited nature of human comprehension, however, they cannot always foresee the possible consequences of their actions, sort out their own conflicting motives, or rise above the culture that formed them. Take, for example, Lucy's decision to wait for her parents' forgiveness. As self-appointed scapegoat for what are essentially the failings of others (Horahan and his friends' decision to set Lahardane afire; the Gaults' failure to deal sensitively with the feelings of a child, their too-hasty decision to abandon the search, and their choice to remain out of contact with Ireland), Lucy injures Ralph as well as herself, in a way for which no clear restitution could be made. To end Ralph's suffering by agreeing to marry him after a divorce, even if Lucy would agree to do so, would involve injuring his wife and child. But not marrying him has also led to the failure of the Gault line, as an unmarried Lucy has not provided an heir, resulting in the property being as much lost to the Gaults as if the intruders in the night had indeed burned it down.

The theological theme of the novel comes to a climax in the scene in which Lucy, speaking to Ralph, relates the grief of the keening women on the seashore to that of her parents (118–20). Lucy sees her life as defined by a single irrevocable choice: running away. Because she sees this as a trespass against her parents, only they can forgive her. Until such time as they do, she must deny herself ordinary human happiness. Because she caused her parents to suffer as the keening women are suffering, she cannot do otherwise than suffer herself. The irony of this scene is that Lucy is in effect confessing her sin to Ralph; but were she to have this same discussion with Canon Crosbie, the clergyman, he, with a theological education superior to Lucy's own, might well point out the error of her belief that an eight-year-old child under extreme emotional stress is morally responsible to the extent that she believes herself to be. The canon might also point out the mitigating circumstances—the impossibility of a child's foreseeing the consequences of her act, the responsibility shared by the adults around her—and encourage her to seek the forgiveness of God and equally important, to forgive herself. She might then in good conscience await her parents' return as a married woman, perhaps a mother. She thinks of herself as the first Mrs. Rochester in *Jane Eyre,* the madwoman in the attic (118), and this self-perception is closer to the truth than she realizes. Like Hanrahan, too, who hallucinates a murder when none took place, Lucy imagines her degree of responsibility to be far, far greater than it is.

The moral universe of the novel is nowhere near as simple as Lucy imagines it to be. In her focus on her own feelings of guilt, she cannot see how others are less than perfect. Many choices in the novel are morally ambiguous. Everard Gault, by being a loving husband and respecting his wife's wishes to avoid all contact with Ireland, inadvertently abandons his daughter. Heloise, though she loves her husband, appears unaware of Everard's longing for home. Everard realizes only upon his return to Lahardane that in making their decision to leave, "a child's anxieties had been impatiently ignored," resulting in unintentional "cruelty" (156). Ralph, by marrying a woman whom he knows to be his second choice, gets on with his life, but at the same time perpetrates an injustice that will set up its own chain of consequences no matter what Lucy chooses to do. And these are all good people. Perhaps the only truly negative character in the book is the loathsome Miss Chambré, who makes the decision not to tell Heloise Gault's aunt about Lucy's survival. But even she is a prisoner of her own ignorance, as well as of the childrearing practices of her day (such a "home of correction" [59] as she suggests for Lucy did exist in Ireland at the time).

The key moral event in the play—the shot in the night—is literally triggered by a chain of events begun long before. Had England not established plantations in Ireland, taking away the land rightly belonging to the native Celts, Hanrahan and his fellows would not be aggrieved nor Gault defensive. But even if Gault, a good man, were to repent, how would he begin to make restitution, and to whom? His efforts to do so focus on the gunshot wound and are repulsed by the Hanrahans, and rightly so, as the issue is larger than that. But what would suffice? Lahardane does return to what Nationalists believe to be its rightful owners when Bridget and Henry move permanently from the cottage to the Big House. When, even upon Gault's return, they refuse (albeit politely and with the valid excuse of Lucy's well-being) to move back to their cottage and position of subordination, Gault accepts that decision as the right and just one. On the psychological level, the novel deals with the vexed issue of collective guilt. Assuming that, as the Englishwoman in Bruges tells Everard, the British have treated the Irish badly in the past (147), who is to make reparation for this? And to whom? If one is tracing rivers of guilt back to their sources, what of the brothers at Holahan's school, who taught them that "the big house is the enemy" (184), with little apparent thought for the consequences of these lessons?

Despite the all-pervading sorrow of this novel, the ending holds out some hope for reconciliation. Members of the conflicting groups in Ireland make not just peaceful but loving connection. Everard Gault makes Lahardane home to Henry and Bridget, who maintain a lifelong commitment to the family. Henry and Bridget raise Lucy in the faith of her family rather than their own. Lucy visits Holahan in the asylum, though his own family members, "ashamed" (220), do not. The two nuns visit Lucy as much to learn "redemption" and "mercy" from her as to provide her with food and companionship (224). At the same time, Trevor portrays Ireland as a place where, in Gault's words, "the past was the enemy" (10), a place where long-dead sinners poison the lives of their descendants. The Big House, Lahardane, still stands, but Ireland itself is more like another house, "Paddy Lindon's tumbled-down cottage," with its leaking roof, a dwelling fit only for a "wild man" (10).

In her old age, Lucy Gault confides in the two nuns "a thought that came in the night" about the fate of Lahardane after her death: "I think what will happen . . . is that they'll make a hotel of the house. She lay sleepless and the transformation lingered: a cocktail bar, a noisy dining-room, numbers on the bedroom doors. She doesn't mind. It doesn't matter. People coming from all over, travellers like never before; that is the way in Ireland now" (225). Of the Big Houses that survive, many are maintained by foundations, trusts, government agencies, and historic preservation associations. Others still are home to descendants of the original owners but are at least partially financed by fees paid by visitors. Still others have become hotels, just as Lucy imagined. The great irony of her life is that she dedicated it to preserving a heritage for the enjoyment of transients.

While Big House fiction is often critical of the Ascendancy culture that produced the houses, readers must keep in mind that fiction is a relatively inexpensive art form, available to them for the cover price of a book, and often for less than that. The visual arts—interior design, landscape design, architecture, painting, sculpture, furniture design, art patronage, art preservation—are expensive and depend, in Ireland as elsewhere, on the wealthy, the leisured, the well-educated, the well-connected. Such were the Anglo-Irish in their time. But their legacy lasted far beyond the descent of the Ascendancy. Elizabeth Bowen was right: "Nothing in Ireland is ever over." Sharp social class divisions continued to generate tensions and hostilities festered due to religious differences throughout the twentieth century. These too are known in Ireland as the Troubles.

Chapter 7

"Fanatic heart"

A Legacy of Violence

In Charles Townshend's *Ireland: The Twentieth Century*, a reader can keep the chronology of events in order by means of a time line in the back of the book. Considering the book's title, one would expect the time line to begin in 1900; but in fact it begins in 1782.[1] This is one historian's way of acknowledging what is a continuing theme in contemporary Irish literature as well: no event takes place in isolation; all present-time events are tied to and often caused by earlier events. The same term, the Troubles, is used to describe two periods of political unrest in Ireland: that period following partition in 1921 that formed the setting for Trevor's *The Story of Lucy Gault,* and a time from the late 1960s to the 1990s in which paramilitary groups of both Loyalists and Nationalists wreaked havoc in Northern Ireland, killing more than three thousand people.[2] Historian R. V. Comerford defines the latter period as "three decades of civil unrest and terror."[3] William Trevor's "Beyond the Pale" and Bernard MacLaverty's *Cal,* both of which take place in the 1970s, both in the North, one in the country, one in the city, connect these second Troubles with their historical antecedents.

In "Beyond the Pale" a distant historical event (the establishment of the Irish Pale in 1495) is echoed by political unrest in the 1970s. The present-time action of the story involves the disrupted vacation of a British foursome: Strafe and his wife, Cynthia; their friend Dekko; and Strafe's mistress, Milly, who is the narrator. The vacationers stay with English innkeepers in the north of Ireland, expecting a known, comfortable environment, pleasant routine, good food, and bridge. This pleasant hiatus is disrupted when a young Irishman, his own life destroyed by Ireland's sad history, tells his story to Cynthia, then drowns himself. Having read Trevor's "Beyond the Pale," the reader is prepared to continue with the reading of Bernard MacLaverty's *Cal,* a coming-of-age story in which the young protagonist copes with problems specific to the Northern

Ireland setting. As with many other works of Irish literature, the cumulative influence of the past on the present is central to both story and novel.

"Unpleasantness": William Trevor's "Beyond the Pale"

The modern idiomatic meaning of "beyond the pale" is "irrevocably unacceptable or unreasonable" (*American Heritage College Dictionary*), and the phrase has a long history. First used in Ireland in 1495, the Pale designated a small area around Dublin in which English law prevailed. Beyond the Pale lay the rest of Ireland, which was at the time under the control of the native Celtic population. From the point of view of the British, their Pale was a land of peace as order, as opposed to the chaos beyond. Since the Pale was small, most of Ireland was deemed by the British to be "beyond the pale," out of control, beyond the rule of law. The term establishes the following set of analogies: English/Irish = within the Pale/beyond the Pale = order/disorder = rational/irrational. The Pale, then, becomes a metaphor for the relationship between the English and the Irish, past and present. The British characters think of themselves as rational, controlled, and correct and of the Irish characters as the opposite: irrational, uncontrolled, impulsive.

Adding to the complexity of this story is the fact that Trevor, himself of Anglo-Irish background, has filtered his understanding of the Irish, the Anglo-Irish, and the English through a narrator, Milly, an Englishwoman. Milly is an example of the fictional technique of the unreliable narrator, that is, a narrator whose perceptions are incomplete, distorted, or biased; while she is telling the truth as she sees it, the reader is not to assume that the character's viewpoint equals the author's. It becomes increasingly apparent that Milly is historically ignorant and insensitive to her contemporaries, especially Cynthia; therefore she is ill prepared to empathize with the suffering of the young man who tells his story to Cynthia.

Since by their standards much of Ireland is beyond the pale, the British foursome in the Trevor story should expect to encounter some deviation from their sense of order when they leave England for Ireland. Stereotypical traits appear in these four vacationers: all are, at least on the surface, highly controlled and regular in their habits, which makes them think of themselves as reasonable and right. Their vacation habits are orderly: they take the same vacation every year, to County Antrim in Northern Ireland; there they stay at the same hotel, Glencorn Lodge, and each day of their visit is carefully patterned along familiar lines. Since they think of Northern Ireland as much like England, the last thing they want on vacation is a new experience.

The four stay at a hotel run by the Malseeds, an English couple; neither Irish nor Anglo-Irish, they are newcomers rather than descendants of Planters. Glencorn Lodge is a Georgian-style house, its architecture reminiscent of the

Anglo-Irish Big Houses. Everything there appears to be as it should be. The inn might well be in England, except that Mr. Malseed plays at being Irish, wearing Donegal tweed and greeting them with a traditional Irish welcome (in English). Ironically the vacationers find Malseed's Britishness reassuring evidence that "all was well with [Glencorn's] Irish world."[4] Like everything else in the story, this comment is from Milly's viewpoint; but Trevor has already undercut Milly's opinion in naming the innkeepers. The Malseeds, superficially charming, are a bad seed, a modern iteration of the Planters whose usurpation caused so many later problems.

Milly, Dekko and Strafe, stereotypical Britons themselves, stereotype the Irish to one another. Dekko tells "an Irish joke about a drunk" (752). Strafe "does a good Co. Antrim brogue," mocking Irish speech (758). Milly regards the Irish police as being slow of intellect. She knows that there is violence in Northern Ireland and notes how "people in England thought us mad" for vacationing there (751); but to her the Troubles are distant from and irrelevant to Glencorn Lodge. Milly regards political violence as trivial, and the terms she uses to describe it—"the unpleasantness," "a particularly nasty carry-on" (751)—testify to her emotional detachment. According to journalist John Ardagh, some rural areas in Ireland have "never known terrorism."[5] So Milly is right that the Glencorn Lodge area may have been spared; but her comment that she and her companions had never heard any discussion of it has to be specious. The fact that the four vacationers did consider "finding somewhere else, in Scotland perhaps, or Wales" (751), shows that they were aware of possible problems. Milly accepts Dekko's reassurance that "nothing could be further away from all the violence than Glencorn Lodge" (751–52). Consoled by this thought, she sees the problems of the Irish as easily avoided or ignored.

Milly is similarly, but again erroneously, reassured by the fact that she and her companions had "never seen a thing, nor even heard people talking about incidents that may have taken place" (751). But to whom would she have spoken, and who would have spoken to her? Commentators on the Irish situation agree that there is a "sectarian identifier process" by which it is determined who is Protestant or Catholic, Loyalist or Nationalist, which must be completed before any interaction may take place.[6] These four would be immediately identifiable as outsiders by their accents alone, precluding any real communication with regard to the political situation. On vacation the quartet mainly interact with each other and with those employed in the tourism industry, all of whom have a vested interest in avoiding any reference to what Milly terms "the unpleasantness." Tourist Ireland camouflages political Ireland.

Unlike her companions, Cynthia is sympathetic to the Irish. Despite the vacationers' repeated visits, only Cynthia has made a significant effort to learn about the country. As a result, even to Milly, in whose eyes she can do no right,

Cynthia "is extremely knowledgeable about all matters relating to Irish history" (755). She has read the guidebooks, but also history, politics, biography, autobiography. This background gives her a context in which to place the young man's story, thus making her responsive to it. Like the young man, Cynthia is vulnerable, if in a different way: her husband is unfaithful, her children (at least according to Milly) do not respect her. Lacking the self-protective shell of her fellow vacationers, she identifies with the Irishman.

The intersection of the lives of Cynthia and the Irishman—representatives of alien cultures who are unexpectedly responsive to each other—is the key plot event. When the young man appears, Milly sees him as "uncouth-looking . . . not at all the kind of person one usually sees at Glencorn Lodge," "red-haired," thus obviously Irish (752). The Malseeds react as Milly does, perceiving him as lower-class, an outsider, beyond the pale; the Malseeds feel that they have to apologize *for* him (not, of course, *to* him). Dekko does not want it to be thought that he "was objecting to the locals" (754) when in fact he is doing just that. Not much has changed since the days of the Big House. The Malseeds and their fellow British think Ireland is theirs and the locals are inferiors fit only to serve them. The young Irishman believes that the English, the Malseeds and their guests, are trespassers.

The young man's story as told to Cynthia is another perfect illustration of how, in Elizabeth Bowen's words, "nothing in Ireland is ever over."[7] The young man is the storyteller, and although he is too young to have the authority of an authentic shanachie, he has participated in at least some of the events and is himself Irish. In addition the storyteller chooses Cynthia as the sole member of his listening audience, as if sensing that she is the only one who will listen carefully, who can place the story in the context of the terrible history of the Irish.

The young man's story is a montage of smaller stories that cumulatively constitute his personal interpretation of Irish history. He believes in a lost Eden, the heroic Celtic past "of scholars and of heroes, of Queen Maeve and Finn MacCool. There was the coming of St Patrick to a heathen people. History was full of kings and high kings" (761–62). He sees the arrival of the British as the end of this heroic age, and so his stories take a darker turn. Cynthia repeats the young man's stories, "chant[ed] in a singsong way that sounded thoroughly peculiar, 'the Statutes of Kilkenny. The Battle of Glenmama, the Convention of Drumceat. The Act of Settlement, the Renunciation Act. The Act of Union, the Toleration Act. Just so much history it sounds like now, yet people starved and died while other people watched. A language was lost, a faith forbidden. Famine followed revolt, plantation followed that. But it was people who were struck into the soil of other people's land, not forests of new trees; and it was greed and treachery that spread as a disease among them all'" (763). These tragic stories connect, like links on a chain, to the story of the two young lovers. This last story and, worse, the young Irishman's suicide, devastates Cynthia.

But when Cynthia becomes a storyteller in turn and tells the young man's story to her husband, Strafe, and to Dekko and Milly, they prove themselves to be unsatisfactory listeners. Each of her companions, then Mr. and Mrs. Malseed, tries to discourage her from finishing her story, thus bringing her back within their own pale of repression and denial. Each behaves as if Cynthia's response constitutes not just a disproportionate reaction to the horrors of the Irish past but an actual mental breakdown. Her companions believe that she has been foolish to get involved with the young man at all. Had she not listened to his story, he would have killed himself anyway, but they would not have been involved in it. They could have gone on with their vacation. They could have continued to pretend that the slogan "Brits Out" does not refer to them, when Cynthia knows that it does (765). She recognizes that "'Brits out' . . . does not just mean British forces and British government, but also the entire Northern Ireland population that identifies itself as British—and Protestant."[8] This includes the Malseeds and their clientele.

Trevor clearly means the reader to see Cynthia's reaction—"My God, it's terrible" (757)—as the right one. If one does not experience emotion as she does, one has not truly understood Ireland's history. All her companions' efforts to return Cynthia to what they believe constitutes admirable British reserve fail. Milly, Strafe, and Dekko will not return to Ireland because she has ripped off the veneer of propriety that covers atrocity. Cynthia understands that to suppress emotion is to falsify Ireland and its people. Strafe in particular is angry not because terrible events have happened but rather because Cynthia has talked about these events. That, to him, is beyond the pale; she should have, as the Ulster proverb warns, said nothing. At this point his decades-long affair with Milly becomes public; once restraint has vanished, anything might be revealed.

Cynthia tries to form some sort of an emotional bond with Kitty the waitress. She, not the Malseeds, represents the real Irish; the fact that she is a maid and Cynthia a guest is incidental to the fact that Kitty represents her people and the Malseeds, like the Planters before them, are usurpers. The function of this minor character is to represent the native Celtic population that has for centuries lived as inferiors in Northern Ireland. Earlier in the story, Kitty's conventional hospitality-industry chitchat soothes the visitors, creating a superficial atmosphere of well-being. This is one of the many factors that contributes to Milly's notion that "all was well" with the "Irish world" of Glencorn Lodge. By the end of the story, that same Kitty comes to represent the true Irish, with whom Cynthia has come to empathize and whose forgiveness she now must seek. But the emotional response that Cynthia needs might well place Kitty's job at risk, so she cannot respond as Cynthia wishes.

Only Cynthia reaches a new understanding that the situation in Northern Ireland is more than merely unpleasant. In "Beyond the Pale" Trevor suggests that anyone who understood the history of Ireland would have to react as Cynthia did, at the risk of being regarded as mad by those who feel nothing at all. The issue of rationality and control is related, though in a complex fashion, to another issue: Can those alive in the present do anything to right historical wrongs, and if so, what? Trevor's story suggests that at least some progress can be made through fiction. The function of storytelling—whether the young Irishman's, or Cynthia's, or Trevor's own—is to generate empathy. But the odds that this will happen are not favorable: only one in four, Cynthia, can feel for the sufferings of others.

"Great hatred, little room": Bernard MacLaverty, *Cal*

When John Ardagh describes the 1970s Troubles as "an outdated sectarian confrontation that is less about religion than nationality, territory and political power, laced with sheer gang warfare,"[9] he might well have been identifying the key issues in *Cal* by Bernard MacLaverty (b. 1942). The novel is told in the third person, with the central consciousness being Cal (né Cahal) McCluskey, a nineteen-year-old lower-class Catholic coming of age in the 1970s, in "a country town" with social divisions similar to those in the novelist's native Belfast.[10] The language Cal uses to deal with the world around him illustrates the way a young person's thought processes are shaped by his environment. Having spent his formative years amid ancient enmities, he assumes that confrontation, sectarianism, nationalism, territoriality, and gang warfare are givens of life rather than peculiarities of his environment. Inexperienced and undereducated, he also does not comprehend how many and how complex are the factors that exacerbate the town's problems and how typical they are of all of Northern Ireland.

In the novel the role of religion is less as a belief system, and far less as a code of ethics, than as a tribal marker. For example Cal's reaction to an incident in town shows the deep divisions within this small community:

> Cal detested the condescension of some of the Protestant men he met about the town.
> "You're Shamie McCluskey's boy? A good man, Shamie."
> And implied in everything they were saying was "for a Catholic."[11]

Here again is the sectarian identifier process at work. Having identified each other as the Other, members of both communities then shift into the kind of dialogue that seems innocuous but, because of the historical enmity between the two, invites negative interpretation. Cal's habit of identifying people by their religion, of imputing hostile motives to them and assuming that they in turn judge him and his father in the same way, is not his personal idiosyncrasy but rather a characteristic of his culture.

In *Breaking Enmities: Religion, Literature and Culture in Northern Ireland, 1967–97*, Patrick Grant weighs how much of the rivalry between Protestants and Catholics in Northern Ireland is truly based on religious differences and how much is political, social, and economic. Both sides claim to be Christians yet "engage in murderous hatred and violence."[12] Since this cannot be squared with the tenets of Christianity, some look to the roots of the conflict in Protestants' seeing themselves, because of their connection with England, as of a higher social class than Catholics. Protestants' desire that the situation remain that way fuels their political decision-making and leads to educational, social, and housing segregation. Such separation of the two communities means that Catholics and Protestants seldom know each other personally.

Cal's situation in the 1970s, like that of his historical counterparts, has its roots in the Anglo-Irish Big House culture discussed earlier, which was itself shaped by its own historical past. The equation Protestant = upper class = landowner = Loyalist was already well established by the nineteenth century. In the twentieth, middle- and working-class Loyalist Protestants like Cal's neighbors in the housing estate had no Ascendancy connections themselves, but still they wanted the terms of this equation maintained. Their fear that a Catholic state would have allegiance to Rome was neatly summarized in the slogan "Home Rule is Rome rule."[13]

Catholics, on their side, also see themselves as a separate community, regardless of whether or not they actually practice the religion with which they so fervently identify. As Grant sees it, "During the past thirty or so years, worldwide media attention has by and large latched onto the religious label, going on them to explain that Catholics want a united Ireland, whereas Protestants want to remain part of Britain. One result of this widely disseminated account is that Northern Ireland frequently seems a curious backwater, caught up in religious disputes that by and large were resolved in Europe some hundreds of years ago."[14] Because Protestants are still in the economic and social ascendancy in Northern Ireland, a Catholic such as Cal can easily feel patronized by the Protestant men of the town. His father's first name, Shamie (for Seamus), is a Catholic name, a tribal marker; to Cal the Protestant men seem to stress this by their repetition of it. Even the men's expression of approval is undercut by what he believes to be their assumption that for Catholics the bar for decent behavior is set low. Cal's heightened sensitivity causes him to find condescension in a possibly innocuous comment because it was made by a Protestant. But Cal, all unaware, sets a low bar of his own, faintly praising Cyril Dunlop, Mrs. Morton's foreman, for being "affable enough for an Orangeman,"[15] just a little better than a Nationalist Catholic would expect an Orangeman to be. The Orange Order, a militant Loyalist movement with a strong anti-Catholic component, is, according to John Ardagh, "the mass movement whose influence remains one obstacle to a reasonable political compromise in the North."[16] The problem posed by the Orange Order is real; the insult perceived by Cal may or may not be.

A superficially friendly exchange can be as fraught with innuendo as this one is because the two communities live separate existences, which makes communication between them rare and, when it does happen, stilted, artificial and tense. Working with members of other faiths is a commonplace elsewhere in the world. Shamie's working with Protestants and Cal's having tea with Cyril would be, in many another country, an unremarkable event; even in Northern Ireland, it could have been a small step toward the two communities' learning to understand each other. But their constant consciousness of their differences makes for tense encounters.

A related issue for the Catholic and Protestant communities is the ancient lust for land. Obsessed with the power that control over territory confers, the two communities mark their turf via signs and symbols. These markers indicate pride of ownership (or at least occupation, as most seem to be renters), but they also suggest barriers, each tribe attempting to keep the other at bay. Cal "could not bear to look up and see the flutter of Union Jacks, and now the red and white cross of the Ulster flag with its red hand. Of late there were more and more of these appearing in the estate. It was a dangerous sign that the Loyalists were getting angry. The flags should all have been down by now because the Twelfth of July was long past."[17] The flags—the British flag and the Ulster flag—announce that Loyalists claim the estate (housing development) and warn Catholics away.

Territorial struggle comes to the foreground during Marching Season, a period beginning in March and culminating on July 12, on which date each year the Orange Order commemorates the 1690 victory of William of Orange over James II in the Battle of the Boyne. The Order sees this event as the triumph of Protestantism over Catholicism, and so it is celebrated every year by means of Orange parades through areas in which Catholics live. To its defenders the Orange Order and its marching season is a way of maintaining local tradition;[18] to its critics the parades constitute yet another invasion of territory that Catholics define as theirs, hence a blatant reminder of the British presence in Northern Ireland. Apparently deliberately designed to stoke hostilities between the two groups, the parades are often accompanied by violence: they "still have the potential to open half-healed sores about territorial conquest."[19] Journalist and historian Tim Pat Coogan makes a further point about these parades: they "divide Catholics from Protestants so that the working classes of either sect will never unite to overthrow the Protestant ascendancy."[20] Here the term *ascendancy* seems to mean socioeconomic dominance, not the ownership of Big Houses. Far from it: the humbler the neighborhood, it seems, the greater the potential for July 12 violence. Sectarian hatred is largely a working-class problem; in more affluent areas, "the mixing is fairly easy."[21] Their hostilities focused on each other, the Protestant and Catholic working classes never address the barriers to their common advancement.

To guard their low-value turf, some resort to anonymous hate mail: "GET OUT YOU FENYAN SCUM OR WE'LL BURN YOU OUT. THIS IS YOUR 2ND WARNING. THERE WILL BE NO OTHER. UVF."[22] Catholics ("Fenyans" is a misspelling of "Fenians," alluding to a nineteenth-century Nationalist organization) are forcefully reminded that certain areas are Loyalist. Threats such as these were intended to drive Catholic families from such areas. In this case the territory under contention is an estate, but even these modest housing developments have a political history, since they were often built in places where Protestants were needed to vote in favor of pro-British candidates.[23] The Ulster Volunteer Force (UVF), an ultra-Loyalist paramilitary organization, has been responsible for just such acts of arson as MacLaverty depicts in the novel.[24] Another aggravating factor is the communal pressure deterring people from selling property to members of the other faith. The resulting religious homogeneity intensifies spatial segregation and vice versa.

Separate housing discourages casual social interaction. Journalist Sean O'Hagan cited a startling statistic: in a 2002 study, the researchers found "68% of 18- to 25-year-olds admitting that they had never had a meaningful conversation with anyone from the other community."[25] In Cal's demographic in the 1970s the same lack of contact prevails. All Cal's associates are Nationalist Catholics; he and Seamus are the last Catholics in their estate. But even those who live in mixed areas "might be divided by the so-called peace-lines (twenty-foot-high reinforced walls to keep Catholic and Protestant—at their own desire—apart)."[26] The website of an organization called Geography in Action, quoting journalist Henry McDonald, examines what it calls "ethnic interfaces." An example of such interfaces is a north Belfast wall that bisects a public park, "creating Protestant trees and Catholic trees; Protestant grass and Catholic grass; Protestant flowers and Catholic flowers."[27] While McDonald's comment about sectarian foliage is humorous, the consequences of the peace lines are not. Leaving aside the negative aesthetic impact, these walls and gates reinforce the concept of separateness.

Physical barriers may be demoralizing, but psychological barriers can be even more so. Catholics often feel safe only within their own areas. The effects of poverty are exacerbated by religious and political discrimination with regard to the few jobs that do exist.

"Any jobs in the paper today?" asked his father.

Cal shook his head, his mouth full. When he had swallowed he said, "A couple in Belfast."

"You're safer away from the city."[28]

The Opsahl Commission, an international human-rights commission reporting in 1993, "found ample evidence of . . . self-imposed segregation in working-class areas, with young males in particular fearful of traveling outside their own community, even to take up much-needed employment," which is one reason that "Catholics were twice as likely to be unemployed as Protestants."[29] If a job is located in a Protestant area, Catholic job-seekers often do not apply, assuming, in many cases rightly so, that they will be the victims of discrimination, perhaps even violence. So Catholics stay in their own areas, which are often, as Shamie says to Cal, away from the city, away from the Troubles, but also away from the jobs.

Since Catholics assume that only Protestants will get jobs, they do not apply, while Protestants do. Unemployed Catholics remain on the dole, which reinforces the Protestant assumption that they lack a work ethic and are "devious, untrustworthy, lazy, slovenly."[30] Protestants then "sometimes see Catholics as inveterate whingers and scroungers on the state, perfectly happy to live on the dole. In fact, research has shown that Catholic attitudes to work differ little from those of Protestants."[31] Frustration develops into a Catholic "grievance culture."[32] But if Catholics attempt to break the mold and apply for what are regarded as Protestant jobs, they "[risk] the old accusation of 'selling out' or of becoming 'Castle Catholics,'"[33] like a latter-day version of Thomas Dunne in Sebastian Barry's *Steward of Christendom*.

Some Catholics, Cal's father being one of them, accept the situation and work within it. But Shamie's passivity makes him a poor career adviser to Cal. Because of the lack of job opportunities for Catholics, he thinks that Cal should remain at the abattoir. Though brutal and poorly paid, it is a job; moreover it is a job in a Protestant-controlled organization. Among the few token Catholics, Shamie seems to assume that he and his son exist on the sufferance of Protestants and so must make no trouble. Underlying his speech is the assumption that Cal should be grateful for his father's efforts to get him the job (over, it is suggested, Protestant applicants) and should stay in it, regardless of his unpromising future there and his antipathy to killing.

After leaving the abattoir job, Cal receives public unemployment assistance— the dole. His father sees this as acceptable, preferable to working abroad, and so advises Cal: "If the dole keeps you living you should stay here."[34] That is a counsel of despair. For young Irish men and women seeking work, emigration had long been an alternative to living on the dole, and contrary to Protestant stereotype, Catholics want to work.[35] So at this point in the novel, Cal is considering leaving Northern Ireland. Geographically his goal is London, which is not far away. Considering the success historically experienced by the Irish abroad, Shamie should perhaps be encouraging Cal to better himself by moving much farther than London. His lesson to his son, however, is to accept the status quo and stay at home. By passively taking his father's advice and doing nothing to ameliorate his situation, Cal dramatically limits his own possibilities.

Part of the problem is common to many cultures. Disaffected young men with nothing to do, nothing to lose, no jobs, and no ambition are a potential menace anywhere in the world. Such young men are found on both sides of the Northern Ireland equation: Skeffington, Crilly, and associates on one side and "four youths in denim" on the other. The element of sheer gang warfare to life in Cal's neighborhood involves symbols of sectarian politics serving as gang insignias: "Four youths in denim were lounging against the garden wall at the far side of the street. One of them, wearing a red, white and blue scarf knotted at his neck, was looking over at the McCluskeys' house."[36] Denim is the youth uniform worldwide, but the symbols of Loyalist identity, the scarves in the color of the British flag, attest to their political justification for their scapegoating the one Catholic family in the housing development. But the problem lies not with religious conflict so much as with lack of employment in the North of Ireland. If the members of either group had jobs or were educating themselves to obtain them, they would have less time and energy for causing trouble.

The scarves, like the peace lines, mark ethnic interfaces, points at which ethnic tensions meet and clash. The concept of the "ethnic frontier zone"[37] is similarly useful in understanding the mentality of these four young men. At points "where stability is already disturbed," conflict is usually avoided by means of elaborate "rituals of civility"; thus "people in Northern Ireland manage to lead 'normal lives' by concealing the hard issues of confrontation and choice."[38] On the other hand, flaunting "ethnic tribal identity"[39] exacerbates hostilities. Much like street gangs in American cities, their loyalty is to any group that will accept them as members, and their hostility is directed toward anyone outside that group. In Northern Ireland the labels are religious and political, but the dynamics of late-adolescent male behavior remain the same as in other parts of the world.

Cal's story follows the typical trajectory of the coming-of-age story, in which the young person seeks to define himself in the terms provided to him by his culture. He identifies with being Irish, Catholic, and male. As an Irishman he tries to provide for himself what the educational system in the North has for political reasons failed to provide: a grounding in the Irish language. "For the sake of the Movement he had tried to teach himself some Gaelic out of a book he had bought at a jumble sale but he never knew how to pronounce the written form of the words."[40] Had Cal been a student in the Republic, he would have studied Irish as a required school subject. In Northern Ireland he could have learned Irish only through independent effort. Learning from a book is not a particularly effective way of learning any language, and the fact that the book is a discarded one is a commentary on the sorry state of Irish language learning in Northern Ireland as well as on Cal's own poverty. His attempt to learn Irish nevertheless "for the sake of the Movement" is an acknowledgement that speaking Irish is a political/religious statement, "a Catholic code . . . a weapon" indicating support for Republicanism.[41]

Like much else in twentieth-century Irish writing, Cal's beliefs about the relationship between the Irish language, Catholicism, and Republicanism can be traced to Patrick Pearse (even if Cal himself does not explicitly make the connection). As was discussed with regard to the Easter Rising, Pearse saw the Irish language as a way of furthering the Republican cause but also, perhaps even more important, as a way of emphasizing Celtic identity. Using Irish was for Pearse a crucial element of the "theme of a pure Gaelic Catholic race finally being restored to what is rightfully theirs, not by overnight victory, but by endurance and sacrifice."[42] Others, like Cal, find it impossible to learn the language. Another course of action was possible: Celticizing one's name or those of one's children. Naming customs are one of the many signs by which identity is expressed and reinforced throughout Ireland as it is in the United States, where ethnic-sounding names of all sorts connect people to their heritage. But in Northern Ireland, Irish-origin names could be disadvantageous in that they "marked the bearer as Catholic" and thus "acted as an effective bar to Catholic employment in certain areas."[43] When Skeffington, the novel's representative of the physical-force brand of Irish Nationalism, addresses Cal by his real name, Cahal, he simultaneously celebrates Celtic Catholicism and scorns economic pragmatism.

Cal's sense of himself as an Irish male is also reinforced by the rebel songs, a form of Irish music that celebrates dying for Ireland's freedom. He literally learned these songs as a child at his mother's knee: "She had a good voice and knew countless songs off by heart, rebel songs, and she would bounce him on her knee and sing with gusto, 'As Roddy McCorley goes to die / On the bridge of Toome today.'"[44] This particular song celebrates the brief life and early death of an Irish hero, Roddy McCorley. McCorley was hanged in 1799 for his part in the destruction of the Bridge of Toome by a secret society, the Defenders, in protest of the Penal Laws then restricting the civil rights of Catholics. Rebel songs such as this one appear on many of the albums of such stars of Irish music as the Dubliners and the Clancy Brothers. In *Angela's Ashes* Frank McCourt frequently mentions his father Malachy's habit, when in his cups, of rousing his young sons late at night with this particular rebel song and many

others, exhorting the boys to pledge themselves to "die for Ireland."[45] Mc-
Corley's short life exemplifies the warrior ethic glorified by Pearse. The song
teaches Cal that young men must be willing to give up their lives so that others
(Skeffington, perhaps) might live in freedom. The converse of that proposition,
however, is that young men must also kill for Ireland. Cal, passive and peaceful
by nature, is a reluctant rebel hoping to distance himself from the Republican
paramilitaries who involved him in the murder of Robert Morton.

In the world of the novel, long-ago battles are refought on a daily basis.
The presence and sometimes-discriminatory behavior of the police—the Royal
Ulster Constabulary (RUC)—and the British army keep the Catholic population in a state of fear and resentment. The news report Cal and his father watch
is a typical example: "The Army had shot a deaf mute, saying that he had been
seen carrying a weapon, but by the time they had reached the dead man an
accomplice had removed the gun."[46] According to historian Marianne Elliott,
such confrontations lent credence to the Nationalist cause and exacerbated
existing tensions.[47] John Ardagh, who takes a position on the police and the
army similar to Elliott's, says that while the government of Northern Ireland
has been effective in "redressing past injustices," the behavior of the police and
the army "can be extremely unjust *and* plain stupid."[48] So they are portrayed
in MacLaverty's novel. No solution is apparent. An obvious one, encouraging
more Catholics to join the police force, does not work: "few will do so, as they
know that it could turn them and their families into targets for IRA intimida-
tion."[49] Paramilitary organizations on both sides operate on the principle of
"representative violence," so retaliatory killings of "representative" Loyalists
by "representative" Nationalists continue the cycle.[50] Extreme stances on both
sides preclude compromise.

Skeffington's beliefs illustrate the ideological intractability on the Republican side of the conflict. Presumably Loyalists would be similarly rigid, but no
such characters can be included in the novel since Cal would never have met
them. Skeffington frames the issue in mathematical terms: "'The problem with
this kind of thing is that people get hurt.' Skeffington leaned forward. 'But
compared with conventional war the numbers are small. I know that sounds
callous but it's true. In Cyprus the dead hardly came to three figures. That's
cheap for freedom.'"[51] Because he defines the group to which he belongs as the
duly constituted military of a sovereign state, he regards their actions as justifiable in the same way as those of any other army in wartime. Following Skeffington's logic, if loss of life is the price of war, the number of people killed in the
Troubles in Northern Ireland (estimated at about three thousand) is freedom
bought at a bargain price. Cal is unconvinced. He may be unable to verbalize
the flaw in Skeffington's argument, that loss of human life can be equated to
and quantified in the same way as loss of money, but he senses the weakness

of the analogy. The death of unspecified people is also easier to accept than the death of a particular individual. As Cal comes to know the Morton family, he learns that accepting the death of a family member is hardest of all. Marcella suggests that her marriage to Robert had soured, but Robert's mother, his severely injured father, and his child are all collateral damage from Cal's own actions.

To persuade Cal to engage in those same actions, Skeffington had urged him to "think of the issues, not the people. Think of an Ireland free of the Brits."[52] Here again is that issue of the situation of Irish Protestants in a theoretically united Ireland. Loyalists fear that the ultimate goal of the Republican movement is to render them, in the short term, a powerless minority[53] and, in the long term, to drive them out of Ireland altogether. If Skeffington or his equivalent were in charge, these fears would have some basis. Skeffington's military strategy rests on the willingness of "the hard men and the bandits . . . the real revolutionaries,"[54] men such as Crilly, muscle to lay the groundwork for the political intellectuals (as Skeffington sees himself) to take over as the official face of Republicanism. It is not up to Crilly to think; that, Skeffington assumes, is his job as chief theoretician of the revolution. He seems to plan to rise to power in the new Republic once the hard men have won the war. He appears not to see himself as dying for Ireland as did Pearse and James Connolly, but as having a future in a united nation. Such men as he might be great leaders or they might be political opportunists using others to facilitate their own ends. It is fairly obvious to the reader if not to Cal that Skeffington sees him as more like Crilly than like Skeffington himself and expects to do Cal's thinking for him while Cal drives getaway cars, a role in which he is not a hard man but not innocent either. He is not in a leadership role but also is not able to withdraw from a movement that he never planned to join.

Cal's confused thought processes have placed him in this situation and demonstrate his intellectual and maturational limitations. As a Catholic he has been taught to think in theological terms, but the complexities inherent in the moral judgments he faces elude him. Thinking about his past actions—a Catholic pre-Confession practice known as examining one's conscience—Cal makes distinctions that seem valid to him: "Mortal and venial sins. Red for sex and murder, white for working while you were collecting the dole."[55] In Catholic theology sins are considered mortal, deadly, when they are radically destructive of an individual's relationship with God, as opposed to venial sins, which faults, flaws, or imperfections in that relationship. Influenced by the Puritanism of the Irish Catholic Church, Cal, absurdly, sees murder and sex as in the same category of seriousness and thus equally sinful. On the other hand, he sees the widespread practice of "doing the double," accepting off-the-books employment while collecting the dole, as improper but excusable. Because he does not understand the economics of the larger situation, Cal does not realize that the issue is more complex than simply fitting the practice into the theological category of the venial sin. His fellow Catholics typically do have "greater readiness (and indeed necessity) to 'do the double,'"[56] so extenuating circumstances in a given situation may at least partially mitigate guilt from a moral standpoint. But from a political standpoint, playing the system exacerbates sectarian tensions, which has serious social consequences.

Cal, ill equipped as he is to deal with complexity, finds himself in a situation fraught with moral ambiguity. Some Catholics are not as good as they could be (Cal himself, Skeffington, Crilly); some Protestants are not as bad as they might be (Mrs. Morton, Cyril Dunlop); and victims of sectarian violence (Robert Morton) exhibit an array of human failings, none warranting the death penalty. Cal never comes to understand the roots of his problems: how his passive acceptance of his father's inadequate advice traps him in marginal employment; how his desire to be accepted by his peer group leads him into criminal associations from which he finds it impossible to extricate himself; how his choice of a wildly unsuitable love object ties him to the scene of the very crime for which he hopes to escape punishment. His tragedy lies in his inability to see a way out of his own troubles; in that he resembles his country. The "fanatic heart" of which William Butler Yeats wrote in his 1931 "Remorse for Intemperate Speech" still beats in Northern Ireland.

So far the discussion here has focused mainly on political problems generated by the troubled relationship between Ireland and England. Private life, divorced from politics, has its own set of issues. One recurrent subject in Irish literature is the drinking habits of the Irish. It is rare to find a piece of Irish fiction or drama that does not include some reference to "the drink." The pub setting is one of the most convivial and appealing in Irish literature, as in Irish life. It is not only the drink but the sociability, the animated conversation, and often the music that make for the *craic*, the pleasure specific to the pub experience. For some, however, alcohol is not just one aspect of an evening's entertainment but a destructive way of life.

Chapter 8

"Lots of fun at Finnegan's Wake"

The Drinking Life

Seven nights in a row, an Irishman comes home drunk. Each night, he finds increasingly irrefutable evidence that another man has been in his house. On the seventh night, he finds the man himself in his bed. But each night his wife concocts increasingly implausible explanations. Drunk, the husband is in no condition to argue and so takes the adulterous wife's explanation at face value. A woman devotes herself day in and day out to "the sup"; she drinks it constantly; never will she stop this habit. A tipsy hod-carrier falls off a ladder, suffers a head injury, and dies. His wake occasions still more drinking, as is the custom. As a sign of respect for the deceased, the mourners place samples of his preferred beverages at his head and feet. Whiskey (in Irish, *usquebaugh*) is the "water of life";[1] so the mere proximity of it revives him, and the erstwhile corpse joins in the celebration.[2] Merry tunes such as those accompanying these lyrics make the use of alcohol among the Irish seem endearing, part of their fabled charm; but unlike the unnamed imbiber in "Seven Drunken Nights," Dicey Reilly, and Tim Finnegan, some characters in Irish fiction go over to the dark side via "the drink."

Alcoholism researchers have studied the stereotypical association between the Irish and alcohol thoroughly, but without definitive results. A survey of work done in the field shows that many researchers see strong ambivalence in the attitude of the Irish to alcohol. Even trying to discover whether the Irish do in fact drink more than other ethnic groups seems fraught with complications. First there is the question of what group is to be used to serve as a basis for comparison: natives of other European Union countries, or the Irish abroad as opposed to the Irish at home? Then there is the surprising piece of information that there are more teetotalers in Ireland than there are in other European countries. This complicates matters statistically, in that if A has four drinks and B has none, then their average consumption is two drinks, which seems moderate—except that A, having consumed four drinks, might be drunk. Multiply the drinking habits of both A and B over a whole population, and statistical complexities ensue.

Then there is the problem that the Irish tend to drink away from home rather than at home, which means that (statistically again) the Irish pay more of their income for alcohol than at-home drinkers do; but this does not necessarily mean that pubgoers in Ireland drink more than dinnertime drinkers in, say, Italy. And then there is the perennial problem of self-reporting; it is said that American doctors automatically double a patient's self-reported alcohol use. But given the acceptability of alcohol consumption in Ireland, it is possible that, like boastful fraternity brothers on a Monday morning, Irish self-reporters may attempt to measure up to the national reputation and thus exaggerate their drinking in morning-after tales. With all these factors operating, it is hard even for the expert to say definitively how much the Irish drink.

There does, however, seem to be a consensus among alcohol researchers that the Irish drink differently from some other ethnic groups. In *A Hair of the Dog: Irish Drinking and American Stereotype,* sociologist Richard Stivers suggests that drinking rituals of all sorts not only mark life's milestones (birth, marriage, death) but also are part of everyday life in Ireland. Drawing on evidence from eighteenth- and nineteenth-century Ireland, England, and Scotland, Stivers cites evidence that alcohol was used to reward children for good behavior, to validate "bargains and transactions . . . especially at fairs and markets," and, referring to his title, "to relieve the effects of past drinking episodes."[3] So, like Dicey Reilly of song, some Irish people mark not only rites of passage but daily events with a dram (or two). Further the custom of drinking apart from meals, often instead of meals, exacerbates the effects of alcohol in a way that, for example, wine drunk with a meal may not.

Of the many drinking rituals that Stivers describes, the one with most relevance to fiction and drama involves the pub. The pub serves as both "meeting place" and "recreation center" for a community,[4] and its regulars are connected by both trade and neighborhood ties. In the pub there are many rules and rituals, but the most important of them is treating or buying rounds: "This norm of reciprocity made all men equal and bound them to each other. A man was obligated to buy drinks for his friends, as they were for him. The norm of treating cut across class boundaries and occupational lines and permeated both the public and the private sectors of life. It was a symbol of group integration and an affirmation of male identity."[5] This custom is almost a guarantee of consumption to excess, not to mention wasteful spending. If two men walk into a pub, each must treat the other; if only one treats, the rule of reciprocity is broken and the recipient of the treat is diminished in his companion's eyes and in his own. So at least two drinks per man must be consumed in any given pub visit. Then should a third man walk in, a third round must commence, followed, perhaps, by a fourth, fifth, or sixth as more arrive; as the ritual continues, the first two drinkers are particularly in danger of drinking too much. Ending the ritual is difficult, as it should ideally be done at a point at which all the men in the group have measured up to the "norm of reciprocity," thus asserting their membership in what Stivers calls the "bachelor group"[6]—a group made up, for various complicated reasons, of married men as well as single.

In addition to gender solidarity, class solidarity is also maintained by not only the pub rituals but also the practice of drinking itself, especially public drinking, and there are historical, sociological, and psychological factors dating back at least two centuries that cause this to be so. Historian George Bretherton explains how, particularly in the rural areas, the nineteenth-century temperance movement was associated with the Protestant Ascendancy and with the landowning classes. Rural landowners had a great deal to gain if their tenants remained sober, and so the point of temperance became to provide reliable workers. Anything beloved of the landlords was anathema to the tenants; plus Protestant reformers defined abstinence in terms of banning the drinks that the Catholic lower-class population drank, while permitting the drinks favored by upper-class Protestants. Thus, abstinence, or even moderation, came to mean allying oneself with the landholding classes and their religion and against one's own class and faith—clearly an unacceptable situation.[7]

In urban areas, according to sociologist Joseph Gusfield, attempts to limit drinking were also class-based and economics-based. Gusfield begins his essay with Oscar Wilde's witticism "Work is the curse of the drinking class." The drinking class (the urban proletariat, lower-class, and Catholic) resented the attempts of the urban equivalents of those temperance landlords, the business and factory owners (middle- to upper-class and Protestant) and their minions, to control their celebratory rituals in the interest of increased productivity. Social controls on drinking imposed from above were intended not to benefit the individual drinker but to provide for a docile and efficient urban working class. One big problem, according to Gusfield, was "the Saint Monday phenomenon, absenteeism or drunkenness of workers after the weekend. Unaccustomed to a time sequencing that required planning and pacing of the total daily agenda, workers continued to declare holidays and sought to work when they saw fit rather than follow the systematic organization of daily and weekly time that the industrial process made dominant."[8] So not only was drinking, for the urban worker, a chance to relax with his mates in the pub, it was also a way of asserting class solidarity and defying the employer's control over the worker's after-hours time. Moreover drinking was the worker's way of asserting his right to carnival, "with its licensed release from . . . prohibitions,"[9] instead of the perpetual Lent required by the business model of behavior.

Removing from the office to the pub had not only gender and social implications but anthropological ones as well, according to psychologist and anthropologist Marianna Adler: "Before the 1830s, the shared practice of daily drinking was a primary symbolic vehicle for the generation and affirmation of the social relations of community that formed the basis of English preindustrial society."[10] The ritual of shared drinking reasserts the group solidarity involved in the "reciprocity and communality" of treating.[11] Had the landlords and the industrial tycoons understood the anthropological meaning of drinking to the drinkers, their better course of action might have been to share in the ritual rather than try to control it. Adler points out that "the mutual obligation to treat at drinking extended beyond the community of status equals. Employers were also expected at ritually defined times to supply drink to their employees," and this process "linked men of unequal status in relations of exchange."[12] Disrupting this link by placing landlords and management on the opposite side of tenants and workers made abstinence or moderation look like an attempt by the former to control the latter, which had the paradoxical effect of making the latter drink more to assert group solidarity.

The conversation on the Irish and alcohol involves writers and artists as well as medical, historical, anthropological, and sociological investigators. For the purpose of discussing fictional characters, whose blood alcohol levels cannot be tested, alcohol abuse can be defined as a character's drinking to a point that affects other characters, triggers plot events, and/or develops a theme of the work. Two well-known literary examples are a pair of stories in James Joyce's *Dubliners,* "Counterparts" and "A Little Cloud." The central characters, Farrington and Little Chandler, respectively, fit the definition of alcohol abusers. In addition the drinking habits of each of them develop one of the central themes of Joyce's work, the inferiority of Dublin life.

The Lesser Life: James Joyce's *Dubliners*

One of the key themes in *Dubliners* by James Joyce (1882–1941) is the limited way in which his characters live, for which Joyce blames Ireland. Even in Ireland's principal city, he felt, there was no possibility of living fully. The sobriquet of the main character of "A Little Cloud," "Little" Chandler, calls attention to this recurrent theme in the collection: "He was called Little Chandler because, though he was but slightly under the average stature, he gave one the idea of being a little man."[13] During the course of the story, Chandler comes to believe himself a man of small mind and spirit, in contrast to the greatness he perceives in his old acquaintance, Ignatius Gallaher, recently returned from London.

The key term, however, is *perceives.* The story is told from the third-person limited viewpoint; the viewpoint character is Little Chandler himself, so the reader knows only what he thinks. Chandler believes that in his eight-year absence from Dublin, Gallaher has "got on," experienced the kind of success that would be possible only to those who leave Ireland. In Ireland Gallaher had been "shabby and necessitous"; in England he "had become a brilliant figure on the London press" (57). Chandler believes this because Gallaher says so; there is little corroborating evidence other than his "travelled air, his well-cut tweed suit and fearless accent" (57). His pose of worldly sophistication is swallowed whole by Chandler, who has little experience of the world and therefore little basis for evaluating the truth of Gallaher's traveler's tales. All that is really known about Gallaher is that he can afford one well-cut tweed suit and an evening of drinks; everything else is Chandler's interpretation of what he says and does.

As Chandler ponders the self-proclaimed achievements of his old friend, he thinks with "gentle melancholy" (57) of the ambitions that he once had to become a prominent literary figure himself. He owns a collection of books of poetry and often considers reading some of his favorite poems to his wife, "but his shyness had always held him back" (58). The reader has no way of knowing how his wife would have reacted to this poetry reading, and neither does Chandler. But his wife and their baby become convenient scapegoats for his unfulfilled ambitions. Like Joyce himself Chandler comes to believe that living in Ireland is antithetical to artistic accomplishment: "There was no doubt about it: if you wanted to succeed you had to go away. You could do nothing in Dublin" (59).

Instead of attempting the hard work of artistic creation, Chandler thinks gloomily of what might be his "poet's soul" (60) and what of his (possible) talent might yet be developed at his ripe age of thirty-two. He imagines rave reviews of his yet unwritten poetry and tries to decide which formulation of his name would be "more Irish looking" (60), thus more likely to connect him with the greats of the Irish Literary Revival then in the process of putting Ireland on the world's literary map. He does not, however, write any poems. He leaves his office as a poet manqué resigned to his fate as an office functionary. In this spirit he enters Corless's bar, where Ignatius Gallaher awaits him. His reveries about his supposedly lost literary career deepen his regret, and by the time he returns home from the bar, he is in a state of suppressed rage, which triggers an angry outburst directed toward his infant son. His experiences in Corless's bar explain why this happens.

Chandler tells Gallaher that he, Chandler, "drinks very little as a rule" (61), and his reaction to the crowd at Corless's suggests that at least he drinks at Corless's very little. He thinks of the bar as a sophisticated place, attracting a sophisticated, multinational clientele of theatergoers; this is not Chandler's "local," where he is comfortable and the habitués familiar. Thus he is out of his element as he enters the bar, and Gallaher has the advantage on him. Their meeting at the bar, combined with Gallaher's boisterous gregariousness, initiates the drinking ritual, with no possibility of Chandler's ordering a milder drink than even the "very much diluted" whiskey that Gallaher aggressively orders for him (61). Gallaher drinks his own whiskey undiluted, which—along with the rapidity with which he causes the drinks to be placed before them, his thirst masked as bonhomie—marks him as a hard drinker, unlike the more abstemious Chandler.

The inevitable toast ensues, and the drinking begins. Gallaher finishes the first drink rapidly, while Chandler "sipped a little" (62). But the time spent on just one drink is too short a visit for old friends, and neither Gallaher nor Chandler suggests a meal. So the second drink follows hard upon the first. As does the third. This intake is excessive for a small individual such as Little Chandler. But Chandler matches Gallaher drink for drink, lest he be thought of as less manly than his friend. And during these three drinks, consumed in rapid succession, his manhood is taking a battering. Gallaher's competitive stance when Chandler enters the bar—"leaning with his back against the counter and his feet planted far apart" (60)—is paralleled by his verbal aggression, demonstrated in all his conversational topics. His goal seems to be to prove himself the bigger man in every way: better traveled, more sexually experienced, worldly wise. This, of course, puts Chandler in the role of the provincial, the hometown boy, married young, monogamous, reliable, and therefore, to Gallaher (and soon to Chandler himself), a failure. Chandler does not have the emotional distance—or, after the first drink, the sobriety—to evaluate Gallaher's grandiose claims and takes them at face value.

Chandler's moderate alcohol consumption has heretofore made him a decent companion (he has "an odd half one or so" with old friends [61]); but mainly it allows him to be a reliable worker and a passable husband and father. But once Chandler is outside of three whiskies, these virtues seem tepid indeed. So when the work/pub/home triangle is complete, his self-perception is irrevocably altered. Hearing about Gallaher's sexual adventures, he compares his wife, Annie, to the supposedly more erotic, certainly more exotic, European women of what might be Gallaher's imagination only and finds her wanting. It is no accident that Chandler thinks about the English poet George Gordon, Lord Byron (1788–1824), who was indeed the embodiment of at least one form of the artistic life: testing the limits of experience, especially with regard to sexuality. Living dangerously, as Byron did, does not necessarily produce great art in and of itself; but neither, Joyce's story suggests, does living tepidly.

Although Joyce himself believed that Dublin and creativity were mutually exclusive, the case of his character is much more complicated. Chandler may not be the possessor of a great talent, and Gallaher may not be an exemplar of the creative life. Corless's bar is surely not the locus of male conviviality but is a battlefield on which alcohol is as much of a weapon of male self-aggrandizement as is bragging speech designed to establish pecking orders. His own ego battered, Chandler takes out his frustration as the lower man in a hierarchy on one even lower than himself: a young boy. Such behavior is "little" indeed.

The short story "Counterparts" has a similar structure to that of "A Little Cloud." Farrington moves from office to pub to home, with a similar result. Low-level office work (he is a law copyist) unmans him; his size and strength is disproportionate to the unchallenging nature of his job. It is as if the urban desire for middle-class respectability has trapped a big, strong man, who would be more at home under the open sky, into wielding a pen as a scrivener. Worse, he is under the thumb of Mr. Alleyne, urban remnant of the Protestant Ascendancy, his "piercing north of Ireland accent"[14] the voice of authority in Farrington's work life.

Unlike Little Chandler, Farrington shows signs that he is a problem drinker already. His anger at his situation in the office triggers "a sharp sensation of thirst. The man recognized the sensation and felt that he must have a good night's drinking" (71). The connection between Farrington's emotions and his alcohol consumption is thus established. Rendering the situation more serious is the fact that Farrington, husband, father, and sole support of his family, cannot afford the number of drinks that might be involved in buying rounds. He hopes to complete his work so well that he can get an advance on his salary but undercuts that very plan by sneaking out of the office to the bar on the pretext of using the bathroom. At O'Neill's he is clearly a regular, on a first-name basis with the waiter; his fast glass of porter is followed by a caraway seed serving the function of a breath mint. It is clear that there is no social gratification to this visit but rather a gratification of his need for alcohol only. The time is midafternoon, and Farrington has no justification for interrupting the workday with this leisure activity, which has become a compulsion. This is just the sort of behavior that the temperance movement in Ireland sought to discourage, as it made for inefficient workers and thus unprofitable businesses.

Upon his return to the office, the impact of the porter makes him "confused" and so less capable of completing his assigned copying task (73). It is then that he conjures his fantasy of the bar as great good place, as compared with the gloomy environs of the office and even of twilight Dublin itself: "The dark damp night was coming and he longed to spend it in the bars, drinking with his friends amid the glare of glass and the clatter of glasses" (73). Fiscal reality intervenes as he considers possible ways to bankroll this venture. He has spent his last money on the earlier glass of porter. He has lost hope of the advance on his salary, as the task he has been set is clearly impossible to complete, what with the time of day and the influence of the porter. Could he borrow enough from the waiter, Pat, to subsidize his drinking? Probably not. Why not, then, pawn his watch chain?

Borrowing money to drink in a pub is clearly a poor move economically. But in order for the pub visit to perform its designated function—bolstering Farrington's increasingly shaky sense of self—he must have enough money to engage in two key pub rituals: storytelling and standing rounds. Farrington is to this story as Ignatius Gallaher is to "A Little Cloud": the barroom braggart. In the story he tells to the appreciative audience in the pub, Farrington casts himself as a veritable hero of the Celts in challenging the authority of Mr. Alleyne. This triggers the appreciation of one Nosey Flynn, which he expresses by treating Farrington, which in turn sets up a reciprocal obligation in Farrington to treat Flynn. Then two more drinkers, O'Halloran and Paddy Leonard, come in, hear the story again, and begin a new round by treating the group. Not to respond to this ritual of reciprocity requires the drinker to leave the group or, if he accepts drinks without himself treating, to be considered a "sponge" like Weathers (79). Farrington, then, the man of the hour, "told the boys to polish off that and have another" (77). Then Higgins comes in, hears the story, and the whole process begins anew. Like Ignatius Gallaher, whose meeting with Little Chandler was only the first of the evening, the men regroup and go on to several other pubs for more rounds. At this point Farrington has had much more to drink than Chandler did. In the former story, it is easy for the reader to count Chandler's drinks (three); but with all the treating and pub-crawling, it is not easy to determine how much alcohol Farrington has consumed, and that is the point—neither can he. Farrington has certainly drunk more than he should have and much more than he can afford.

The point of all this activity has been to bolster Farrington's shaky sense of himself as a man, threatened as it is by his lack of success on his job and Mr. Alleyne's bullying. But at this point events occur that threaten his manhood in ways that even alcohol cannot soothe, sending him home furious. First there is the perceived rejection by an English girl. Then there is his loss at the pub game of arm-wrestling; worse still, he loses to Weathers, the sponge (80). Farrington's position in the bachelor group had already been challenged by O'Halloran, who, regarding a proposed trip "behind the scenes" at the theater to meet "some nice girls," says that "Farrington wouldn't go because he was a married man" (78). All these affronts have a cumulative effect. He can now prove himself a real man only by continuing to drink. The night of drinking concludes with, yes, another drink, the custom being to take one for the road; then all head to their various homes.

Farrington does so in the worst possible mood: "He was full of smoldering anger and revengefulness. He felt humiliated and discontented: he did not even feel drunk and he had only twopence in his pocket. He cursed everything. He had done for himself in the office, pawned his watch, spent all his money; and he had not even got drunk" (80). He may not feel drunk, but he is drunk, and with consequences: loss of prestige within the peer group; loss of the watch, as he does not have enough money left to redeem it; and perhaps loss of his job. The violent feelings spill over into an act of domestic violence directed against his young son at home. Like Little Chandler's son, Farrington's child is a scapegoat, a target of booze-fueled rage.

Twenty Drunken Years: Roddy Doyle's Paula Spencer Novels

Much has changed in Dublin from the time of publication of Joyce's *Dubliners* to the beginning of the literary career of Roddy Doyle (b. 1958). But alcohol still figures in the lives of the Dubliners of fiction, as does ambivalence about the drinking life. In Doyle's novel *The Snapper*, the second of his Barrytown Trilogy, the pub plays the role described by Richard Stivers in *A Hair of the Dog*. It is the center of public life in Barrytown, the go-to destination for men to gather and escape the crowded conditions (and the world of women and children) in their tiny homes. But in the Dublin of Doyle's fiction, the pub is also frequented by young women, and Sharon Rabbitte's excessive drinking on a certain night leads to a situation in which she is incapable of giving consent to a sexual encounter and is raped. Such is the lure of the pub that Sharon continues to drink to excess throughout her resulting pregnancy. On the one hand, the Barrytown pub is warm, convivial, lots of fun; on the other hand, it is the breeding ground for all manner of social ills, including unplanned pregnancies.

Nevertheless the overarching message of all three Barrytown novels is a positive one. Despite the difficulties the characters face (some of which they create themselves), this is a community that pulls together and offers its members hope. All three novels show characters drinking to excess but managing the consequences in a way that is relatively harmless and, in the case of Sharon's "snapper," even life-affirming. These three novels are not, however, Doyle's only work dealing with alcohol use and abuse. In his paired novels *The Woman Who Walked into Doors* and *Paula Spencer,* the microhistory of the Spencer family reflects larger and more ominous social trends with regard to alcohol use, especially among the urban poor.

Since *The Woman Who Walked into Doors* is told in the first person, Paula is the reader's only source of information. Her ability to express herself is limited by a number of factors, however: her lack of education, her inability at this point in her life to understand her own role in her fate or to comprehend causes of her own behavior, and, of course, her drunkenness, which impairs her judgment at the time and her recollection thereafter. She does understand that her drinking has become problematic, in that she takes steps (largely unsuccessful) to control it. She sets herself rules for when and how much she drinks, for example, not until after her youngest child Jack goes to bed—resulting, predictably, in Paula's efforts to get Jack to bed earlier and earlier. She also concocts elaborate schemes for locking away the alcohol and "losing" the key. Nevertheless her drinking has reached the point of physical dependency: "I don't enjoy it, the drinking. I need it. I shake. My head goes; I have small blackouts. I start sweating patches of sweat."[15] And later: "My eyes are glueing. I have to scream. My joints are stuck. I'm made of sore cement" (113). If the definition of literary alcohol abuse is drinking that has consequences for the drinker and others, triggers plot events, and/or develops a theme of the work, then Paula is by all three measures, as she often describes herself, an "alco." Moreover the novel is thematically concerned with the role of alcohol in Irish life in general as well as Paula's own.

Other family members drink, and little if any disapproval is expressed, nor are social sanctions imposed on the drinker. Except for her sister Carmel, who, according to Paula, saved her (188), concern for privacy appears to trump concern for Paula's well-being and that of her children. Even the doctors and other members of the hospital staff who examine and treat her after her many emergency-room visits for domestic abuse inquire only casually into the circumstances of her life. The behavior of these medical professionals suggests that "this kind of abuse is deeply embedded in the very fabric of a patriarchal Irish culture."[16] The doctors and nurses do not ask Paula directly if she has been abused (which would, in her mind, leave her free to answer; volunteering the information is against her idiosyncratic personal ethics). The emergency room staff members accept her excuse of her own drunkenness to account for her injuries as if it were the most natural thing in the world, if a failing at all a venial one, for a young mother to have such "accidents." Not only do they "indirectly endorse abusive behavior,"[17] they do not even appear to see the drinking as an issue. The Irish medical system treats her and releases her as if her condition were equivalent to a bout of influenza, regrettable but inevitable. Indeed the whole society colludes in "'turning a blind eye' . . . to domestic violence."[18] The same blind eye is turned to her and Charlo's drinking.

Because of the first-person narrative viewpoint, the reader is never in the mind of Charlo, so there is never a definitive answer to the question of why he drinks or why he batters his wife. Paula is too drunk herself to register much that is implied by Charlo's actions. Her own problem drinking develops over the course of the marriage, but her problem with Charlo's drinking begins on their wedding night. His behavior is absolutely stereotypical. Excessive alcohol use in rite-of-passage rituals means that there is no possibility of his drinking moderately enough to make the night a memorable one for Paula (or even for himself). Paula waits for Charlo with no certainty that he will actually appear to consummate their new marriage: "I went up to the room upstairs and sat on the bed. I wanted Charlo to come in now. Before it was too late. Before he got too drunk. Before he went off somewhere *with the brothers*" (143; emphasis added). Instead of devoting himself to his bride, Charlo allies himself with "the brothers," the bachelor group, drinking so much that he "came in at about three o'clock and blacked out before he hit the bed" (147). Granted the wedding night was not a sexual initiation for either of them; nevertheless Charlo's spending it with the boys rather than with his wife sends a clear message of her relative importance in his life. No surprise, then, that he will spend many a night at his local, Campions, leaving Paula home alone with the children.

As the novel continues, it is never quite clear, as if Paula does not actually know, what Charlo does for a living. He does not seem to have a steady job and so must get money for alcohol from pickup jobs, the dole, criminal activity, or a combination of all three. That the last two are the most likely is suggested by the episode of the burning money. It is hard to imagine that a person of limited means who had worked hard for his cash, digging ditches, say, would burn it to torment his wife. In addition whatever Charlo does for a living cannot be time dependent, as his alcohol use renders him unfit for any sort of labor involving punctuality or time management. Charlo's failure in the world outside the home, combined with his socializing with the bachelor group, accounts for his domestic violence. As in Joyce's two short stories, the same pattern applies: a man goes from work to pub to home; at work he is underemployed and dissatisfied; in the pub he finds some satisfaction; but even there he is only one of many, not the dominant male. Only at home is he the strongest person. His misguided efforts to prove his own masculinity lead to violence. The alcohol lowers his inhibitions against his anger, the only emotion men like him allow themselves to acknowledge.

The question arises, is Paula a facilitator of Charlo's drinking and the ensuing violence? When she first meets him, she discounts the significance of his alcohol use: "He'd been drinking. I could smell it but it didn't matter. He wasn't drunk" (4). She even sees drinking as a sign of affluence: "He had money, I knew he did. The smell off his breath told me that" (10). The first time they make love, they are both drunk (21). Later she finds his drinking part of his charm: when he has a hangover, she sees him as "funny . . . a laugh"; when he misbehaves while drunk, she forgives him—"No bother" (148). Only eighteen, she does not see his drinking as part of a larger pattern of deviant behavior, including his being "a skinhead . . . up in court three times and in St. Pat's once" (22). The "St. Pat's" reference is explained to her later. While Paula regards it as "not really jail" because it is "only for kids" (52), Charlo explains that it is indeed jail and that he had been there for robbery. So St. Pat's must be juvenile detention, a harbinger of future trouble for Charlo. Paula's father picks up the signals, but like eighteen-year-olds everywhere, she thinks she knows better. So it is only a matter of time until she is on the floor, looking up at "Charlo's feet, then his legs, making a triangle with the floor" (5).

Why would a woman stay in a violent situation such as this? Not only does Charlo face no consequences for his behavior either in terms of his marriage or the larger society, Paula implicitly condones it by continuing to have reproductive sex with him, resulting in five pregnancies, one of which is lost to the violence and the other four of which result in children who further tie her to their father. Depression makes her drink; alcohol makes her more depressed. Paula endures the abuse for seventeen years. At no point does she seek outside help, whether from the legal system (she fails to prosecute, for example, for the loss of the baby Sally), from the mental health system, or from the medical system. In blaming herself and in seeing her situation as hopeless, she plays out the script of an abused woman, trying to placate her abuser while simultaneously further arousing his anger. When Paula is finally driven to act to protect Nicola, the way in which she gets rid of Charlo increases his hostility, thus perpetuating the cycle of violence.

Divorce is not possible for Paula. The events of *The Woman Who Walked into Doors* begin with her and Charlo's first meeting in 1973 and continue through the seventeen years of her marriage, until 1990; the referendum legalizing divorce in Ireland passed in 1995. Paula could have separated from Charlo and fails in her responsibility to her children by not separating them from him. But does she have any responsibility to the larger society to alert someone in authority to Charlo's capacity for violence? When he kills the hostage, it is clear from the way he does it that Charlo's uncontrolled anger has been displaced onto Gwen Fleming. Is Paula at some level responsible for Gwen's death? Apparently she does not think so, because the murder and subsequent killing of Charlo by the police do not set her on the path to recovery, at least not for a long time.

At the beginning of *Paula Spencer*, it is 2005, Paula's forty-eighth birthday, and she has only been sober for "four months and five days."[19] The year covered by the book, to her next birthday, chronicles the changes in Paula's life as she tries to stay away from the bottle. Due to her disease, she has missed a good many maturational stages, and this year is a time of accelerated psychological growth as she tries to make up for lost time and repair damaged relationships. One commonly accepted measure of competence is the ability to perform independently the basic activities of daily living appropriate to one's situation. For Paula her year is devoted to mastering time, which in her case means earning money; to developing a healthy relationship with food instead of a sick dependence on drink; and to repairing the family relationships broken by her alcohol use.

Large blocks of time have gone missing for Paula, and like an Irish Rip Van Winkle, she reenters a world that is very different from the one she left when she married Charlo. Since she has for all practical purposes lost those years, she is in perpetual catch-up mode. She is astounded, for example, to realize that Phil Lynott, front man for the rock band Thin Lizzy, has been dead for nearly twenty years and that Bono and U2 have long since picked up that musical torch. The reference to Lynott and Thin Lizzy is more important than it may first appear. For one thing the band was mentioned in *The Woman Who Walked into Doors* by way of a poster in Paula and Charlo's kitchen (166); apparently both were fans. For another thing Thin Lizzy's breakout hit was a rock version of the Irish drinking song "Whiskey in the Jar." And for a third, Phil Lynott died young, at thirty-six, of the combined effects of drugs and alcohol. Paula is not as far behind the times in never having taken the Luas, at the time a new tram system supplementing the buses and trains upon which she depends; it opened to passengers in 2004, only a year earlier. Her life experiences have been few and narrow; she has, for example, never ventured far afield from Dublin, not even to Belfast, about two hours by train. A larger issue is that she has missed not only her peak earning years but also her peak mothering years.

So one of Paula's main developmental tasks at age forty-eight is to master time. As a member of the lower class in service to higher classes, she must accommodate herself to her superiors' schedules. Her cleaning jobs are planned around the activities of her bosses: daytime for the private houses, evening for the offices. The time management skills necessary to complete these cleaning jobs were beyond her when she was drinking, and a drunk is useless to any part of the economic system other than as a consumer for the liquor industry. Now she can manage a complex schedule and get to the right houses on the right days. She can take on extra side jobs (like cleaning the arena) and even experiences a modest degree of success in being promoted from cleaner to cleaning supervisor. Though this may be a distinction without much of a difference in terms of salary and job prestige, it does reinforce her efforts at sobriety. Paula notices repeatedly that in the Ireland of 2005, eastern Europeans have largely replaced the Irish in these jobs; but she understands that her low status is a consequence of her own behavior. Mastering time enables her to make money, which in turn makes her proud. She knows she has enough money for food shopping; she is saving for a computer, and "her work is going to pay for it" (44). A more complex task is to make up, as far as she can, for lost time. Paula's alarm clock is set for seven-thirty during the week, so she can wake up Jack and even see Leanne before she goes to work on the weekends. These activities reassure her that she is "still a mother" (11). But Jack and Leanne are really too old to benefit from the organized, child-centered household that Paula is trying to institute now. So her second line of defense is to mother them through food.

A big part of Paula's recovery has to do with redefining her own relationship with food, which would help her with her belated goal of mothering her children properly. One of the key tasks of a mother at which she noticeably failed was to see to it that her children were fed regularly and appropriately. If a mother makes the food herself, so much the better, as the whole process of selecting food and preparing it in the children's preferred ways is a major way to express love and food is at the heart of many people's fondest childhood memories. But the whole task of feeding a family is more complex than it might seem to anyone not accustomed to doing it. One must have the money to buy nourishing food and if that basic need is met, the time management skills to keep the refrigerator stocked. Then there is the issue of the food preferences of each member of the household. Organization is more important as the complexity of a recipe increases: one must have not some, but all the ingredients to hand and be able to manage time sequencing in such a way as to prepare a dish correctly. One cannot do any of these things effectively when drunk.

Heretofore Paula has failed miserably at this central task of motherhood. At the height—or depth—of her alcohol abuse, a pathetic scene occurs involving her "local," now resurrected as Finnegan's Wake, and Jack when he was a "little fella": "He stood outside that pub . . . waiting for her to come out. He stood in the rain. He often did it. She brought crisps out to him, and Coke with a straw. Like it was a treat. There you are, love" (16). Potato chips and Coke hardly constitutes an appropriate dinner for a child, and this episode would be a grievous abnegation of maternal responsibility even if it only happened once; but Paula remembers that Jack *often* did this (and in the rain). Now she feels guilty, as she should; and in her recovery she tries to do penance for this sin of omission by reasserting her position as a mother in the kitchen.

Her ambivalence about this role centers on her refrigerator. A housecleaner by trade, Paula is something of an authority on the subject of refrigerators, and she knows that the one given to her by her oldest child, Nicola, is a fine one, better than those of many of her clients. But the refrigerator's presence in her household rankles. "It's a good fridge. . . . It takes up half the kitchen. It's one of those big silver, two-door jobs. Ridiculous. Twenty years too late. She opens it the way film stars open the curtains. Daylight! Ta-dah! Empty. What was Nicola thinking of? The stupid bitch. How to make a poor woman feel poorer. Buy her a big fridge. Fill that, loser. The stupid bitch. What was she thinking?" (3). The fact that the fridge is too big underlines her lost mothering years. Then the fact that it was a gift from Nicola underlines the daughter's greater financial success and reverses the roles of parent and child in that Nicola is implicitly instructing Paula in her domestic role rather than vice versa. Paula also suspects that one of Nicola's motives in buying the refrigerator is to give the daughter an excuse to spy on her mother by looking not for alcohol—both

Paula and Leanne are alcoholics and so would hide it—but for the mixers that would betray its presence. Finally a large, fully stocked refrigerator requires more money than Paula has or has ever had at any one time, so the refrigerator always seems empty despite her best efforts.

Despite these difficulties Paula takes upon herself the task of making soup. She has found that, since she stopped drinking, her appetite has improved, and she has learned for the first time as an adult to appreciate the taste of food. But her main inspiration for the soup is her belated desire to care for Leanne, whose malnourished state terrifies her. As a culinary task, soup is a good choice, as the only indispensable component of soup is water; the rest of the project involves whatever suitable ingredients are in the refrigerator, in any order. And while the chopping, mixing, and cooking certainly require time, time management is more flexible in making soup than in making other dishes. Soup can simmer for an hour, or two or three, once all the ingredients are in the pot and on the stove. It is hard to fail at soup-making.

But it is certainly possible to fail at completing the emotional transaction that the soup is intended to generate. When a cook has undertaken a complex culinary project, the reinforcement for that would be the diners' conspicuous gratitude for and enjoyment of the meal. Family dinners, however, can be disappointing in this way; the beneficiaries of the kind act are often less appreciative than they might be, distracted, uninterested, or simply not hungry. They may even choose to engage in acts of passive aggression by refusing to eat the food. In Jack's case any of the above could be true. Instead of responding enthusiastically to Paula's offer of the soup, he eats bread and cheese (93), which certainly appears to be a rejection of her efforts. He could merely not be in the mood for lentil soup, but he could also be wary of responding to this overture of maternal love. Having been disappointed in this relationship many times in the past, it is possible that he does not trust his mother in that long-neglected maternal role. His refusal of Paula's penitential offering shows that he is not ready to forgive her for that long-ago pub "meal."

Worse still is Leanne's reaction. Paula's initial impetus for making the soup is her fear for her daughter's health: "Leanne is skin and bone. . . . Leanne is dying" (86). Providing homemade soup for Leanne is Paula's attempt at giving her "alco" daughter an opportunity to eat rather than drink. Leanne, however, comes home with an "off-licence bag" (98), a bottle of Smirnoff's vodka for drinking at home, an indication that she has a different agenda. Like her brother Leanne rejects Paula's effort, observing that the soup smells like "something burning" (98). When the encounter becomes violent, the evening deteriorates into a major disaster.

One of the prime tenets of Alcoholics Anonymous is that the recovering alcoholic must, to the extent possible, make amends to those damaged by his or her drinking, and Paula is trying to do this. Not only did she have the soup ready for Leanne, she had it in Leanne's "special bowl," her favorite one (100). Paula understands the significance of what she is doing: "The bowl wasn't the point. The soup wasn't even the point. The woman bringing the soup to Leanne, holding the bowl in front of her, not shaking—the woman was the point" (100). There is no guarantee, however, that the damaged person will be in the mood to forgive at the moment that the recovering alcoholic is ready to ask forgiveness. Leanne eventually drinks the soup, but her behavior, like Jack's, undercuts Paula's attempt at making amends. Similarly with John Paul, her attempts to establish a relationship with him, overcome her revulsion for his partner, Star, and become a conventional grandmother to their children are efforts to correct the wrongs of the past.

With Nicola, however, Paula is at a loss. Unlike the others she seems to need nothing that Paula can give; indeed Nicola gives to Paula. Nicola's self-sufficiency, and even her generosity, grate on Paula. For her to remake the film of the past, revising the mothering process, her children have to play their part in the drama of repentance. Nicola, it is clear, has no desire to do so, has in fact sealed herself off from any feelings regarding either of her parents. This self-protective mechanism works well for her but not for Paula, who would like to have another chance to mother this unmotherable young woman. Nicola's competence as wife, mother, and professional means she has somehow managed to travel far beyond any point of meaningful connection with Paula.

As the novel ends, Paula has improved in her ability to do ordinary life activities and made efforts to repair her relationship with her children and sisters. She looks almost ready to take a first step into the rest of her life. Yet she is still organizing her life around alcohol; the *not* drinking is as absorbing to her as the drinking was, and she will never be as she would have been had she been able to drink moderately or abstain. She is still living with the consequences of her own and Charlo's alcohol abuse. Her old injuries still hurt: three of her four children are obviously damaged, and one, the baby Sally, is dead. Because she has missed years of possible financial and educational development, poverty and low social class seem to be her lifelong fate. Apparently the "Celtic Tiger economy . . . has not benefited underprivileged groups" such as marginally employed cleaning women.[20] Others, however, are doing better than Paula is. Her daughter Nicola seems to have transcended the limitations imposed on her by nature and nurture and is living a middle-class life, and one of Paula's sisters is buying an investment property in Bulgaria; they can grab the tail of the Tiger, but Paula cannot.

The remaining question is this: given Paula's dismal history with her husband, can or should she take a chance on Joe? In the earliest stages of this relationship, she is more assertive, more in control, than she was with Charlo.

She is not nearly as sexually attracted. She will not be having children with Joe. She is honest, disclosing her alcoholism up front. But her recovery is still, and possibly always will be, fragile. And Joe is himself the survivor of a failed marriage. Paula knows very little of him as the novel ends, and so it is not clear whether he represents hope for the future. Perhaps the new name of Paula's local, Finnegan's Wake, suggests rebirth for Paula, as it did for Tim Finnegan. Doyle has written trilogies before and may again to trace the further development of this character.

According to James Joyce, the solution for the limited life available to his characters in *Dubliners,* as to himself, was to leave Ireland. Little Chandler and Farrington believe themselves to be trapped where they are, but Joyce's own life demonstrates that they were not. However, for the real-life counterparts of Chandler, Farrington, and Paula Spencer, emigration will not help and perhaps may exacerbate their alcohol abuse. Habits, social customs, and genetic tendencies are all packed in the emigrant's baggage. For others not so burdened with debilitating problems or able to overcome the ones that they do have, the emigration experience offers as much hope as it ever did. And with travel more convenient than ever, a return to Ireland is more likely than not. Emigration was once an act of desperation; now international travel is so commonplace that, at least for the most successful, it can almost be seen as commuting. The decision to leave is still difficult, the pain of those left behind is still real, but all of it can be reversed with the purchase of a ticket. Emigrants can go home again. But when they return from America, they return in a new incarnation of themselves as "Yanks."

Chapter 9

"But come ye back"

The Yank

"The women fished for their sons in the sloe-black river that ran through the small Westmeath town, while the fathers played football, without their sons, in a field half a mile away."[1] The opening sentence of "Fishing the Sloe-Black River," a short story by Colum McCann (b. 1965), captures the longing of those left behind in Ireland in the wake of emigration. The great tide began with the Great Famine, but though the Famine ended, emigration did not. When success rather than survival is the motivation, it makes sense to emigrate when young. This obvious fact is the premise of McCann's story. Ireland has become a land of old people only, "not a brat around";[2] the elders, ludicrously, are engaged with each other in activities that would usually be done with children. "Ever since the children had begun their drift," instead of coaching their children's sports teams, fathers play against each other, while the women of the town cast their lines fishing for sons, but "cast in vain."[3] The pathos is made all the more poignant by the fact that, while the spatial setting is specified (Westmeath), the temporal setting of the story at first appears vague. But the cars the characters drive were available from the 1960s on. This places the story in a time when the emigrant children probably could return easily; thus the parents' longing becomes all the more pitiful. McCann's empathetic portrayal of these parents is, however, not universal in contemporary Irish literature. In some works older family members constitute at least part of the reason for the young to want to escape. The conflict experienced by the younger generation in deciding whether to emigrate or, having emigrated, whether to return or, having returned, whether to stay is often exacerbated by an adult child's relationship with a parent. This is true in Benedict Kiely's short story "Homes on the Mountain," Brian Friel's play *Philadelphia, Here I Come!*, and Colm Tóibín's novel *Brooklyn*.

The Famine-era emigrant was fortunate to survive the grueling journey across the ocean. The difficulty of the journey all but ensured that he or she would never return; and so for those left behind, departure was the equivalent of death. Hence arose the custom of the American wake, a leave-taking ceremony that resembled a funeral in all respects except that the person mourned was alive. The pain of such an event is captured in the description in Joseph O'Connor's *Ghost Light* of the last dance of a father and daughter at the latter's American wake: "And you recall the waking held for a neighbour's girl on her last night in Dublin. Her father and mother and the gathering of relations. . . . 'Get up with me, Bridget,' said the father, late in the night, 'and face me in a step. Will you do that for me, girl? For likely it's the last dance we'll ever have in this world.'"[4] This is an old story, not original to O'Connor but recounted also in Kerby A. Miller's *Emigrants and Exiles.* This historian's version of the story (which he traces through two other sources, in typical folkloric fashion, to "an old woman") describes the dance as between a father and a son and adds the telling detail: after this last dance, "there wasn't a dry eye in the house."[5]

Despite the pain of separation, young people continued to leave for America for opportunity, to get away from the lesser life available to them in Ireland, to free themselves from the stultifying effect of tradition, to lift the weight of the Catholic Church's heavy moralism, and for assorted personal motives. Kerby Miller describes how post-Famine emigrants could count on the "emigrant chain": one emigrant gets established in the United States, then sends passage money home to another, who in turn sends money home to another. This system not only financed the trip but ensured that each succeeding group of emigrants had some sort of support system on the other side. Representatives of the Catholic Church, as well as family members, often filled this role as well. Once in the United States, the emigrant was expected to live much as he or she would have in Ireland, maintaining ties to other Irish emigrants and to the church and, most important, sending "American money" home, money to be spent in Ireland to support the family there, plus passage money for other emigrants.[6]

Under the influence of the "streets paved with gold" theory of limitless American possibility, the emigrant hoped to become so rich that he could return triumphant. Emigrant ballads depict the intense longing for home and the desire to return in glory. A common theme in the ballads is idealization of the people left behind, imagined as a virtuous rural peasantry. In the ballads Ireland is imagined as fixed in amber; nothing changes in the emigrant's absence. The ballads further assume that when the emigrant did come home, he himself would be essentially unchanged (except for his wealth). In the works discussed here, however, the folks back home are ambivalent about the character type known as the "returned," "returning American," or "Yank." The feelings of abandonment and longing expressed in McCann's story might have been dealt with in such a way as to suppress those painful emotions and replace them with a feeling of scorn for the one who comes back with uppity ways, getting above himself, distinguishing himself from the family in ways perceived as negative.

"The Elysium of the Emerald Isle": Benedict Kiely's "Homes on the Mountain"

The returned Yanks in "Homes on the Mountain" by Benedict Kiely (1919–2007) are examples. The adult narrator remembers his twelve-year-old self watching as his godmother and her husband fulfill the emigrant dream by bringing the money they earned in Philadelphia back to "the bleak side of Dooish Mountain,"[7] where they build a house. The narrator remembers how impressed he was by his godmother's wealth; she carries "more half-crowns in her patch pockets than there was in the Bank of England" and distributes them generously (673). Looking back at the experience, he wonders why these Yanks returned and attributes it to the same "nostalgia" that motivates his own interest in sentimental Irish songs. The narrator's mother, however, "who was practical and who had never been far enough from Ireland to feel nostalgia, deplored" the return of these Yanks and scorns these "lost people" who "live between two worlds" (673). Construction of the house, involving a bibulous local contractor and a batch of other returning Yanks "who came in their legions to watch the building, to help pass the bottle and to proffer advice" (674), similarly draws his mother's scorn. The result, according to her, is "an American apartment on the groundwalls of an old cabin. Living in the past" (675).

But the Yanks' house, inauthentic though the locals perceive it to be, is preferable to the second of the two homes on the mountain. On the day of the Yanks' housewarming, the family visits "the falling house of John and Thady O'Neill": "Once it must have been a fine, long, two-storeyed, thatched farmhouse, standing at an angle of forty-five degrees to the roadway and built backwards into the slope of the hill. But the roof and the upper storey had sagged, and, topped by the growth of years of rank decayed grass, the remnants of the thatched roof looked, in the Christmas dusk, like a rubbish heap a maniacal mass-murderer might pick as a burial mound for his victims" (677). If the house is bad, the brothers O'Neill are worse. Their condition has, like the house itself, deteriorated from the halcyon days when their mother was alive. Not the Yanks' nostalgia, nor the sentimentality of the narrator's songs, but the O'Neill brothers themselves represent the authentic Irish character, at least as it exists here on the unforgiving mountain. The story ends with the narrator remembering his youthful self, caught between his mother's scorn for those who leave and come back and his father's pity for those who stay.

The two old men in Kiely's story illustrate some of the reasons why many left and were loath to return. In *The American Irish* historian Kevin Kenny describes the conflicts emigrants experience in terms of what he calls the "push factor" and the "pull factor."[8] That which potential emigrants dislike about the native country pushes them out of it; that which they are attracted to in the receiving country pulls them to it. When the narrator of Kiely's story thinks about Ireland, he remembers the O'Neills' dilapidated house as a symbol of the nation's decline and the dreadful brothers as an example of the consequences of limited opportunity and ambition; and these factors might push him out of Ireland. The example of the affluent godmother, bringing pots of money home from America, enough to squander on an inefficient construction project, will pull him toward America.

While historians such as Kenny point to mass trends in emigration history, imaginative writers such as Kiely, Friel, and Tóibín portray the complex motivations of individuals. For a particular character, an ambivalent relationship with another character may push and pull simultaneously. Ireland itself pulls its children back, maintaining a tight emotional hold over the most determined would-be Yank. In Kiely's story the narrator's nostalgia for the Ireland depicted in sentimental songs, well-developed when he is only twelve, will bring him back both in thought and in reality to "the Elysium of the Emerald Isle" (681), even if the episode recounted in the story has caused him to question it. All these factors become part of the emigration decision, and because, in the twentieth century and beyond, improved transportation makes it possible for many departures and returns to take place, the conflicts may recur over and over again.

"Whatever you say, say nothing": Brian Friel, *Philadelphia, Here I Come!*

The emigration decision is so intellectually complex and emotionally fraught in Brian Friel's play, *Philadelphia, Here I Come!* that the playwright has to invent a new solution to representing internal conflict onstage. Unlike fiction, wherein the unspoken thoughts of a character may be described by a narrator, drama only allows for speech (and, as is crucial in this play, silence). If they are speaking, characters must talk either to themselves, to one another, or to the audience. To make dialogue realistic onstage, protagonists in traditional drama are often provided with a confidant, perhaps a character who has been away and now needs to be filled in on events that took place in his absence. Another dramatic convention, the soliloquy, allows characters ostensibly to talk to themselves, as if unconscious of the audience.

Here Friel has used an innovative technique to express the central character's private thoughts: splitting him into two separate characters, Public Gar and Private Gar. Public Gar equals the young man Gar seems to be and wants people to believe he is, "the Gar that people see, talk to, talk about."[9] Private Gar equals the fears, the emotions, the thoughts Public does not care to share or cannot admit even to himself because they are unacceptable even in private; this Gar is "the unseen man, the man within, the conscience, the alter ego, the secret thoughts, the id" (xi–xii). Private says what Public cannot say. However the two cannot be automatically labeled "real" Private and "phony" Public Gar. Private does not necessarily equal the "real" Gar; the public face of Gar is also part of his character. The real Gar is a combination of Private and Public.

The time is "the present," the first time the play was performed (1964) and every time thereafter. The play is set on the night before and morning of Gar's planned departure, the time when, in the past, the American wake would take place.[10] The absence of the wake hovers in the background of the play; it is the main thing that is *not* happening. The wake, with its "harrowing" release of emotion,[11] often facilitated as much by consumption of alcohol as by the impending "death" of the emigrant, at least served as a way—in an emotionally reserved culture—to give the young person a sense that he has been loved. By 1964 the departure to America was no longer the nearly irrevocable act it was in the nineteenth century. As the likelihood of the Yank's return increased, the wake custom faded. But Gar and his father should observe the custom, or at least some variant of it, anyway; not to do so is, for both of them, a missed opportunity. Each of them holds back the words that need to be spoken, complicating Gar's emotional state.

For Gar the pull of the United States is adventure, excitement, money, success, and sex; America is "a fantasy world of libidinal and consumer fulfillment."[12] Both Public and Private envision the jet that will take them to America as a warplane, then imagine themselves as sports heroes. Only Private can think about even higher ambitions: "President of the United States. . . . Chairman of General Motors. . . . Boss of the Teamsters' Union. . . . The U.S. Senate!" (38–39). Private salivates over imagined American women: "Great big sexy dames and night clubs and high living and films and dances and—" (36). The silence that follows *and* is meant to suggest sex, but even in private, a good Catholic boy is not supposed to think about that. Clergy in Ireland often inveighed against the moral risks of emigration, the "frightful dangers" of America, the place where "the devil himself holds sway, and lust—abhorrent lust—is everywhere indulged in shamelessly" (5). Private can only hope that America is just such a hotbed of sin as he has been told.

Each of the visitors on Gar's last night in Ireland, surrogates for the typical attendees at the American wake, represents a feature of the Ireland that Gar is trying to escape. The situation of his former girlfriend, Kate, is like Gar's in that she is subject to the authority of her father as well as to the strict sexual morality of Catholicism. Were she to have a "Private" version as Gar does, hers would also be warning her against "long passionate kisses in lonely places" (15). Impelled as much by sexual frustration as love, "randy boy" Gar wants to get married right away; Kate's father, however, has already selected Francis King as her husband, based on the new son-in-law's ability to boost the Doogans' social status, and Kate has bought into the plan. Gar's father also controls when and if his son will marry through setting his salary; the custom, common in farming families, of keeping a young man waiting until the father dies to inherit the farm is extended into the mercantile situation, but the results are the same: Gar's father expects him to act like an "old boy" and wait to marry until his father is ready.

Kate's apparent regrets associate her in Gar's mind with his mother, and his mother's story he associates with the harshness of life in Ireland. As he is packing an old suitcase, he finds the newspaper for January 1, 1937, the day his parents were married. The old suitcase is a visual image of Ireland as repository of tradition; what is in it—his connection to his mother—is part of the emotional baggage he will carry with him. The connection is all the stronger because to Gar his mother's story is incomplete. It comes to him from several tale-tellers: Master Boyle, who loved and lost her; Lizzy, her sister, who was present at Maire's wedding; and Madge, who to some extent has replaced her. The one person who never tells the story of Gar's mother is her husband.

Weaving together the fragments provides a narrative of a girl, Maire, "small . . . and wild, and young" (11), who could have married one man but marries another, much older and somewhat more affluent man. The young girl's behavior on her wedding day is unusual enough for her sister to attempt to describe it years later; but the sister is silenced by the inhibiting presence of Maire's son, Gar. The young girl becomes pregnant shortly after her marriage but dies three days after her son is born, under such circumstances that Madge thinks that "maybe it was good of God to take her away" (12). As in the case of Mary Kinsella in John Millington Synge's "An Autumn Night in the Hills," another young mother mysteriously dead before her time, questions abound but are never answered: Why did she marry S. B. and not Master Boyle? Did she love either of them? What is meant by the description of her as "wild"? Was Maire laughing or crying at her wedding? Why would Madge think that Maire was better off dead than alive? The incompletely narrated story of Gar's mother is an example of a prevailing theme in the play: that which is unsaid sends a stronger message than that which is said.

Gar's mother's early death places Madge in the substitute mother role. Because she is a paid employee of the household, her grief at Gar's departure is never acknowledged, even by her. Only Madge admits that "this [is] the last night we'll have you" but adds "to torment us" (79)—undercutting the emotion she must feel. Her relationship with the Mulhern family is clearly a way of dealing with her frustrated desire to have children of her own. Somehow if the Mulherns had named this new baby after her—which they do not—she would have been compensated for her childlessness. Later in the play, the canon seems to suggest that S. B. could have married her, formalized her relationship with Gar, and perhaps given her children of her own. Now these opportunities are gone forever. She will not even have the name of a child, much less an actual child, and she is losing the child she raised. In losing Madge, Gar is also losing an important piece of his past. She is one of the few remaining people who could help him fill in the gaps in his mother's story. Just as she is about to leave, Public tries to get Madge to tell him why his mother married his father instead of Boyle. Even Private thinks this is going too far in the way of opening oneself up to emotion and so attempts to quash Public's effort: "We want no scenes tonight" (80).

If Madge's story, like Maire's, is one of frustrated hopes, so is Master Boyle's. The vehemence of his rejection of Ireland and enthusiasm for the United States—"Don't keep looking back over your shoulder. Be one hundred per cent American" (34)—suggests regret that he did not emigrate himself. Now he has lost his opportunity for love, and at work he is enmeshed in job problems. His conflicts with the canon demonstrate the control of the church over the educational system. Boyle's poetry remains unpublished; his (perhaps fictitious) job offer in Boston underlines his regret for having stayed despite the lack of opportunity in Ireland. Gar might well feel pity for his mentor, but Private discourages this emotion by saying (probably truthfully) that Boyle is "a drunken aul schoolmaster—a conceited, arrogant wash-out!" (35).

Now as the evening passes and his departure nears, Gar needs something to be said between father and son. Enter the canon for his evening ritual: a game of cards with S. B. The tradition of the American wake had also included "a visit to the parish priest's house."[13] Because this is a play with a single stage set, the priest must visit Gar; but the visit loses meaning insofar as it is made under the guise of the card game. Again Gar feels the absence of the American wake tradition; no one is acting as if this night is different from any other. Routine and repetition prevent the expression of emotion. The canon and S. B. talk about the weather rather than the momentous event. What the canon does not say is, to Private, a dereliction of his duty as a priest. If he were doing his job correctly, he could act as a conduit between father and son; this is his last chance. The role of a priest in small-town Ireland is multifaceted, and here Private expects him to be something like a psychologist as well as a theologian: Private feels that the canon "could translate all this loneliness; this groping, this dreadful bloody buffoonery into Christian terms that will make life bearable for us all. And yet you don't say a word. Why, Canon? Why, arid Canon? Isn't this your job?—to translate? Why don't you speak, then? Prudence, arid

Canon? Prudence be damned! Christianity isn't prudent—it's insane!" (82). For Friel, "the idea of translation" is crucial; and the word has a range of meaning, including "the desire to understand, to find meaning, to make meaning if that is necessary."[14] "Translation" at this point in this play means acting as a facilitator of speech between father and son. Why should the canon do this? Why does he fail to? Does he assume they have done it already? Is he making himself available in case they want to have his help? Private cannot tell.

Gar's problems in dealing with his father are to some degree typical. Like all young people on the brink of adulthood, he must weigh his baggage, the pieces of the past that he will bring into his own future as well as those he will discard (the suitcase serving as a visual reminder of this typical developmental task as well as of Gar's imminent departure). Like all young men, he must individuate from his father. He resembles his father in that he too has difficulty expressing emotion. A mother might help them communicate; instead two taciturn men out-stonewall each other. All these problems might be overcome, or at least diminish, with the passage of time, but the deadline placed on them by Gar's emigration exacerbates the situation. His complicated relationship with his father pushes him away from Ireland, but at the same time it pulls him back in unexpressed hope of finally hearing the words that will convince him that his father loves him; Gar is waiting for something similar to the emotional outpouring of the American wake.

But they have already developed a wide repertory of mechanisms for placing emotional distance between them. Instead of openly discussing his problems at work, Gar expresses his resentment of his father in little acts of passive-aggressive defiance such as oversalting the salted fish (3). This sort of rebellion is probably too subtle for the father even to notice and leads nowhere. Gar also rebels by means of the secret egg deal, his idea of an adventurous business practice; but S. B. never knows (or never admits to knowing) about this. Private's tension increases as time passes and the hour of actual departure grows near; he wants the father to talk about something important rather than what the father actually does discuss (store details and clichés).

Private's long monologue outlines the problems in the father-son relationship, which he attributes exclusively to S. B. The father's lack of spontaneity, his inability to express emotion, and his failure to adjust his behavior to the increased maturation of his son all push Gar away. Yet they pull him back, as Gar keeps trying to get some response out of his father. Gar wants S. B. to show some regret that his son is leaving or ask him to stay: "say, 'Gar, son—' say, 'Gar, you bugger you, why don't you stick it out here with me for it's not such a bad aul bugger of a place.' Go on. Say it! Say it! Say it!" (28). Does Gar really want to stay? Or does he really just want his father to ask him to stay? Or does he want his father to express love for him, whether he stays or goes? Even Private Gar does not really know.

Contrary to the Ulster proverb, Gar wants his father to say something, no matter what it is, about something important. For example Private would like to be able to talk to his father about whether Gar's own sexual feelings are normal (30). Of all the difficult topics, this is the most difficult. To whom can one talk about such private matters in Ireland? Both Private and his father are prisoners of emotional inhibitions. At one point Gar fears that his father is going to cry, and his reaction—"Please, please don't cry, Screwballs" (30)—demonstrates that Gar too fears the expression of emotions. Emotional control requires unspoken words, and ironically, since this is theater, unspoken words are more powerful than spoken words. It is as if a musician were to advocate for silence.

One possible way of getting S. B. to talk would be for Gar to bring up a shared memory. He has a happy childhood memory of a fishing trip with his father when he was ten or eleven years old. Fishing is a typical male activity with the special advantage that speech, so difficult for the O'Donnell men, is discouraged; fishermen should not talk and do not even need to look at each other. Gar wants reassurance that his father remembers the episode and that it was as important to the father as it was to the child. But Gar can only think about this memory, not talk about it: "between us at that moment there was this great happiness, this great joy—you must have felt it too—it was so much richer than a content—it was a great, great happiness, and active, bubbling joy—although nothing was being said—just the two of us fishing on a lake on a showery day—and young as I was I felt, I knew, that this was precious." Gar understands that, though his father did not express his love verbally, he did so in small behaviors: "you had given me your hat and had put your jacket round my shoulders because there had been a shower of rain." This sufficed for him at the time, as the hat and the jacket make him feel safe, secure, protected: "your hat was soft on the top of my ears—I can feel it—and I shrank down into your coat" (74). What is Gar trying to say here? That he fears being without the protection of his father? For a young man, this would be a most damning admission, even to himself. He must, therefore, speak in emotional code, which he is hoping (contrary to past experience) that his father will be able to interpret. His father, however, will not do this. Instead S. B. acts as if his son's last day in Ireland were an ordinary day.

Would it help if there were a woman in the home to act as an interpreter of the language of emotion? Early in the play, Madge attempts to fill this role by acting as a conduit between Gar and his father: "just because he doesn't say much doesn't mean that he hasn't feelings like the rest of us. . . . He said nothing either when your mother died" (6). Late in the play, S. B. confides in Madge that he has doubts about his ability to "manage rightly" without his son; he uses the van as the ostensible subject, but it is really "managing by himself" that he fears (93). Neither of the two men can communicate his needs and fears to the other, but they can to Madge. Since she is not S. B.'s wife or Gar's mother, however, she can do only so much to repair the two men's damaged relationship.

Later that night the father and son have a last chance. Neither of them can sleep; now they have privacy (no canon, no Madge), and the wee hours encourage confidential discussions. But what do they talk about? A tire for the van, fencing posts, pliers, plug tobacco, a window lock, and the buying and selling of cans. The cans remind S. B. of selling cans in the past for cooking, at a time when other cooking utensils were luxuries: "'Maybe you'd sell a kettle at turf-cutting or if there'd be a Yank coming home . . .' *Pause*" (89). The pause is significant. S. B. stops here because they are on dangerous turf; he might be about to say something like "Please come home. I will miss you." But he does not. Missed opportunities for human connection abound in this play. Yet S. B.'s advice to Gar about sitting in the back of the plane sends a message of its own: "I fear for your safety. Take care of yourself!" Private appears to understand this, as the airplane comment causes him to urge Public to bring up the fishing episode at that point: "Now! He might remember—he might. But if he does, my God, laddo—what if he does?" (90). Merely thinking about the possibility for emotional expression is fearsome. What might be the consequences to Gar if S. B. does remember?

Private need not have worried. This abortive conversation continues the adversarial mode within which father and son have interacted throughout. Discussing the episode, they disagree about details (like the color of the boat or which song the father might have been singing, assuming that this event really happened at all). Is there any way to salvage the conversation? Public seems to think not; he gives up and withdraws by running into the shop. Could he have handled it any other way? Is he being fair to his father? Is Gar considering the possibility that, given the subjective nature of memory, there might be a difference between not remembering at all and not remembering in the same way—especially given the age discrepancy between father and son?

S. B. tells Madge, not Gar, his own memory of Gar as a child. Just as the fishing episode expresses what Gar needs from S. B., the little boy in the sailor suit story tells what S. B. needs from Gar. At that time Gar fulfilled S. B.'s need for admiration and emulation. Little Gar wanted to go to work with his father and not to school, and so his father was walking him to school. This occasion—significantly, like the fishing trip, one in which the two need not face each other—is a satisfying memory: "the two of us, hand in hand, as happy as

larks—we were that happy, Madge—and him dancing and chatting beside me
—mind?—you couldn't get a word in edge-ways with all the chatting he used to
go through" (93). They used to be able to talk when Gar was a child. And Gar
did seem to be ready to fulfill his father's needs when he left college to work for
the family business. S. B. cannot understand what has happened to change the
little boy into the young man. He blames the distance that has come between
them on their difference in age: "Maybe, Madge, maybe it's because I could
have been his grandfather, eh?" (93). S. B. was an older-than-usual father, but
all fathers and sons have generation gaps. This father and son have a communication gap as well.

The play ends as it must, in ambiguity. One possibility is that Gar "has not
decided to leave Ireland for America after all" despite "hostile feelings about his
hometown."[15] Another is more likely: the play ends at a moment in time when
Gar is still his divided self, inclined both toward leaving and toward staying. In
a stage play, as opposed to a film, it would be impossible to show his making
his final decision to get on the plane and go to America; and even if it could be
shown, the scene would no longer connote the same finality that the emigrant
ballads portrayed. In the final scene, Private is still conflicted about leaving,
because Public has unfinished business in Ireland. The play ends with unan-
swered questions: Will Gar leave? Should Gar leave? If he leaves, will he return?
Should he return? Will he come back in triumph, the very model of the returning Yank, "driving a Cadillac and smoking cigars and taking movie-films" (68),
as Public boasts to Kate? What might he find when he gets home? Will anyone
be any different from the way they are now? What would make them change?
What is there for him in Ireland if he changes his mind at the last minute, as the
dialogue between Private and Public at the end seems to suggest that he might?

Conflicts, misunderstandings, and memories shared and unshared are inevitable between fathers and sons, but the drastic change of emigration makes
them come to a head. The young person must individuate, and the parent must
let him—a hard developmental task for both, and one that is by its nature per-
petually incomplete. The long tradition and practical necessity of emigration
exacerbates this already difficult rite of passage for parents and children.

You Can Go Home Again: Colm Tóibín's *Brooklyn*

In *Brooklyn*, by Colm Tóibín (b. 1955), the typical emigrant push/pull situation
focuses on a young girl, Eilis Lacey. Her weak employment prospects plus her
sister's influence push her from her home in Enniscorthy, and the encourage-
ment of a priest pulls her to Brooklyn. In Eilis's case, a new element is added,
which might be called pullback: duty and guilt call her back again to Ireland.
Unlike Gar she does not initially want to emigrate but succumbs to family
pressure. Once in Brooklyn, however, her love life and her work life develop in

ways that would not be possible in Ireland. The perceived needs of her mother, however, cause Eilis to retreat from the progress she has made in fashioning a new American self. A product of her time and place, she remains between two worlds, symbolized in Tóibín's novel by the image that has figured so often in the Irish writing discussed here: the ocean voyage.

Financial problems afflict Eilis as they had so many before her. American money will help support her widowed mother, and this need is the impetus for the emigration plan. As the novel opens, "as their mother's pension was small, they depended on Rose" to support the household: Rose herself, Eilis, and their widowed mother.[16] Rose has taken the initiative to position Eilis for greater success in Ireland; she "had tried to find her work in an office, and Rose was paying for her books now that she was studying bookkeeping and rudimentary accountancy, but there was . . . no work for anyone in Enniscorthy" (11–12). Eilis's job situation is dim and her prospects worse. She only has a low-level part-time job in Miss Kelly's grocery store, with a demanding and demeaning boss. The situation of her coworker, poor downtrodden Mary, is even worse, showing how meager were the options for young Irish girls in that time and place. Without significant monetary or psychological rewards or the prospect of advancement, Eilis's job is not enough to hold her in Enniscorthy. Yet she had made no plans herself, "had never considered going to America" or even England, despite the fact that such journeys were "part of the life of the town" and that "people who went to America could become rich" (25–26).

The role that Rose's illness plays in her encouraging Eilis to emigrate is unclear because the novel is told from the third-person limited point of view, which allows for the expression of Eilis's thoughts and feelings but not Rose's. The reader never knows if Rose pushes Eilis out of Ireland because she knows that her income cannot be relied upon indefinitely. The intervention of Father Flood adds another "push" factor to that supplied by Rose. In small-town Ireland the priest plays multiple roles, and tradition is carried on, even in the United States, in the person of Father Flood. He is a financial adviser, a travel agent, a realtor, an educator, a psychologist, a social worker, and a career and relationship counselor. Eilis's mother, "listening with cowed respect" to the priest (24), accepts his authority in all areas of life without question, as if priesthood conveys universal expertise, and Eilis herself behaves as if Father Flood's recommendations have the force of law.

It is tempting to read Father Flood as a busybody. In a small town, he might well know where and for whom Eilis works, but the fact that "he had found out about her pay . . . expressed shock at how low it was . . . [and] inquired about her qualifications" (24) seems intrusive. But there are many other instances in the novel illustrating how little privacy small-town life affords, and at least Father Flood, unlike the town gossips, is attempting to solve a real problem. To his credit his efforts on Eilis's part are innovative, and his effect on both her career and her education is almost totally positive. Via his connections within the secular community in Brooklyn, he arranges an entry-level job for her at Bartocci's Department Store and negotiates the terms of her employment there. When she experiences homesickness, he enrolls her in a challenging two-year bookkeeping program at Brooklyn College, using his personal contacts to get her admitted after the formal registration date and arranging payment by a wealthy benefactor. Surprisingly he does not steer her toward a Catholic college, of which there were many in New York at the time. In return for all this, he seems to expect little, only asking her to work one day per year at the parish Christmas dinner for the poor—and even this is more a response to Eilis's loneliness on the holiday than it is a favor to him.

But in his involvement in her love life, it becomes clear to the reader, if not to Eilis, that Father Flood expects a quid pro quo: in return for his assistance, she is to remain close to her Irish roots, a good Catholic, connected to the parish and, above all, virginal. The boarding house he chooses for Eilis, run by Mrs. Kehoe, provides chaperonage rather than privacy; Eilis is supposed to support herself and send money home like an adult but is supervised like a child. Through his local connections, Father Flood performs what amounts to a background check on Eilis's boyfriend, Tony, and, although the priest approves of him, he reinforces Eilis's assumption that marriage is the inevitable goal. Once Father Flood becomes aware of the sexual aspect of Tony and Eilis's relationship, she senses a pressure to marry and soon, as morality is more important to the priest than education or career development. Thus Father Flood, albeit with the best of motives, is sending Eilis a double message: look at the big multiethnic and multidenominational world and consider all its possibilities, but an active sex life requires prompt retreat into the smaller Catholic world of the wife and mother.

Father Flood's expectations complicate Eilis's psychological task of creating a new American self. As Gar notices in *Philadelphia, Here I Come!*, America is a land in which one can design oneself anew. Being a young man, he does not imagine these changes in the drama of his life as involving costume changes, but a young woman such as Eilis does. The clothing details in the novel constitute her tentative steps toward self-fashioning. Here too she shows herself to be malleable, easily influenced by others, as she was with regard to accepting the emigration plan devised by Rose and Father Flood. Georgina, her shipboard roommate, takes Eilis in hand, beginning the process of reshaping her via her wardrobe. Georgina chooses the clothing in which Eilis will begin her new life in America, clothing that must project an image neither too experienced, "like a tart," nor "too innocent" (51). The makeup Georgina applies is intended to bolster Eilis's confidence in this new land; an unspecified "they" will "be afraid to stop" this version of Eilis from entering the United States (51–52). Eilis understands fashion, and particularly makeup, as armor, shielding her from the gaze of strangers: "It would be much easier, she imagined, to go out among people she did not know, maybe people she would never see again, if she could look like this" (52). Yet she senses at the same time that she is wearing a disguise. Georgina's actions suggest that Eilis's real self is inadequate and that an invented self will be more acceptable to those who look at her. Her inner conflict over clothing is, then, an expression of her divided self, and it will recur when she returns to Ireland, at which point her mother will attempt to reverse the process that begins with Georgina on the ship. Clothing images throughout the novel trace this difficult process of self-definition.

Her external appearance is only one area in which Eilis experiences dramatic change. Life in America opens intellectual doors. At Brooklyn College she is introduced to an intellectual world far beyond bookkeeping. Her instructor is Joshua Rosenblum, whose Holocaust experience, as described to her by the bookseller, introduces her to a more complex twentieth-century world than was presented to her by her ethnocentric Irish education. The diverse urban environment presents her with other opportunities for growth. At the department store, though her job is humdrum, she has a variety of transformative experiences, among which are the sexually charged encounter with her supervisor, Miss Fortini, and the then-controversial desegregation of Bartocci's customer base. This is indeed a new world for her.

Via her job, her schooling, the denser population of New York and environs, and the social opportunities available in Brooklyn, it is inevitable that Eilis meets a greater variety of men than she would have at home in Ireland. Tony, an Italian American, is an exotic to her. There are many pros and cons to her relationship with him. In his favor he seems to love her and wants to marry her. He has a good disposition, a generous nature, and a facility for empathy. He comes from a close and affectionate family, who—after some initial reservations—accepts Eilis; he carries little baggage. As a plumber he is below Eilis socially as it is, and far below what she might hope to achieve by remaining in the work force or marrying a professional man. But his essential and potentially lucrative skill, combined with his practical plan to develop land in what were then the outer reaches of Long Island, bodes well for his financial future. He would be following hard on the heels of real estate developer William J. Levitt, who built and sold 17,500 houses from 1947 to 1951, immortalizing in Levittown his vision of suburbia as well as his name. Eilis's idea of doing the bookkeeping from home on a part-time basis for Tony's real estate development business is feasible, likely to contribute to its growth and their family's prosperity.

The idea of marriage, however, frightens Eilis and pushes her away. It is clear to the reader if not to the character that, while she loves Tony, she is psychologically incapable of making a permanent commitment, either to him or to Brooklyn. She appears to be about twenty years old; by the standards of her time in Ireland as well as in America, she is of marriageable age. But Eilis is simply not ready to commit to a definite path in life. Tony's detailed plans for their future simultaneously charm and frighten her, and she is dishonest with him in withholding her doubts about marriage: "She did not want to say she would think about it because she knew how that might sound" (175). In this situation not saying no is equivalent to saying yes, and so she leaves Tony with the incorrect impression that she too believes that "marriage had been already tacitly agreed between them" (175). While Eilis is in this ambivalent state, Rose dies.

The death of Eilis's sister triggers a series of events. In her grief she has sex with Tony for the first time. Psychologically this is understandable, an affirmation of the life force in the face of death. But because Eilis and Tony are Catholic, they both believe that they have sinned. For Eilis this means that she feels even more obliged to marry Tony than she did before. It is important to note that the priest to whom she goes to confession does not require this commitment of her as a condition of forgiveness. Even more than Father Flood, this priest is presented positively, though briefly. "His tone sympathetic," his questions exploratory, the priest elicits Eilis's honest response about the nature of her feelings for Tony: "'I would like to marry him,' she said hesitantly, 'but I am not ready to marry him now'" (198). Due to the nature of the confessional experience, he can have no knowledge of anything else about Eilis than her status as repentant sinner (and likely recidivist). The process of going to confession takes only a few minutes and does not allow for subtleties. This priest cannot know that Eilis thinks she should want to marry Tony because having sex with a man with whom she was not in love and had no intention of marrying would make her an even worse sinner than she already is. Her own guilt over losing her virginity—not the priest's counsel, during confession or when she returns to him the following month—leads her to accede to Tony's request to enter into a civil marriage before she returns to Ireland.

Canon law regarding civil marriages is clear: for Catholics such marriages are invalid, the only valid or sacramental marriage being the one witnessed by a priest according to specified church ritual. In the eyes of the church, after participating in a civil ceremony, Eilis and Tony are not married and cannot legitimately have sex, which both of them acknowledge. The civil ceremony is more in the nature of an engagement to them. The consequence of this is that neither of them would need a Catholic annulment to undo the civil marriage;

they would only need a civil divorce, which was much easier to obtain. So when Eilis continues to date in Ireland as if she were a single woman, although she is violating the spirit of her commitment to Tony, she is not violating the letter of Catholic law. Ironically she is using a fine point of Catholic canon law to justify a pattern of behavior that surely constitutes personal betrayal. On the other hand, if Tony did the same thing back in Brooklyn, he would be in the same position as she is with regard to the civil versus sacramental marriage issue.

It is at this point in the novel that Eilis returns to Ireland, thus becoming, albeit unwillingly, a returned Yank. Arriving in Enniscorthy, she is immediately perceived, and even perceives herself, as having changed. Of real as opposed to fictional emigrants, sociologist Mary P. Corcoran observes that this may be the whole point of emigration and return: to "reinvent the self"[17] and then present the new self for inspection. This self-reinvention, however, places the returnees at odds with family and friends. In this section of the novel, the conflict between Eilis and her mother dramatizes this process. Mrs. Lacy shows herself to be not the fragile widow lady of Eilis's imagination but rather a woman with an agenda and the ability to implement that agenda via the manipulative deployment of speech and silence.

The ostensible issue is clothing. Eilis's independent clothing purchases during the time she lived in Brooklyn represent "the extent to which Eilis is altered and her identity refashioned . . . by her immersion in American consumer culture."[18] Mrs. Lacey wants to undo this process. Her agenda is to reshape Eilis's self-image into that of a traditional Irish girl rather than a Yank. Her strategy is to express disapproval of Eilis's (American) wardrobe; to foist Rose's (Irish) wardrobe on Eilis; and to ignore Eilis's protestations that she is in fact going back to America. Via her clothing Eilis is trying to make a statement about her new, and hard-won, American identity, a statement that her mother chooses to ignore. Via Rose's wardrobe Eilis's mother is saying: you have not changed; you belong in Enniscorthy, replacing Rose in this home. For a while Eilis resists.

But with the offer of Rose's old job, a good one, and her developing relationship with Jim Farrell, who, by Enniscorthy standards, is as much of a catch as Tony if not more, the elements of a successful Irish life start to fall into place. Like the emigrants Corcoran studies, Eilis, though unconsciously, seeks in Ireland "anchorage . . . attachment to others and a sense of continuity."[19] Homecoming affords her the satisfaction of taking on a respected traditional role in caring for her widowed mother (especially since the two brothers feel no compulsion to do so and dispatch themselves for England at the first opportunity after Rose's wake). Homecoming allows her to dodge the guilt she would feel if she did not behave as expected. Part of the appeal of Ireland is familiarity and security, and this was true even before her time in America, when she "has always presumed that she would live in the town all her life, as her mother had done, knowing everyone, having the same friends and neighbours, the same routines in the same streets" (29). Now, because of Jim, she would not be the pathetic "old girl" living with her mother all her life but rather would assume an enviable position in the community as the wife of an established, prosperous pub owner, "a great catch, a young man in the town with his own business" (243). This seems to be a safer bet than continuing the difficult process of acclimating to the United States and eventually becoming the wife of an Italian American plumber and real estate developer in training. Eilis, in 1952, cannot know that Long Island real estate would soar in value over the next twenty years, while her small Irish town would continue to lose population. More significant, she assumes that her choice is a binary one: Jim (and Ireland) or Tony (and America). She never seriously considers an obvious set of alternatives: marrying neither of them and living in neither place. She is still framing her life choices as if she were the heroine in a traditional marriage plot, who must choose this man or that one; this country or that one. As she makes the decision to return to Brooklyn, she assumes that she is also opting for Tony.

As the narrator's mother observes in Benedict Kiely's "Homes on the Mountain," "returned Americans . . . are lost people. They live between two worlds."[20] The novel ends with Eilis literally between two worlds, aboard ship. Just as the emigrants in the nineteenth-century ballads expected those left behind in Ireland, and the country itself, to remain unchanged, so Eilis imagines Tony in a state of suspended animation, waiting for her back in Brooklyn. But earlier in the novel, a hint of an abruptly terminated relationship—the vomiting girl on the Ferris wheel—reminds the reader that if Eilis has other options, so has Tony. How might Tony have interpreted her desultory correspondence? The unopened letters might mean that he has ended the relationship. If so Eilis is left between two men, one of whom she has rejected and one of whom has rejected her. This may not be a bad outcome for a twenty-year-old whose sense of herself is still so clearly in flux.

Tóibín's decision to end the novel while Eilis is on the sea is of a piece with his use in earlier novels of what literary critic Liam Harte terms "marine geographies." Harte calls these ocean settings "liminal landscapes," points of transition, neither here nor there. In *The South* (1990), *The Heather Blazing* (1992), and *The Blackwater Lightship* (1999), Tóibín demonstrates his "subtle geographical imagination in which space, place, and landscape are active determinants of identity and experience."[21] In *Brooklyn* the three ocean voyages undertaken by Eilis operate as metaphors for stages in the developing personality of a young girl. On her first voyage to the United States, her seasickness connects her to the difficult journeys of the emigrants before her from the time of the Great Famine to the present-time action of the story (the early 1950s). In the 1950s sea journeys were difficult but not as dangerous as they were in the

Famine years. This means that the ties connecting the emigrant to the old country can be pulled tight in times of crisis. The second sea journey, from Brooklyn to Ireland following the death of Rose, is not described; for Eilis this is not as difficult a transition as the previous journey. She is merely reaffirming the ties of duty and love that connect her to her life in Ireland, and this is easy to do. It is what is expected of her and, more important, what she expects of herself.

Eilis's third journey is an indicator of her increased maturity, as she is no longer allowing decisions to be made for her but chooses, despite her mother's disapproval, to return to Brooklyn. But braving her mother's rejection does not guarantee the rightness of her choice. Herein lies the significance of the symbolism of the ocean. Harte reads Tóibín's marine spaces in the earlier novels as "metaphors for the transitional and malleable condition of contemporary Ireland itself."[22] In this novel the transitional and malleable element is Eilis herself. Like the heroines of the fairy tales, she is a young girl in the liminal state between childhood and marriage. The message sent to her by both Irish and American cultures at the time is that the marriage choice is imminent and urgent, that she should put an end as soon as possible to the state of liminality. The novel is set in a socially conservative time in the United States as well as in Ireland, before the impact of feminism in either country, and Eilis cannot imagine that seeking closure on the issue of marriage might not be the best choice for her at this time. She needs to learn, as do Tóibín's earlier protagonists, "the liberating potential of ambivalence,"[23] the rightness of in-betweenness. On the water it might be possible to Eilis to begin to release herself from the social expectations that she has internalized and accept the ambiguity of her situation.

The novel ends with Eilis's not having opened Tony's letter, a perfect example of the ambivalence Harte describes. Should this be a breakup letter, she would be devastated, but the (presumably older and wiser) reader might extrapolate from the novel and imagine a future for her. Learning to tolerate and even enjoy this state of tension between two worlds (single and married, Irish and American) might be the best possible outcome for her at this point in her life. Instead of unconsciously identifying with the heroine in the marriage plot, she might identify with the young boys in fairy tales who go forth from the place of their birth to seek their fortunes in strange lands, face down giants and ogres, and return triumphant. In her liminality she could explore the male fairy-tale hero within her and have her own independent adventures before (or instead of) settling down to the role of wife and mother in Ireland, America, or anywhere else in the world.

All over the world, no Irish ballad is better known than "Danny Boy." This classic emigrant ballad dramatizes the pain of emigration from the point of view of a parent left behind in Ireland. The parent longs for Danny's return but fears that he or she will not live long enough to see him again. In imagination the parent sees him visiting his or her grave and feels at peace at this evidence of his lasting love. The pathos of the situation reflects the emigrant situation in the same way as does the American wake story retold by Joseph O'Connor in *Ghost Light:* until the recent past, the emigrant's trip west to America felt like a death to those left behind.

At the risk of treading on sacred ground, it is possible to read the works discussed here as the antithesis of the "Danny Boy" situation. The ballad is sung from the parent's point of view, not Danny's, so it is impossible to imagine Danny's feelings toward his parent as he kneels at the gravesite. The ballad conveys the parent's longing for the absent child but can say nothing about the emigrant's feelings toward the parent. In each of the works discussed here, the relationship between parent and child is much more complicated on both sides. Colum McCann's parent characters in "Fishing the Sloe-Black River" are, like the parent in "Danny Boy," pure images of abandonment and loss, but that is because the story is told from their perspective only. In Benedict Kiely's "Homes on the Mountain," the boy's mother is contemptuous of and cynical toward the returning Yanks and presumably would take the same attitude toward her son should he one day make the same decision. In Brian Friel's *Philadelphia, Here I Come!,* the older generation simultaneously pushes their children away by their cold and controlling behavior and pulls them back via chains of guilt. If emigrants do in fact return, the living parent may not be anywhere near as helpless and forlorn as she pretended to be but instead may be manipulative and domineering, like Eilis's mother in *Brooklyn,* resentful of her daughter's new self and determined to roll back her progress.

Unlike the Famine generation, the twentieth-century emigrant can go home again easily; the emigration decision is eminently reversible. When these Yanks return, they are likely to find living parents with their own sets of demands and expectations. And the situation is both facilitated and exacerbated by the speed of transportation. Even the ship only takes a week in the Tóibín novel, and the plane is of course even faster, so the adjustment back and forth can be made over and over again. The either/or dichotomy that the ocean once symbolized is no longer a useful concept. What might replace it is a definition of self that incorporates, and perhaps even celebrates, living between (at least) two worlds.

Conclusion

One of the risks in writing about living authors is that their next book or play can, and in fact should, challenge all one's theories about the arc of their literary careers. Even so the historical events and cultural themes discussed here can be expected to continue to stimulate Irish writers' creativity for the foreseeable future and to offer readers many more opportunities for extending their experience of Irish writing. A few examples from recently published fiction come to mind, in that experiencing fiction is entirely within the reader's control. Unlike drama, which depends on performance, fiction is as accessible as the nearest library, bookstore, or home computer.

Consider the new fiction related to the 1916 Easter Rising, such as Roddy Doyle's Henry Smart trilogy, consisting of *A Star Called Henry* (1999), *Oh, Play That Thing* (2004), and *The Dead Republic* (2010). The protagonist, born with the twentieth century, participates in the Easter Rising as a sixteen-year-old, an experience that shapes his own future as well as his country's. Emma Donoghue's short story collection *Astray* (2012) examines the experience of emigration from a multitude of angles. Its title suggests a psychological subtext as well, in that readers familiar with Seamus Heaney's 1983 *Sweeney Astray,* his translation of the medieval Irish poem *Buile Suibhne,* will know that *astray* is a translation of a word that can also mean *mad.* Another living writer worth studying is Joseph O'Connor, whose *Ghost Light* (2010) is the story of the relationship between the actress Maire O'Neill (née Molly Allgood) and playwright John Millington Synge. In the background of the novel is Synge's classic drama *The Playboy of the Western World,* first staged in 1907, which as an added bonus is available in a film version.

Infinite possibilities exist, but a final suggestion is to consider the evolution of a living writer from his earliest works to the present. Discussed earlier in the book, but too briefly, is Colum McCann. From his early short story collection *Fishing the Sloe-Black River* (1994) to his universally acclaimed *Let the Great*

World Spin (2009) to his most recent novel *Transatlantic* (2013), McCann's work has an impressive range. *Transatlantic,* as its title implies, picks up where the discussion of the final chapter leaves off, with the journey across the ocean as its central metaphor. Similarly at the top of his profession is Colm Tóibín, whose *Brooklyn,* discussed here, represents only one dimension of this multi-talented writer. An essayist and playwright as well as novelist, Tóibín is one of the great contemporary masters. What McCann and Tóibín have in common is a shared Irish heritage combined with an imaginative scope that encompasses much more than their native land.

These suggestions may bring readers to greater appreciation of a fine body of work. Other contemporary writers can be studied this way, in the context of the history and culture of their home countries, as well. In the meantime the literary tourist can come along for a visit to Ireland.

Notes

Chapter 1. "Nothing can happen nowhere": A Place in the World

1. Bowen, "Notes on Writing a Novel," 253.

2. Joyce, "Dead," 187–90. See also the film version, directed by John Huston (DVD, Channel 4, 1987).

3. Smyth, *Space and the Irish Cultural Imagination*, 37.

4. Ibid., 36.

5. Éamon de Valera, "On Language and the Irish Nation," speech on Raidió Teilifís Éireann, March 17, 1943. Accessed October 2, 2014. http://www.spinnet.eu/images/2014-04/devalera1943.pdf.

6. Smyth, *Space and the Irish Cultural Imagination*, 36.

7. O'Toole, "Going West," 111.

8. Dezell, *Irish America Coming into Clover*, 2.

9. Bew, *Land and the National Question*, 1.

10. Miller, *Emigrants and Exiles*, 388.

11. Bew, *Land and the National Question*, 5.

12. Ibid., 234.

13. Ibid., 235; italics in original.

14. Ibid., 236–37.

15. Ibid., 15.

16. See Miller, *Emigrants and Exiles*, 48–49.

17. Bew, *Land and the National Question*, 9.

18. Boyle, "Pastorale," 338–39, 343. Subsequent page numbers are given parenthetically in the text.

19. Trevor, "Kathleen's Field," 1246. Subsequent page references are given parenthetically in the text.

20. O'Brien, *Wild Decembers*, 1. Subsequent page references are given parenthetically in the text.

21. Ingman, "Edna O'Brien," 1.

22. *The Quiet Man*, directed by John Ford (DVD, Argosy Pictures, 1952).

23. Fitzgerald-Hoyt, *William Trevor*, 180.

24. Valiulis, "Neither Feminist nor Flapper," 154.
25. Shannon, "Changing Face of Cathleen ni Houlihan," 258.
26. Ingman, "Edna O'Brien," 254.
27. MacPherson, "Ireland Begins in the Home."
28. Ingman, "Edna O'Brien," 263.
29. Lindahl-Raittila, "Negotiating Irishness," 83.

Chapter 2. Just Tell Them the Story: Tradition Bearing

1. Binchy, "Writers on Writing."
2. Harvey, *Contemporary Irish Traditional Narrative,* 21.
3. Lysaght, *Pocket Book of the Banshee,* 64.
4. Harvey, *Contemporary Irish Traditional Narrative,* 12–13.
5. Ibid., 5.
6. White, *Remembering Ahanagran,* 51; cf. Zimmermann, *Irish Storyteller,* 358.
7. Zimmermann, *Irish Storyteller,* 450.
8. White, *Remembering Ahanagran,* 49.
9. Zimmermann, *Irish Storyteller,* 446.
10. Synge, "Autumn Night," 85.
11. Ibid., 86–87.
12. Carey, *Mermaids Singing,* 278.
13. Ó Corráin, "Prehistoric and Early Christian Ireland," 8.
14. Kerrane, "Structural Elegance," 106.
15. Als, "Men at Work."
16. McPherson, author's note, in *Weir,* n.p.
17. A. O'Connor, "Faeries," 370.
18. Johnston, "Pre-Christian Religions," 892.
19. Brantley, review of *The Weir.*
20. Lojek, *Spaces of Irish Drama,* 43.
21. Brantley, review of *The Weir.*
22. Ibid.; cf. Kerrane, "Structural Elegance," 114, and Lojek, *Spaces of Irish Drama,* 49.
23. Grene, "Ireland in Two Minds."
24. Lojek, *Spaces of Irish Drama,* 62.
25. McPherson, *Weir,* 27. Subsequent page references are given parenthetically in the text.
26. Gregory, *Visions and Beliefs,* 35. Subsequent page references are given parenthetically in the text.
27. McPherson, *Weir,* 30. Subsequent page references are given parenthetically in the text.
28. Grene, "Ireland in Two Minds."
29. Kerrane, "Structural Elegance," 110.
30. McPherson, "Late Nights and Proclamations," 46.
31. Brantley, review of *The Weir.*

Chapter 3. "The abuse of language": Irish, English, American

1. Spenser, *A View of the Present State of Ireland*. CELT: *The Corpus of Electronic Texts*. Accessed October 2, 2014. http://www.ucc.ie/celt/published/E500000-001/index.html.

2. "A Statute of the Fortieth Year of King Edward III . . . ," *CELT: The Corpus of Electronic Texts*. Accessed October 2, 2014. http://www.ucc.ie/celt/published/T300001-001/text001.html.

3. Ibid., preamble and article 3.

4. "Remarks by President McAleese at the Commemoration of the Battle of Kinsale—Fort Hill, Summer Cove, Saturday 22 September 2001." Accessed April 12, 2005. http://www.ccrowleyclan.com/events/mcaleese_kinsale.html.

5. O'Reilly, *Irish Language in Northern Ireland,* 14.

6. Jones, *Brian Friel,* 59.

7. Friel, *Translations,* 307. Subsequent page references are given parenthetically in the text.

8. Quoted in Purdon, *Story of the Irish Language,* 34.

9. Amador-Moreno, "Remembering Language," 78.

10. Lojek, *Spaces of Irish Drama,* 35.

11. Pilkington, "Reading History," 500.

12. Seamus Heaney, quoted in Lojek, *Spaces of Irish Drama,* 25.

13. Lojek, *Spaces of Irish Drama,* 17.

14. Ibid., 33.

15. *The Commitments,* directed by Alan Parker (DVD, Beacon Communications, 1991).

16. See, for example, Booker, "Late Capitalism Comes to Dublin"; Moynihan, *"Other People's Diasporas";* Onkey, "Celtic Soul Brothers"; Piroux, "I'm Black and I'm Proud"; and Taylor, "Living in a Postcolonial World," all of which discuss the matter in detail.

17. Doyle, *Commitments,* 13. Subsequent page references are given parenthetically in the text.

18. Quoted in Piroux, "I'm Black and I'm Proud," 50.

19. Ibid., 47.

20. Quoted in McGonigle, "Rednecks and Southsiders," 164.

21. Amador-Moreno, "Remembering Language," 85.

22. Synge, *Playboy,* 103.

23. Synge, preface to *Playboy,* 453.

24. O'Toole, "Going West," 112.

25. Ibid., 111.

26. Piroux, "I'm Black and I'm Proud," 51–52.

27. McGonigle, "Rednecks and Southsiders," 164.

28. McGlynn, "Why Jimmy Wears a Suit," 232.

29. Quoted in McGonigle, "Rednecks and Southsiders," 167.

30. Quoted in ibid., 167.

31. Booker, "Late Capitalism Comes to Dublin," 30.

32. *Thin Lizzy the Rocker: A Portrait of Philip Lynott,* directed by Shay Healy (DVD, Standing Room Only, 1995); and Putterford, *Phil Lynott.*

33. McGlynn, "Why Jimmy Wears a Suit," 236.

34. Thin Lizzy, "Whiskey in the Jar," *Vagabonds of the Western World.* Deram Records, 1973.

35. Kevin McKenna, "Sorry, Phil Lynott, I'm Sticking with the Scots." *Observer,* April 9, 2011.

36. See Jason O'Toole, "Philomena Lynott Overcame Extraordinary Odds to Raise Her Beloved 'Only Boy.'" *Daily Mail,* July 25, 2010. http://www.dailymail.co.uk/femail/article-1297458.

37. Doyle, *Paula Spencer,* 123.

38. Doyle, "Guess Who's Coming for the Dinner," 6.

39. Ibid., 8.

Chapter 4. *An Gorta Mór:* Hunger as Reality and Metaphor

1. For purposes of comparison, the Irish Central Statistics Office (www.cso.ie) estimates the 2014 population at 4.6 million.

2. Quoted in Woodham-Smith, *Great Hunger,* 162.

3. Kinealy, *Death-Dealing Famine,* 1.

4. Woodham-Smith, *Great Hunger,* 75.

5. Kinealy, "How Politics Fed the Famine."

6. Kinealy, *Death-Dealing Famine,* 2.

7. Waters, "Troubled People," 103.

8. Coogan, *Famine Plot,* 83.

9. The lyrics to "The Fields of Athenry" are available at www.petestjohn.com/works/the-fields-of-athenry/ (accessed March 8, 2015); the lyrics to "Black 47" are available at www.metrolyrics.com/black-47-lyrics-black-47.html (accessed March 8, 2015).

10. L. Trevelyan, *Very British Family,* 40.

11. Kinealy, *Death-Dealing Famine,* 4.

12. Quoted in Woodham-Smith, *Great Hunger,* 156.

13. C. Trevelyan, *Irish Crisis,* 184. Subsequent page references are given parenthetically in the text.

14. Kinealy, *Death-Dealing Famine,* 38.

15. Mitchel, *Last Conquest of Ireland.*

16. Quoted in L. Trevelyan, *Very British Family,* 44.

17. Ibid., 46.

18. Ibid., 47.

19. Quoted in ibid., 44.

20. Quoted in ibid., 45.

21. Trevor, "News from Ireland," 884. Subsequent page references are given parenthetically in the text.

22. Estévez-Saá, "Interview with Joseph O'Connor," 165.

23. Laxton, *Famine Ships,* 102.

24. J. O'Connor, *Star of the Sea,* xvii. Subsequent page references are given parenthetically in the text.

25. Laxton, *Famine Ships,* 49; Tóibín, "Irish Famine," 14; Kinealy, "How Politics Fed the Famine."

26. Laxton, *Famine Ships,* 111–12.

27. Kinealy, "How Politics Fed the Famine."

28. Tóibín, "Irish Famine," 14.

29. Laxton, *Famine Ships,* 28–29.

30. Ibid., 31.

31. Quigley, "Grosse Île," 134.

32. Ibid., 135.

33. Ibid., 136; see also Mark Cardwell, "When the Coffin Ships Arrived . . . ," *Medical Post* 33, no. 36 (1997): 9.

34. Laxton, *Famine Ships,* 50.

35. Estévez-Saá, "Interview with Joseph O'Connor," 175.

36. C. Trevelyan, *Irish Crisis,* 2.

Chapter 5. "Terrible beauty": The Easter Rising

1. Yeats, "Easter, 1916."

2. Wills, *Dublin 1916,* 108.

3. Ibid., 218.

4. O'Toole, *Tom Murphy,* 148.

5. Poulain, "Playing Out the Rising," 163.

6. Murphy, *Patriot Game,* 100. Subsequent page references are given parenthetically in the text.

7. Poulain, "Playing Out the Rising," 163.

8. Quoted in Edwards, *Patrick Pearse,* 116.

9. Ibid., 117, 119, 123, 133.

10. Poulain, "Playing Out the Rising," 164.

11. O'Toole, *Tom Murphy,* 153.

12. See, for example, Murphy and MacKillop, "Poets of 1916," *Irish Literature,* 229–42.

13. Poulain, "Playing Out the Rising," 163.

14. O'Toole, *Tom Murphy,* 150.

15. Ibid., 147.

16. Haughey, "Standing in the Gap," 291.

17. Cullingford, "Colonial Policing," 12.

18. Meche, "Seeking 'The Mercy of Fathers,'" 465; cf. Martinovich, "Ghosts of the Great War," 117–20.

19. Meche, "Seeking 'The Mercy of Fathers,'" 475.

20. Haughey, "Standing in the Gap," 290.

21. J. W. Foster, "All the Long Traditions," 110.
22. Barry, *Steward of Christendom*, 55. Subsequent page references are given parenthetically in the text.
23. Cullingford, "Colonial Policing," 13.
24. Gleitman, "Reconstructing History," 226.
25. J. W. Foster, "All the Long Traditions," 101.
26. Haughey, "Standing in the Gap," 299.
27. Cullingford, "Colonial Policing," 14–15.
28. Haughey, "Standing in the Gap," 292.
29. Barry, "Lies and More Lies," 641.
30. Haughey, "Standing in the Gap," 293.
31. Garvin, "Collins, Michael."
32. Ibid.
33. Garvin, "De Valera, Éamon."
34. Kurdi, "Really All Danger," 42.
35. Cullingford, "Colonial Policing," 22.
36. Wills, *Dublin 1916*, 218.
37. J. W. Foster, "All the Long Traditions," 110.
38. Garvin, "Collins, Michael."
39. Tóibín, "New Ways of Killing Your Father," 5.

Chapter 6. The Big House: Symbol and Target

1. Rauchbauer, "Big House and Irish History," 2.
2. Ibid., 4.
3. Ibid., 3; Kreilkamp, *Anglo-Irish Novel*, 8.
4. R. Foster, "Ascendancy Mind," 21; italics in original.
5. Rauchbauer, "Big House and Irish History," 3.
6. Kreilkamp, *Anglo-Irish Novel*, 17.
7. Fehlmann, "Historical Survey," 15.
8. Ibid., 16.
9. R. Foster, "Ascendancy and Union," 190–91.
10. Kreilkamp, *Anglo-Irish Novel*, 21.
11. Rauchbauer, "Big House and Irish History," 10.
12. Rudd, "Cast a Cold Eye," 38.
13. Bowen, *Bowen's Court*, 19.
14. Rauchbauer, "Big House and Irish History," 11.
15. Kreilkamp, *Anglo-Irish Novel*, 18.
16. Ibid., 2.
17. Rauchbauer, "Big House and Irish History," 9.
18. Kreilkamp, *Anglo-Irish Novel*, 11.
19. Ibid., 20.
20. Goodby, *Irish Studies*, 31.
21. Kreilkamp, *Anglo-Irish Novel*, 22.

22. Ibid., 23.

23. Edgeworth, *Castle Rackrent,* 48. Subsequent page references are given parenthetically in the text.

24. Neill, "Mantles, Quirks, and Irish Bulls," 85.

25. R. Foster, "Ascendancy Mind," 21.

26. Smith, note 10 to the edition of *Castle Rackrent* in Smith, *Two Irish National Tales,* 31.

27. Kowaleski-Wallace, *Their Fathers' Daughters,* 149.

28. Corbett, *Allegories of Union,* 40.

29. Butler, "Edgeworth's Ireland," 267.

30. Trevor, *Excursions,* xiii.

31. Trevor, "Distant Past," 349. Subsequent page references are given parenthetically in the text.

32. Bowen, *Collected Impressions,* 173.

33. Mallon, "Fools of Fortune."

34. Trevor, *Lucy Gault,* 3. Subsequent page references are given parenthetically in the text.

35. R. Foster, "Ascendancy Mind," 28.

36. Kreilkamp, *Anglo-Irish Novel,* 24.

37. R. Foster, "Ascendancy Mind," 23.

38. Kreilkamp, *Anglo-Irish Novel,* 4.

39. McWilliams, *Women and Exile,* 150.

Chapter 7. "Fanatic heart": A Legacy of Violence

1. Townshend, *Ireland,* 254.

2. Ardagh, *Ireland and the Irish,* 361.

3. Comerford, *Ireland,* 118.

4. Trevor, "Beyond the Pale," 750. Subsequent page references are given parenthetically in the text.

5. Ardagh, *Ireland and the Irish,* 360.

6. Elliott, *Catholics of Ulster,* 438; cf. Ardagh, *Ireland and the Irish,* 346.

7. Bowen, *Collected Impressions,* 173.

8. Grant, *Breaking Enmities,* 16.

9. Ardagh, *Ireland and the Irish,* 346.

10. MacLaverty, *Cal,* 67.

11. Ibid., 9.

12. Grant, *Breaking Enmities,* 2.

13. Ibid., 4.

14. Ibid., 1.

15. MacLaverty, *Cal,* 56.

16. Ardagh, *Ireland and the Irish,* 416.

17. MacLaverty, *Cal,* 9.

18. Elliott, *Catholics of Ulster,* 440.

19. Ibid., 480.

20. Coogan, *IRA*, 6.

21. Ardagh, *Ireland and the Irish*, 352, 408.

22. MacLaverty, *Cal*, 27.

23. Elliott, *Catholics of Ulster*, 385, 387.

24. Ardagh, *Ireland and the Irish*, 365.

25. O'Hagan, "Belfast, Divided in the Name of Peace," *Observer*, January 21, 2012. http://www.theguardian.com/uk/2012/jan/22/peace-walls-troubles-belfast-feature.

26. Elliott, *Catholics of Ulster*, 342.

27. "Ethnic Interfaces/Peace Lines," *Geography in Action*. Accessed September 26, 2014. http://www.geographyinaction.co.uk.

28. MacLaverty, *Cal*, 15.

29. Elliott, *Catholics of Ulster*, 432, 387; cf. Ardagh, *Ireland and the Irish*, 400–402.

30. Elliott, *Catholics of Ulster*, 437.

31. Ibid., 387.

32. Ibid., 440.

33. Ibid., 384.

34. MacLaverty, *Cal*, 32.

35. Elliott, *Catholics of Ulster*, 387.

36. MacLaverty, *Cal*, 14.

37. Wright, *Northern Ireland*, 10.

38. Ibid., 23–24.

39. Ibid., 12.

40. MacLaverty, *Cal*, 10.

41. Elliott, *Catholics of Ulster*, 453.

42. Ibid., 457.

43. Ibid., 455.

44. MacLaverty, *Cal*, 37. For complete lyrics see "Roddy McCorley." Celtic Lyrics. Accessed October 2, 2014. http://celtic-lyrics.com/lyrics/429.

45. McCourt, *Angela's Ashes*, 40.

46. MacLaverty, *Cal*, 15.

47. Elliott, *Catholics of Ulster*, 441.

48. Ardagh, *Ireland and the Irish*, 350, 366; italics in original.

49. Ibid., 368.

50. Wright, *Northern Ireland*, 15.

51. MacLaverty, *Cal*, 23.

52. Ibid., 24.

53. Grant, *Breaking Enmities*, 5.

54. MacLaverty, *Cal*, 40.

55. Ibid., 39.

56. Elliott, *Catholics of Ulster*, 437.

Chapter 8. "Lots of fun at Finnegan's Wake": The Drinking Life

1. Barrett, "Why Paddy Drank," 156.

2. For a recording of the three songs discussed here, see the following two collections by the Dubliners: "Dicey Reilly" and "Finnegan's Wake" are on *The Ultimate Collection: The Spirit of the Irish*, Sanctuary Records, 2003; and "Seven Drunken Nights" is on *Seven Drunken Nights*, Prism Platinum, 2005.

3. Stivers, *Hair of the Dog*, 16, 18.

4. Ibid., 23.

5. Ibid., 31.

6. Ibid., 76–80.

7. Bretherton, "Against the Flowing Tide."

8. Gusfield, "Benevolent Repression," 405.

9. Ibid., 399.

10. Adler, "From Symbolic Exchange to Commodity Consumption," 381.

11. Ibid., 383.

12. Ibid., 383–84.

13. Joyce, "Little Cloud," 57. Subsequent page references are given parenthetically in the text.

14. Joyce, "Counterparts," 70. Subsequent page references are given parenthetically in the text.

15. Doyle, *Woman Who Walked into Doors,* 89. Subsequent page references are given parenthetically in the text.

16. Persson, "You're Fuckin' Amazing, by the Way," 149.

17. Ibid.

18. Jeffers, "What's It Like Being Irish?," 261.

19. Doyle, *Paula Spencer,* 1. Subsequent page references are given parenthetically in the text.

20. Persson, "You're Fuckin' Amazing, by the Way," 154.

Chapter 9. "But come ye back": The Yank

1. McCann, "Fishing the Sloe-Black River," 53.

2. Ibid., 54.

3. Ibid., 55, 56.

4. J. O'Connor, *Ghost Light,* 185–86.

5. Miller, *Emigrants and Exiles,* 560.

6. Ibid., 271, 273, 520.

7. Kiely, "Homes on the Mountain," 673. Subsequent page references are given parenthetically in the text.

8. Kenny, *American Irish,* 134.

9. Friel, *Philadelphia, Here I Come!,* xi. Subsequent page references are given parenthetically in the text.

10. Miller, *Emigrants and Exiles,* 558.

11. Ibid., 360.

12. Pilkington, "Reading History," 501.

13. Miller, *Emigrants and Exiles,* 558.

14. Lojek, "Brian Friel's Plays and George Steiner's Linguistics," 83.

15. Pratt, "Brian Friel's Imaginary Journeys to Nowhere."

16. Tóibín, *Brooklyn*, 11. Subsequent page references are given parenthetically in the text. A film version, with a screenplay by Nick Hornby and directed by John Crowley, was released in 2015.

17. Corcoran, "Process of Migration."

18. McWilliams, *Women and Exile*, 183.

19. Corcoran, "Process of Migration."

20. Kiely, "Homes on the Mountain," 673.

21. Harte, "Endless Mutation of the Shore."

22. Ibid., 4.

23. Ibid., 9.

Bibliography

Primary Sources

Barry, Sebastian. *The Steward of Christendom*. New York: Dramatists Play Service, 1995.

Boyle, Patrick. "Pastorale." In Forkner, *Modern Irish Short Stories,* 338–52.

Doyle, Roddy. *The Barrytown Trilogy: The Commitments, The Snapper, The Van*. New York: Penguin, 1987.

———. *The Deportees and Other Stories*. New York: Viking, 2008.

———. *Paula Spencer*. London: Vintage, 2006.

———. *The Woman Who Walked into Doors*. New York: Viking Penguin, 1996.

Edgeworth, Maria. *Castle Rackrent*. 1800. Edited by George Watson, with an introduction by Kathryn J. Kirkpatrick. Oxford: Oxford University Press, 1995.

Forkner, Ben, ed. *Modern Irish Short Stories*. Preface by Anthony Burgess. New York: Penguin, 1995.

Friel, Brian. *Philadelphia, Here I Come!* London: Faber & Faber, 1965.

———. *Translations*. In Harrington, *Modern and Contemporary Irish Drama,* 255–308.

Gregory, Lady [Augusta]. *Visions and Beliefs in the West of Ireland*. 1920. Buckinghamshire, UK: Colin Smythe, 1992.

Harrington, John P., ed. *Modern and Contemporary Irish Drama*. 2nd ed. New York: Norton, 2009.

Joyce, James. "Counterparts." In Joyce, *Dubliners,* 86–98.

———. "The Dead." In Joyce, *Dubliners,* 175–224.

———. *Dubliners*. 1914. Edited by Robert Scholes and A. Walton Litz. New York: Penguin, 1996.

———. "A Little Cloud." In Joyce, *Dubliners,* 70–85.

Kiely, Benedict. "Homes on the Mountain." In *The Penguin Book of Irish Fiction,* edited by Colm Tóibín, 673–81. London: Penguin, 1999.

MacLaverty, Bernard. *Cal*. 1983. New York: Norton, 1995.

McCann, Colum. "Fishing the Sloe-Black River." In *Fishing the Sloe-Black River,* 53–56. London: Phoenix House, 1994.

McPherson, Conor. *The Weir*. In *The Weir and Other Plays,* 1–72. New York: Theatre Communications Group, 1999.

Mitchel, John. *The Last Conquest of Ireland (Perhaps)*. Glasgow: Cameron, Ferguson, 1882. https://archive.org/details/lastconquestofiroomitc (accessed March 6, 2015).

Murphy, Maureen O'Rourke, and James MacKillop. *Irish Literature: A Reader*. Syracuse, N.Y.: Syracuse University Press, 1987.

Murphy, Tom. *The Patriot Game*. In vol. 1 of *Plays*, 91–149. 6 vols. London: Methuen Drama, 1992–2010.

O'Brien, Edna. *Wild Decembers*. New York: Houghton Mifflin, 1999.

O'Connor, Joseph. *Star of the Sea*. Orlando, Fla.: Harcourt, 2002.

Synge, John Millington. "An Autumn Night in the Hills." In Forkner, *Modern Irish Short Stories*, 84–90.

———. *The Playboy of the Western World*. 1907. Rpt. in Harrington, *Modern and Contemporary Irish Drama*, 68–112.

Tóibín, Colm. *Brooklyn*. New York: Scribner, 2009.

Trevelyan, Charles. *The Irish Crisis*. London: Longman, 1848. https://archive.org/details/irishcrisi00trev (accessed March 8, 2015).

Trevor, William. "Beyond the Pale." In Trevor, *Collected Stories*, 749–71.

———. *The Collected Stories*. Harmondsworth, UK: Penguin, 1992.

———. "The Distant Past." In Trevor, *Collected Stories*, 349–56.

———. "Kathleen's Field." In Trevor, *Collected Stories*, 1245–61.

———. "The News from Ireland." In Trevor, *Collected Stories*, 881–906.

———. *The Story of Lucy Gault*. London: Penguin, 2002.

Yeats, William Butler. "Easter, 1916." In *The Collected Poems of W. B. Yeats*, rev. ed., edited by Richard J. Finneran, 180–81. New York: Scribner, 1996.

———. "Remorse for Intemperate Speech." In Finneran, *Collected Poems*, 254.

Secondary Sources

Adler, Marianna. "From Symbolic Exchange to Commodity Consumption: Anthropological Notes on Drinking as a Symbolic Practice." In Barrows and Room, *Drinking*, 376–98.

Als, Hilton. "Men at Work: Conor McPherson on the Irish Male." *New Yorker*, June 2, 2008. http://www.newyorker.com/magazine/2008/06/02/men-at-work-2.

Amador-Moreno, Carolina P. "Remembering Language: Bilingualism, Hiberno-English, and the Gaeltacht Peasant Memoir." *Irish University Review: A Journal of Irish Studies* 39, no. 1 (2009): 76–89.

Ardagh, John. *Ireland and the Irish: Portrait of a Changing Society*. London: Penguin, 1994.

Barrett, James R. "Why Paddy Drank: The Social Importance of Whiskey in Pre-Famine Ireland." *Journal of Popular Culture* 9, no. 1 (1977): 155–66.

Barrows, Susanna, and Robin Room, eds. *Drinking: Behavior and Belief in Modern History*. Berkeley: University of California Press, 1991.

Barry, Sebastian. "Lies and More Lies." *Princeton University Library Chronicle* 68, nos. 1–2 (2006–7): 640–48.

Bew, Paul. *Land and the National Question in Ireland, 1858–82*. Atlantic Highlands, N.J.: Humanities, 1979.

Binchy, Maeve. "Writers on Writing: For the Irish, Long-Windedness Serves as a Literary Virtue." *New York Times,* November 4, 2002.

Booker, M. Keith. "Late Capitalism Comes to Dublin: 'American' Popular Culture in the Novels of Roddy Doyle." *Ariel: A Review of International English Literature* 28, no. 3 (1997): 27–45.

Bowen, Elizabeth. *Bowen's Court.* 1942. New York: Ecco, 1979.

———. "Notes on Writing a Novel." In *Collected Impressions,* 249–63. New York: Knopf, 1950.

Bradley, Anthony, and Maryann Gialanella Valiulis, eds. *Gender and Sexuality in Modern Ireland.* New York: American Conference for Irish Studies, 1997.

Brantley, Ben. Review of *The Weir,* by Conor McPherson. *New York Times,* April 2, 1999.

Bretherton, George. "Against the Flowing Tide: Whiskey and Temperance in the Making of Modern Ireland." In Barrows and Room, *Drinking,* 147–64.

Butler, Marilyn. "Edgeworth's Ireland: History, Popular Culture, and Secret Codes." *Novel: A Forum on Fiction* 34, no. 2 (2001): 267–92.

Carey, Lisa. *The Mermaids Singing.* New York: Avon, 1998.

Comerford, R. V. *Ireland: Inventing the Nation.* New York: Oxford University Press, 2003.

Coogan, Tim Pat. *The Famine Plot: England's Role in Ireland's Greatest Tragedy.* New York: Palgrave Macmillan, 2012.

———. *The IRA: A History.* Niwot, Colo.: Roberts Rinehart, 1993.

Corbett, Mary Jean. *Allegories of Union in Irish and English Writing, 1790–1870.* Cambridge: Cambridge University Press, 2004.

Corcoran, Mary P. "The Process of Migration and the Reinvention of Self: The Experiences of Returning Irish Emigrants." *Éire-Ireland: A Journal of Irish Studies* 37 (2002): 175–91.

Cullingford, Elizabeth. "Colonial Policing: *The Steward of Christendom* and *The Whereabouts of Eneas McNulty.*" *Éire-Ireland: A Journal of Irish Studies* 39, nos. 3–4 (2004): 11–37.

Dezell, Maureen. *Irish America Coming into Clover: The Evolution of a People and a Culture.* New York: Doubleday, 2000.

Edwards, Ruth Dudley. *Patrick Pearse: The Triumph of Failure.* London: Faber & Faber, 1977.

Elliott, Marianne. *The Catholics of Ulster.* New York: Basic Books, 2001.

Estévez-Saá, José Manuel. "An Interview with Joseph O'Connor." *Contemporary Literature* 46, no. 2 (2005): 161–75.

Fehlmann, Guy. "An Historical Survey. " In Genet, *Big House in Ireland,* 15–18.

Fitzgerald-Hoyt, Mary. *William Trevor: Re-imagining Ireland.* Dublin: Liffey, 2003.

Foster, John Wilson. "'All the Long Traditions': Loyalty and Service in Barry and Ishiguro." In *Out of History: Essays on the Writings of Sebastian Barry,* edited by Christina Hunt Mahony, 99–119. Dublin: Carysfort, 2006.

Foster, R. F. "Ascendancy and Union." In *The Oxford Illustrated History of Ireland,* ed. R. F. Foster, 161–212. Oxford: Oxford University Press, 1989.

————. "The Ascendancy Mind." *History Today* 38, no. 12 (1988): 20–28.

Garvin, Tom. "Collins, Michael." In Lalor, *Encyclopedia of Ireland*, 219.

————. "De Valera, Éamon." In Lalor, *Encyclopedia of Ireland*, 288.

Genet, Jacqueline, ed. *The Big House in Ireland: Reality and Representation*. Dingle, Ireland: Barnes & Noble, 1991.

Gleitman, Claire. "Reconstructing History in the Irish History Play." In *The Cambridge Companion to Twentieth-Century Irish Drama*, edited by Shaun Richards, 218–30. Cambridge: Cambridge University Press, 2004.

Goodby, John, ed. *Irish Studies: The Essential Glossary*. New York: Oxford University Press, 2003.

Grant, Patrick. *Breaking Enmities: Religion, Literature and Culture in Northern Ireland, 1967–97*. London: Macmillan, 1999.

Grene, Nicholas. "Ireland in Two Minds: Martin McDonagh and Conor McPherson." *Yearbook of English Studies* 35 (2005): 298–311.

Gusfield, Joseph. "Benevolent Repression: Popular Culture, Social Structure, and the Control of Drinking." In Barrows and Room, *Drinking*, 399–424.

Harte, Liam. "'The Endless Mutation of the Shore': Colm Tóibín's Marine Imagery." *Critique* 51, no. 4 (2010): 333–49.

Harvey, Clodagh Brennan. *Contemporary Irish Traditional Narrative: The English Language Tradition*. Folklore and Mythology Studies 35. Berkeley: University of California Press, 1992.

Haughey, Jim. "Standing in the Gap: Sebastian Barry's Revisionist Theater." *Colby Quarterly* 34, no. 4 (1998): 290–302.

Hayden, Tom, ed. *Irish Hunger: Personal Reflections on the Legacy of the Famine*. Boulder, Colo.: Roberts Rinehart/Dublin: Wolfhound, 1997.

Ingman, Heather. "Edna O'Brien: Stretching the Nation's Boundaries." *Irish Studies Review* 10, no. 3 (2002): 253–65.

Jeffers, Jennifer M. "'What's It Like Being Irish?': The Return of the Repressed in Roddy Doyle's *Paula Spencer*." In *Irish Literature since 1990: Diverse Voices*, edited by Scott Brewster and Michael Parker, 258–71. Manchester: Manchester University Press, 2009.

Johnston, Elva. "Pre-Christian Religions." In Lalor, *Encyclopedia of Ireland*, 891–92.

Jones, Nesta. *Brian Friel: A Faber Critical Guide*. London: Faber & Faber, 2000.

Kenny, Kevin. *The American Irish: A History*. Harlow, UK: Longman, 2000.

Kerrane, Kevin. "The Structural Elegance of Conor McPherson's *The Weir*." *New Hibernia Review* 10, no. 4 (2006): 105–21.

Kinealy, Christine. *A Death-Dealing Famine: The Great Hunger in Ireland*. London: Pluto, 1997.

————. "How Politics Fed the Famine." *Natural History* 105, no. 1 (1996): 33–36.

Kowaleski-Wallace, Elizabeth. *Their Fathers' Daughters: Hannah More, Maria Edgeworth, and Patriarchal Complicity*. New York: Oxford University Press, 1991.

Kreilkamp, Vera. *The Anglo-Irish Novel and the Big House*. Syracuse: Syracuse University Press, 1998.

Kurdi, Maria. "'Really All Danger': An Interview with Sebastian Barry." *New Hibernia Review/Iris Éireannach Nua* 8, no. 1 (2004): 41–53.

Lalor, Brian, ed. *The Encyclopedia of Ireland*. New Haven, Conn.: Yale University Press, 2003.

Laxton, Edward. *The Famine Ships: The Irish Exodus to America 1846–51*. London: Bloomsbury, 1996.

Lindahl-Raittila, Iris. "Negotiating Irishness: Edna O'Brien's 1990s Trilogy." *Nordic Irish Studies* 5, no.1 (2006): 73–86.

Lojek, Helen. "Brian Friel's Plays and George Steiner's Linguistics: Translating the Irish." *Contemporary Literature* 35, no. 1 (1994): 83–99.

———. *The Spaces of Irish Drama: Stage and Place in Contemporary Plays*. New York: Palgrave Macmillan, 2011.

Lysaght, Patricia. *A Pocket Book of the Banshee*. Dublin: O'Brien, 1998.

MacPherson, James. "'Ireland Begins in the Home': Women, Irish National Identity, and the Domestic Sphere in the Irish Homestead, 1896–1912." *Éire-Ireland: A Journal of Irish Studies* 36 (2001): 131–52.

Mallon, Thomas. "Fools of Fortune." Review of *The Story of Lucy Gault* by William Trevor. *New York Times*, September 29, 2002, Sunday Book Review.

Martinovich, Kay. "Ghosts of the Great War in *The Steward of Christendom*." *New Hibernia Review* 13, no. 2 (2009): 110–24.

McCourt, Frank. *Angela's Ashes*. New York: Touchstone, 1996.

McGlynn, Mary. "Why Jimmy Wears a Suit: White, Black, and Working Class in *The Commitments*." *Studies in the Novel* 36, no. 2 (2004): 232–50.

McGonigle, Lisa. "Rednecks and Southsiders Need Not Apply: Subalternity and Soul in Roddy Doyle's *The Commitments*." *Irish Studies Review* 13, no. 2 (2005): 163–73.

McPherson, Conor. "Late Nights and Proclamations." *American Theatre* 16, no. 4 (1999): 45–46.

McWilliams, Ellen. *Women and Exile in Contemporary Irish Fiction*. New York: Palgrave Macmillan, 2013.

Meche, Jude R. "Seeking 'The Mercy of Fathers': Sebastian Barry's *The Steward of Christendom* and the Tragedy of Irish Patriarchy." *Modern Drama* 47, no. 3 (2004): 464–79.

Miller, Kerby A. *Emigrants and Exiles: Ireland and the Irish Exodus to North America*. New York: Oxford University Press, 1985.

Moynihan, Sinéad. *"Other People's Diasporas": Negotiating Race in Contemporary Irish and Irish-American Culture*. Syracuse: Syracuse University Press, 2013.

Neill, Michael. "Mantles, Quirks, and Irish Bulls: Ironic Guise and Colonial Subjectivity in Maria Edgeworth's *Castle Rackrent*." *Review of English Studies*, n.s. 52, no. 205 (2001): 76–90.

O'Connor, Anne. "Faeries." In Lalor, *Encyclopedia of Ireland,* 370.

O'Connor, Joseph. *Ghost Light*. New York: Farrar, 2010.

Ó Corráin, Donnchadh. "Prehistoric and Early Christian Ireland." In *The Oxford Illustrated History of Ireland,* edited by R. F. Foster, 1–52. Oxford: Oxford University Press, 1989.

Onkey, Lauren. "Celtic Soul Brothers." *Éire-Ireland: A Journal of Irish Studies* 28, no. 3 (1993): 147–58.

O'Reilly, Camille. *The Irish Language in Northern Ireland: The Politics of Culture and Identity.* London: Macmillan, 1999.

O'Toole, Fintan. "Going West: The Country versus the City in Irish Writing." *Crane Bag* 9, no. 2 (1985): 111–16.

———. *Tom Murphy: The Politics of Magic.* Dublin: New Island Books, 1994.

Persson, Åke. "'You're Fuckin' Amazing, by the Way': Marginalisation and Recovery in Roddy Doyle's *Paula Spenser.*" *Nordic Journal of English Studies* 11, no. 2 (2012): 138–65.

Pilkington, Lionel. "Reading History in the Plays of Brian Friel." In *A Companion to Modern Irish Drama, 1880–2005,* edited by Mary Luckhurst, 499–508. Malden, Mass.: Blackwell, 2006.

Piroux, Lorraine. "'I'm Black an' I'm Proud': Re-Inventing Irishness in Roddy Doyle's *The Commitments.*" *College Literature* 25, no. 2 (1998): 45–57.

Poulain, Alexandra. "Playing out the Rising: Sean O'Casey's *The Plough and the Stars* and Tom Murphy's *The Patriot Game.*" *Études Anglaises* 59, no. 2 (2006): 156–69.

Pratt, William. "Brian Friel's Imaginary Journeys to Nowhere." *World Literature Today* 73, no. 3 (1999): 445–50.

Purdon, Edward. *The Story of the Irish Language.* Cork: Mercier, 1999.

Putterford, Mark. *Phil Lynott: The Rocker.* Rev. ed. London: Omnibus, 2010.

Quigley, Michael. "Grosse Île: Canada's Famine Memorial." In *The Great Famine and the Irish Diaspora in America,* edited by Arthur Gribben, 133–54. Amherst: University of Massachusetts Press, 1999.

Rauchbauer, Otto. "The Big House and Irish History: An Introductory Sketch." In *Ancestral Voices: The Big House in Anglo-Irish Literature,* edited by Otto Rauchbauer, 1–15. Dublin: Lilliput, 1992.

Rudd, Joy. "'Cast a Cold Eye': A Sociological Approach." In Genet, *Big House in Ireland,* 31–42.

Shannon, Catherine B. "The Changing Face of Cathleen ni Houlihan: Women and Politics in Ireland, 1960–1996." In Bradley and Valiulis, *Gender and Sexuality in Modern Ireland,* 257–74.

Smith, James M., ed. *Two Irish National Tales: Maria Edgeworth, Castle Rackrent; Sydney Owenson (Lady Morgan), The Wild Irish Girl.* Introduction by Vera Kreilkamp. New York: Houghton, 2005.

Smyth, Gerry. *Space and the Irish Cultural Imagination.* New York: Palgrave, 2001.

Stivers, Richard. *A Hair of the Dog: Irish Drinking and American Stereotype.* University Park: Pennsylvania State University Press, 1976.

Synge, John Millington. Preface to *The Playboy of the Western World.* In Harrington, *Modern and Contemporary Irish Drama,* 453–54.

Taylor, Timothy D. "Living in a Postcolonial World: Class and Soul in *The Commitments.*" *Irish Studies Review* 9, no. 3 (1998): 291–302.

Tóibín, Colm. "The Irish Famine." In Tóibín and Ferriter, *Irish Famine,* 1–36.

———. "New Ways of Killing Your Father." Review of *Paddy and Mr. Punch: Connections in Irish and English History,* by R. F. Foster. *London Review of Books,* November 18, 1993, 1–6.

Tóibín, Colm, and Diarmaid Ferriter, eds. *The Irish Famine*. London: Profile, 2004.

Townshend, Charles. *Ireland: The Twentieth Century*. London: Bloomsbury Academic, 1999.

Trevelyan, Charles. *The Irish Crisis*. London: Longman, 1848. https://archive.org/details/irishcrisi00trev.

Trevelyan, Laura. *A Very British Family: The Trevelyans and Their World*. London: Taurus, 2012.

Trevor, William. *Excursions in the Real World: Memoirs*. New York: Knopf, 1994.

Valiulis, Maryann. "Neither Feminist nor Flapper: The Ecclesiastical Construction of the Ideal Irish Woman." In *Chattel, Servant or Citizen: Women's Status in Church, State and Society*, edited by Mary O'Dowd and Sabine Wichert, 152–58. Belfast: Institute of Irish Studies, Queen's University of Belfast, 1995.

Waters, John. "Troubled People." In Hayden, *Irish Hunger*, 100–111.

White, Richard. *Remembering Ahanagran: Storytelling in a Family's Past*. New York: Hill & Wang, 1998.

Wills, Clair. *Dublin 1916: The Siege of the GPO*. Cambridge, Mass.: Harvard University Press, 2009.

Woodham-Smith, Cecil. *The Great Hunger: Ireland 1845–1849*. London: Penguin, 1962.

Wright, Frank. *Northern Ireland: A Comparative Analysis*. New York: Rowman & Littlefield, 1987.

Zimmermann, Georges Denis. *The Irish Storyteller*. Dublin: Four Courts, 2001.

Index